W9-CRD-720

GUITO TO
Arizona Backroads & 4-Wheel Drive Trails

By **CHARLES A. WELLS**

Easy • Moderate • Difficult
Backcountry Driving Adventures

FunTreks, Inc.

1

Published by FunTreks, Inc.
P.O. Box 49187, Colorado Springs, CO 80949-9187
Phone: (719) 536-0722
Fax: (719) 277-7411
E-mail: funtreks@pcisys.net

Edited by Shelley Mayer

Cover design, photography, maps, and production by Charles A.Wells

First Edition

Library of Congress Control Number 2001126581
ISBN 0-9664976-3-5

Produced in the United States of America

To order additional books, see order form in back of this book.

DISCLAIMER

Travel in Arizona's backcountry is, by its very nature, potentially dangerous and could result in property damage, injury, or even death. The
scope of this book cannot predict every possible hazard you may
encounter. If you drive any of the trails in this book, you acknowledge
these risks and assume full responsibility. You are the final judge as to
whether a trail is safe to drive on any given day, whether your vehicle is
capable of the journey, and what supplies you should carry. The information contained herein cannot replace good judgment and proper
preparation on your part. The publisher and author of this book disclaim
any and all liability for bodily injury, death, or property damage that
could occur to you or any of your passengers.

ACKNOWLEDGMENTS

I am very much indebted to the following individuals and organizations who helped with this book:

U.S. Forest Service, Bureau of Land Management, Arizona State Parks, Arizona State Land Department, Arizona State Association of 4-Wheel Drive Clubs, Grand Canyon National Park, Organ Pipe Cactus National Monument and Tonto National Monument. I worked with a long list of hard-working staffers who provided courteous and professional advice.

Jack Bushell and Chester May of the Allied Signal 4-Wheel Drive Club. With wives Sue and Janet behind the wheel, they guided me on many trails in the Phoenix area and shared their extensive collection of maps, history books and newspaper articles. Other club members who helped included: Jess Chinn, Nelson Garrison, Brent Philipp and John Griswold.

Robert Witkoff and Eldon Schmidt of the Verde Valley 4-Wheelers who helped me in Sedona, Cottonwood and Flagstaff. Thanks also to Gene Harrison, Charlie McKinnon and Kory McKenley.

Jim Norine, Dave Peterson, Mike List, Phil Klineman and John Hill of the Tucson Rough Riders. They helped me cover a big chunk of southern Arizona. Other members who helped included: Tim Naylor, Mike Acosta, Hal Loy, Bob Peterson, Fred Wilson, John Waack, Earnest Rush, Craig Becwar, Mike Meyers and Rheal Tetreault. Special thanks to Kevin McBride, who helped me repair my Cherokee after Charouleau Gap.

Jim Burns, Warren Breen and Gary Peters of the Havasu 4-Wheelers. They guided me on local trails during a week of 117-degree temperatures. A big thanks to the entire club for their support.

Ken Peterson, Phil Strittmatter and Joan Beck of the Bullhead City 4-Wheelers—a friendly club that's serious about four-wheeling.

Don Munzer, Gordon Grotts and Marty Boetel of the Lo-Rangers 4-Wheel Drive Club, Rodney Hayes of the Parker Four-Wheelers, Gary Snair for help in Quartzsite and Yuma, Brad Jones of the Copperstate 4-Wheelers in Mesa, Gary Keller of the Rim Country 4-Wheelers in Payson, Vern Pierson of the Prescott 4-Wheelers, Gene McKinney for help in Chloride, Michelle Noblet of Colorado Springs, James Howard of Flagstaff, Mike Lagomarsino of the Sedona Red Rock Jeep Tours, Mr. Ed of Mr. Ed's Excellent Adventures, Aaron Dickinson of Macromotive.com, and Bryan Christeson of 4-Wheelers Supply and Off Road Centers in Phoenix.

Thanks to countless others who participated in trail runs and allowed me to take their pictures.

My own club, the Colorado Four-Wheelers in Colorado Springs, who first introduced me to four-wheeling and have supported me over the years.

Shelley Mayer, a respected editor and writer in Colorado Springs, for her thorough editing of this book.

Last but not least, my wife, Beverly, and daughter, Marcia Levault, for their encouragement and assistance.

Montana Mountain (Trail #48), rated moderate.

Contents

Trails Listed by Area

ATV trails shown with asterisk *

Trail Locator Map

● Easy Trails
■ Moderate Trails
◆ Difficult Trails

See individual area maps for more detail.

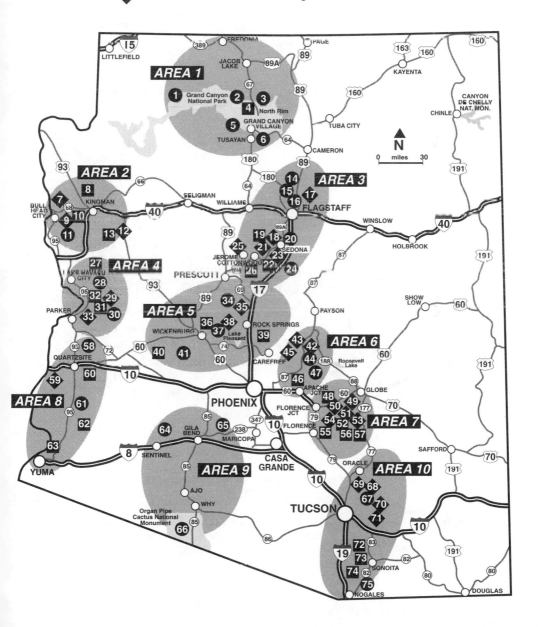

Trails Listed by Difficulty

● Easy

Trails are grouped into three major categories: easy, moderate and difficult. Within each group, trails at the top of the list are easier than at the bottom. If you drive a trail and find it too easy, try one lower on the list. Conversely, if you find a trail too difficult, try one higher on the list. You may have to skip several trails on the list to find a significant difference.

Easier ↑

More Difficult ↓

Pg.	No./Trail
212	61. Palm Canyon
226	66. Organ Pipe Cactus Nat. Mon.
82	15. Schultz Pass
42	3. Saddle Mountain Road
172	47. Apache Trail
50	6. Grandview Lookout
84	16. Elden Mountain
252	75. Patagonia Mountains
222	64. Oatman Massacre Site
80	14. Lockett Meadow
34	1. Toroweap Overlook
92	20. Schnebly Hill Road
230	67. Backway to Mt. Lemmon
38	2. Fire Point, Timp Point
148	37. Castle Hot Springs Road
102	24. Hutch Mountain
136	34. Bradshaw Mountains
68	11. Backway to Oatman
224	65. Butterfield Stage Route
122	30. Swansea Townsite
116	28. Mohave Wash
46	5. South Bass Trailhead
158	41. Belmont Mountain
166	44. Four Peaks
204	58. Plomosa Mountains

Trail Ratings Defined ➡

Trail ratings are very subjective. Conditions change for many reasons, including weather and time of year. An easy trail can quickly become difficult when washed out by a rainstorm or blocked by a fallen rock. You must be the final judge of a trail's condition on the day you drive it. If any part of a trail is difficult, the entire trail is rated difficult. You may be able to drive a significant portion of a trail before reaching the difficult spot. Read each trail description carefully for specific information.

Easy: Gravel, dirt, clay, sand, or mildly rocky road. Gentle grades. Water levels low except during periods of heavy runoff. Full-width single lane or wider with adequate room to pass most of the time. Where shelf conditions exist, road is wide and well-maintained with minor sideways tilt. Four-wheel drive recommended on most trails but some are suitable for two-wheel drive under dry conditions. Clay surface roads, when wet, can significantly increase difficulty.

Moderate   ◆ Difficult

Moderate: Rutted dirt or rocky road suitable for most sport utility vehicles. Careful tire placement often necessary. Four-wheel drive, low range, and high ground clearance required. Standard factory skid plates and tow hooks recommended on many trails. Undercarriage may scrape occasionally. Some grades fairly steep but manageable if dry. Soft sand possible. Sideways tilt will require caution. Narrow shelf roads possible. Backing may be necessary to pass. Water depths passable for stock high-clearance vehicles except during periods of heavy runoff. Mud holes may be present especially in the spring. Rock-stacking may be necessary in some cases. Brush may touch vehicle.

Difficult: Some trails suitable for more aggressive stock vehicles but most trails require vehicle modification. Lifts, differential lockers, aggressive articulation, and/or winches recommended in many cases. Skid plates and tow hooks required. Body damage possible. Grades can be steep with severe ground undulation. Sideways tilt can be extreme. Deep water crossings possible. Shelf roads extremely narrow; use caution in full-size vehicle. Read trail description carefully. Passing may be difficult with backing required for long distances. Brush may scratch sides of vehicle.

Trails Listed Alphabetically

Author's favorite trails are shown in boldface type.

INTRODUCTION

Walnut Canyon (Trail #57), rated moderate.

Introduction

When I left for Arizona to start this book, I wasn't sure what I'd find. Obviously, the beauty of Arizona's highways has been well documented, but would Arizona have the kind of adventure roads my readers want? Having written two books on Colorado and one on Moab, Utah, my standards were very high. I wondered if Arizona would measure up.

It didn't take long to answer this question with a resounding yes! With the help of local four-wheel drive clubs, I quickly discovered the state has hundreds of great roads perfect for SUVs exploration and some of the most challenging hard-core trails anywhere.

Perhaps the biggest surprise was Grand Canyon National Park. I'd been there as a typical tourist years ago and knew it was crowded. I didn't know that most of the five million annual visitors are squeezed into one small portion of the park on the south rim. Few visitors take advantage of bordering Kaibab National Forest where you can camp free in a spacious, quiet setting just minutes from the park. Many forest roads on the north rim lead to outstanding overlooks of the canyon which you can enjoy in virtual seclusion. With more time, you can drive to Toroweap Overlook, far west on the north rim. In my opinion, this dramatic overlook, 3,000 feet above the Colorado River, is the best in the park. It has a beautiful little campground that is rarely crowded. When I was there in September, only two of its 11 sites were occupied.

Another surprise was Sedona. People come from all over the world to enjoy the town's famous red-rock Jeep tours. I assumed the tour businesses had exclusive use of the land. Not so—all the trails are on public lands inside the Coconino National Forest. Although the area is tightly controlled, anyone with a capable vehicle is allowed to drive the trails.

Serious four-wheelers should make a point of getting to Florence Junction east of Phoenix. For the last several years, this spot has been the site of the Arizona State Assoc. of 4-Wheel Drive Clubs' Annual Jamboree. Although the area has some great moderate roads, it is better known for its hard-core trails which include nationally-known *Woodpecker* and *Ajax*.

With one exception, this book does not cover trails on Indian reservations. Since most require special fees and permits, I decided to cover just public lands. If you are interested in the popular four-wheel-drive trip through Canyon de Chelly National Monument, contact the monument directly for details (see appendix). Directions are not needed for this trip because you are required to hire a Native American guide that the monument provides. Clubs often go as a group to share the cost.

I drove most of the trails in this book during the fall and winter months. High-elevation trails, including those around Flagstaff and Grand Canyon National Park, were done first to avoid winter snows. At the recommendation of local residents, I stayed away from desert trails during the summer. However, I was still treated to some hot weather in mid-September when an unusal late hot spell pushed daytime desert temperatures to 117 degrees. Even with an air conditioned vehicle, it was unpleasant when I had to step outside. A mechanical failure, at that point, would have been dangerous had I not been traveling with a group.

Everywhere I went, it was clear to me that four-wheeling is enormously popular in Arizona. People of all ages are involved. Lake Havasu City, a well-known retirement mecca, has perhaps the largest four-wheel-drive club in the state. This club sometimes has 60 vehicles show up for a run. Both Phoenix and Tuscson are big-time four-wheeling cities with many active four-wheel-drive clubs.

Whether you're a tentative new SUV owner or a hard-core four-wheeler, I know you'll be pleased after using this book. I work hard to provide the kind of detail necessary to safely venture into the backcountry. Remember to stay on designated trails and roads at all times. Only through responsible use of our public lands will they remain open to enjoy.

HOW TO USE THIS BOOK

This book has been designed for quick and easy use. Trails are grouped by area. First use the Trail Locator Map on page 7 to determine the big picture, then turn to each area map for more detail. Each trail is shown with photos and a map. All maps are to scale and oriented with north at the top. Scale is indicated using an overall grid. Check the size of the grid at the bottom of each map. A small legend or "Mini Key" is included on each map for quick reference. Find the full map legend on page 30.

The shaded portion of the trail is described in the text. Other roads are for reference only and should be traveled at your own risk. Water crossing and bridge symbols show major stream locations. Most trails are described in one direction; a few, however, are described both ways.

Trails are listed three ways for your convenience: in numerical order by area on page 6, by difficulty on pages 8 and 9, and alphabetically on page 10. Geometric shapes are used to indicate difficulty. A circle indicates easy, a square moderate, and a diamond difficult. Trail ratings are described in detail on pages 8 and 9.

The text for each trail includes: general location, difficulty, special features, length and driving time, how to get to the trail, a detailed trail description, how to get home, location of nearest services, and other maps. Where space allows historical highlights are included.

Mileage readings can vary because of vehicle differences and driving habits. Readings were rounded to the nearest tenth of a mile. The author's odometer was calibrated for accuracy.

GPS waypoints are shown in small brackets in the text and a small square with a dot in the middle on the maps. Waypoint coordinates are found in the appendix. See map for specific page.

Other information in the appendix includes GPS Basics, a glossary, references and recommended reading, helpful addresses and phone numbers, an index, and information about the author.

SELECTING THE RIGHT TRAIL FOR YOUR VEHICLE

Today's modern sport utility vehicles are amazingly well designed for off-highway travel. Modern technology is making the backcountry accessible to ever more capable stock vehicles. More and more people are buying sport utilities and setting out to discover the fun that other SUV owners are having. Sometimes, however, beginners think that once they buy a four-wheel-drive vehicle, it will go anywhere. They soon learn that this is not the case. The following will help you decide which trails are right for your vehicle.

Easy: Suitable for all stock four-wheel-drive sport utility vehicles with high ground clearance and low range. Some trails can be driven in two-wheel drive without low range in dry weather. A few trails, under ideal conditions, are suitable for passenger cars.

Moderate: Suitable for most stock 4WD sport utility vehicles with high ground clearance and low range. For the toughest moderate trails, factory skid plates, tow points, and all-terrain tires are recommended. These options are available from your dealer or local four-wheel-drive shop.

Difficult: Suitable for some aggressive stock 4WD sport utility vehicles with very high ground clearance, excellent articulation, tow hooks, and a full skid plate package. All-terrain tires as a minimum, mud terrains preferred. A winch or differential lockers are recommended for the most difficult trails. Drivers who spend a great deal of time on the most difficult trails may find it necessary to modify their vehicles with higher ground clearance, oversized tires, and heavy duty accessories. A trail is rated difficult if any spot on the trail is difficult. You may be able to enjoy much of a trail before running into the difficult portion. Read the trail description carefully.

STATE TRUST LAND PERMIT REQUIREMENTS

Many of the trails in this book, including trails in the popular Florence Junction area, cross designated state land. Sometimes these lands are posted with no trespassing signs and sometimes they're not. In either case you are required to have a *State Land Recreational Use Permit* to enter. The permit is inexpensive, easy to obtain and good anywhere in the state for a full year. You are required to carry the permit with you at all times while on state land. Responsible four-wheelers who reside in Arizona purchase the permit annually just like a fishing or hunting license. If you are heading to Arizona from another state, you can purchase the permit by mail in advance or in person at the Arizona State Land Department at 1616 W. Adams in Phoenix, AZ 85007. Rates in the year 2000 were $15.00 per individual or $20.00 per family. Permits can also be obtained in Flagstaff and Tucson. For additional information call 1-602-364-2753.

SEDONA RED ROCKS PASS

All trails in the Sedona area require a special Red Rocks Pass if you park for more than a few minutes near or along the trail. No pass is required to drive a trail as long as you keep moving. Passes are available at dispensing machines at the start of most trails. Many stores and government offices in Sedona also sell passes. The cost is $5/day or $15/week. If you plan to picnic or hike, you'll need a pass.

ATVs & DIRT BIKES

This book is not intended to be an all-inclusive guide for ATVs and dirt bikes. However, when an official OHV area corresponds with a four-wheel drive area or when ATVs were seen using a legal area, the author noted this on maps using an ATV symbol (see full legend on page 30). Generally these areas have a concentrated network of roads with centralized parking. It may be officially identified or just a convenient place to leave a trailer. Generally, ATVs and dirt bikes must be street legal when used on any maintained road. Rules for other roads vary across the state. It is your responsibilty to verifiy all regulations with the appropriate Forest Service or BLM office (see appendix). Two four-wheel-drive trails in this book are located in recognized OHV areas: Cinder Hills OHV Area and the Ehrenberg Sand Bowl OHV Area. Cinder Hills, near Flagstaff is the largest and perhaps best OHV area in the state. **ATV trails are identified with an asterisk on Page 6**. Trails without an asterisk may also allow ATVs but none were seen by the author when he was in the area. Make sure to stay on existing trails at all times. Never cross meadows or disturb wildlife. Stay in dry washes whenever possible and never drive on cryptobiotic crust. Irresponsible use of ATVs is one of the biggest concerns of the Forest Service and BLM and a major reason for trail closures. Please do your part to help keep our trails open.

SAFETY TIPS

File a Flight Plan. Determine where you are going and when you plan to return. Be as specific as possible. Inform a friend or relative and call them when you return. If something goes wrong, you'll have the comfort of knowing that at least someone knows where you are and that you could be in trouble.

Travel with another vehicle. Your chances of getting stuck in the back-country are immensely reduced with two vehicles. If one vehicle breaks down, you have a back-up. This could also save you an expensive towing charge.

Carry extra maps. The maps in this book will clearly direct you along the trail. However, if you get lost or decide to venture down a spur road, you'll need additional maps with topographic information. Carry a compass or a GPS unit to orient yourself. At the end of each trail description, I have listed several maps that I found useful. Make sure you have at least one.

I wouldn't go anywhere without my DeLorme *Arizona Atlas & Gazetteer*. Although it's a large-scale map, it has a surprising amount of backroad detail. It covers the entire state and its booklet format is easy to use. Latitude and longitude are printed along the edge of each map. With the simplest GPS unit, you can quickly determine your location. The *Arizona Road & Recreation Atlas* by Benchmark Maps is very similar to the Gazetteer. It has better graphics but doesn't show quite as much backroad detail. Either atlas will work just fine.

The greatest amount of detail is shown on 7.5 minute U.S. Geological Survey Maps; however, each map covers a small area and many maps are required. Since I carry a laptop computer, I buy 7.5 minute maps on CDs. They are extremely economical and easy to use in this format, but they would be useless if something happened to my computer. I use them because they provide maximum detail for GPS tracking. I always carry other maps.

Changing conditions. Arizona's backcountry is fragile and under con-stant assault by forces of nature and man. Rock slides can occur or an entire road can be washed away from a single heavy rainstorm. A road may be closed without notice. Directional signs may be removed or vandalized. Route numbers are sometimes changed. Maps seldom keep up with changes and sometimes have mistakes. Take these factors into consideration when faced with a confusing situation. Rely on your own common sense.

High water, flash floods. Many of Arizona's backroads cross or follow dry washes, small streams, and narrow canyons. Heavy rains can turn these places into raging torrents of water in minutes. Check weather forecasts and keep an eye on the sky. Be conservative and don't take chances. Cut your trip short if necessary. Don't attempt to cross a fast-flowing stream unless you've done it before and know what your vehicle can do. Wait if neces-sary; water levels usually go down quickly after a single rain shower. If you're in a narrow canyon and water begins to rise, drive perpendicularly out of the canyon if possible. If this is not possible, get out of your vehicle and climb to higher ground. Most people who die in flash floods attempt to outrun the rising water in their vehicles.

Inspect your vehicle carefully. Before you start into the backcountry, make sure your vehicle is in top operating condition. If you have a mechanic do the work, make sure he is reliable and understands four-wheeling. Tell him where you plan to take your vehicle. Pay particular attention to fluids, hoses, belts, battery, brakes, steering linkage, suspension system, driveline, and anything exposed under the vehicle. Tighten anything that may be loose. Inspect your tires carefully for potential weak spots and tread wear.

Wear your seat belt. You might think that because you're driving slowly, it's not necessary to wear your seat belt or use child restraints. I've learned through experience that you are much safer with a seat belt than without. Buckle up at all times.

Keep heads, arms, and legs inside a moving vehicle. Many trails are narrow. Brush, tree limbs, and rock overhangs may come very close to your vehicle. The driver must make it clear to every passenger to stay inside the vehicle at all times. Children, in particular, must not be allowed to stick their heads, arms, or legs out the windows.

Cliff edges. Watch children and be extremely careful around cliff edges. Hand rails are rarely provided. Watch for loose rock and stay away from these areas when it's wet, icy, or getting dark. If you climb up a rock wall, remember it's harder to get down than to climb up.

Lightning. During a storm, stay away from lone trees, cliff edges, and high points. Stay low to the ground or in your vehicle. Lightning can strike from a distant storm even when it's clear overhead.

Mines, tunnels, and old structures. Be careful around old mine buildings. Stay out of mines and tunnels. Don't let children play in these areas.

DESERT SURVIVAL

Self-reliance. Most of us live in populated areas and are accustomed to having other people around when things go wrong. In Arizona's remote backcountry, you must be self-reliant. Don't count on anyone else's help. Try to anticipate what can go wrong and prepare accordingly.

Water, water, and more water. I can't stress enough the importance of carrying and drinking plenty of water—at least one gallon per person per day plus extra water for your vehicle. I leave an extra five-gallon container in my vehicle at all times. A canteen is handy if you have to walk out. Running out of water under certain circumstances can be a fatal mistake.

First Aid. Always carry a good first-aid kit. Take a first-aid course and learn the basics. Make sure the kit contains a good first-aid book.

What to do if you have mechanical problems or you get lost. Stay with your vehicle. There's always a chance that someone will come along if you stay near the road. Your vehicle is easier to see than you are. Your car can provide shelter from wind, rain, and cold. The desert can get very cold at night, especially if you get wet. During the day, desert heat will drive you out of your car. Seek shade. You're more likely to find a rock overhang than a shady tree. Don't sit on the hot ground. Dig down to cooler sand below or sit on something at least 18 inches above ground. Create your own shade with blankets or tarp attached to your car or build a lean-to. If necessary, dig a depression under your car and crawl underneath after exhaust pipes and engine have cooled. If you don't have a shovel, dig with a hub cap. Work slowly; don't overexert yourself. Rest as much as possible. Drink plenty of water; don't wait until you're thirsty. Wear light-colored, loose-fitting clothing that covers as much of your skin as possible. Wear a hat and use sunscreen. Collect firewood before dark. Build a fire before you need it. If you get lost or separated from your group, stay in one place.

If you're familiar with the area and know exactly how far it is to hike out and are absolutely sure you can make it, consider walking out as a last resort. Cover up with loose clothing, take plenty of water, food, and rain protection to stay dry. Travel at night when it's cooler if the terrain is not too treacherous. Make sure you can see where you're walking.

Try to draw attention to yourself. Make noise anyway you can—whistles, horns, whatever you have. Don't run down your car battery. Build a smoky fire. Three fires in a triangle 150 feet apart are an international distress signal. Use flares if you have them. Some are designed for day use, others for night. Use a reflective mirror if you see an airplane or anyone in the distance.

Take your cellphone but remember you're usually out of a service area when you are in the backcountry. Sometimes cellphones will work if you can get to higher ground. If you have a CB radio, broadcast on channel 19 or emergency channel 9. Continue intermittently to call out even if no one responds. Make sure you give your location.

Hyperthermia. When your body overheats it's called hyperthermia. Symptoms include dry, flushed skin, inability to sweat, rapid heartbeat, and a rising body temperature. Hyperthermia is often preceded by cramps. They may not go away by drinking water alone. You may need food or salt. If hyperthermia is allowed to progress you could collapse from heatstroke, which is extremely serious and can be fatal if not treated quickly.

To prevent hyperthermia, stay in the shade, don't overexert yourself, wear loose-fitting clothing, and drink plenty of water. If work is required to find or make shade, conserve your energy as best as possible.

Dehydration. As your body sweats to cool itself, it dehydrates. You may be drinking water but not enough. Eating may make you nauseous. You won't want to eat or drink. As symptoms get worse, your mouth will become dry, you may become dizzy, develop a headache, and become short of breath. At some point, you may not be able to walk or care for yourself. You must prevent dehydration before it happens. Drink more than just to quench your thirst. If you must conserve water, rest as much as possible, try not to sweat, and don't eat a lot. Digestion requires body fluids. If you have plenty of water, drink it.

Hypothermia. It gets cold in the desert after the sun goes down. If it rains and gets windy, you could find yourself shivering in no time, especially if you've worked up a sweat during the day. Your hands and feet will become stiff. You may not be able to hold a match and start a fire. Again, prevention is the key. Put on a jacket before you begin to get cold. Stay dry. Change clothes if necessary. If you get too cold, blankets may not be enough to warm you. Build a fire, drink hot liquids, or cuddle up with someone else. Your car is a great shelter—use it.

CHECKLIST. No single list can be all inclusive. You must be the final judge of what you need. Here's a list of basic items:

- ❑ WATER, WATER, WATER. At least one gallon per person per day. It's also wise to carry extra water for your vehicle.
- ❑ Food for normal eating and high-energy foods for emergencies. Energy bars, dried fruit, and hard candy store well.
- ❑ Loose-fitting, light-colored clothing, sun hats, shoes, socks, coats, and boots. Wool clothing keeps you warm when you're wet.
- ❑ Sleeping bags in case you get stuck overnight even if you're not planning to camp.
- ❑ A good first-aid kit including a first-aid book. Other important items include: sunscreen, insect repellent, water purification tablets, safety pins, needles and thread, tweezers, pocket knife or all-purpose tool.
- ❑ Candles, matches, fire starter, and a lighter.
- ❑ An extra set of keys and glasses.
- ❑ Toilet paper, paper towels, wet wipes, and trash bags.
- ❑ A large plastic sheet or tarp.
- ❑ Rain gear, small tent or tarp, nylon cords.
- ❑ Detailed maps, compass, watch, and a knife.
- ❑ If you plan to make a fire, carry your own firewood. Make sure fires are allowed.
- ❑ A heavy-duty tow strap. (The kind without metal hooks on the ends.)
- ❑ A fire extinguisher. Make sure you can reach it quickly.
- ❑ Jumper cables, extra fan belts, stop-leak for radiator.
- ❑ Replacement fuses and electrical tape.
- ❑ Flashlight and extra batteries.
- ❑ Flares, signal mirror, police whistle.
- ❑ Extra oil and other engine fluids.
- ❑ A full tank of gas. If you carry extra gas, make sure it's in an approved container and properly stored.
- ❑ A good set of tools, work gloves, and a complete service manual for your vehicle.
- ❑ Baling wire and duct tape.
- ❑ An assortment of hoses, clamps, nuts, bolts, and washers.

❏ A full-size spare tire.

❏ A tire pressure gauge, electric tire pump that will plug into your cigarette lighter, and a can of nonflammable tire sealant.

❏ A jack that will lift your vehicle fairly high off the ground. Take a small board to place under the jack. Carry a high-lift jack if you can, especially on more difficult trails. Test your jack before you leave home.

❏ Shovel and axe. Folding shovels work great.

❏ Tire chains for winter mountain travel. They can also help if you get stuck in the mud.

❏ CB radio and/or cellular phone.

❏ Portable toilet.

❏ If you have a winch, carry a tree strap, clevis, and snatch block.

Store these items in tote bags or large plastic containers so they can be easily loaded into your vehicle when it's time to go. Some things can be left in your vehicle all the time if you have room. Make sure you tie everything down thoroughly so it doesn't bounce around or shift.

Maintenance. Backroad travel puts your vehicle under greater stress than normal highway driving. Follow maintenance directions in your owner's manual for severe driving conditions. This usually calls for changing oil, oil filter, and air filter more frequently as well as more frequent fluid checks and lubrications. Inspect your tires carefully; they take a lot of extra abuse. After your trip, make sure you wash your vehicle. Use a high pressure spray to thoroughly clean the underside and wheel wells. Automatic car washes usually are not adequate. Do it yourself, if you want your vehicle in good shape for the next trip.

YOUR RESPONSIBILITIES AS A BACKCOUNTRY DRIVER

Make sure you know and follow backcountry, *Tread Lightly* guidelines. Consider joining the national *Tread Lightly* organization (see appendix for contact information). Although much damage is done by deliberate violators, some is done by well-intentioned, ignorant drivers.

Stay on the trail. This is the single most important rule of backcountry driving. Leaving the trail causes unnecessary erosion, kills vegetation, and spoils the beauty of the land. Scars remain for years. Don't widen the trail by driving around rocks and muddy spots and don't short cut switchbacks. When you have to pass another vehicle, do so at designated pull-overs. Sometimes the edge of the trail is defined by a line of rocks. Don't move the rocks or cross over them. Drivers who leave existing trails risk fines and cause trails to be closed. Practice diligently to leave no trace of your passage.

Wilderness Areas. It is a serious offense to drive in a designated wilderness. These areas are usually well marked and clearly shown on maps.

Private Property. Pass through private land quietly and stay on the road at all times. Don't disturb livestock. Leave gates the way you find them unless posted otherwise.

Ruins and archaeological sites. It is a federal crime to disturb archaeological sites. Don't touch them or climb inside. Do not remove or touch historical artifacts. Don't camp or picnic near an archaeological site. Call 1-800-VANDALS to report vandalism.

Cryptobiotic crust. The black jagged crust you see everywhere in the desert is called cryptobiotic crust. It forms a base for future plant growth and is nature's first step to controlling erosion and reclaiming the land. In its early stages, it's nearly invisible. It is extremely delicate and takes decades to form. Never walk, ride, or drive on it.

Pets. Pets are allowed in Grand Canyon National Park but they must be leashed at all times. They are not allowed below the rim. Organ Pipe National Monument allows leashed pets on a couple of hiking trails but nowhere in the backcountry. Pets are permitted in Kofa National Wildlife Refuge but they must be confined unless they are participating in a legal hunt. The more popular trails in Sedona require pets be kept on a leash. Other local regulations may apply across the state. No pet should ever be left in a hot, closed vehicle. Even outside a vehicle, Arizona's heat can be deadly. Under any circumstances make sure your pet has plenty of water. Generally it's best to leave pets at home.

Trash disposal and litter. Carry plastic trash bags and pack out your own trash, including cigarette butts. Where waste receptacles are provided, use them. When possible, clean up after others. Keep a litter bag handy and pick up trash along the trail.

When nature calls. The disposal of solid human waste and toilet paper is becoming a big problem as more visitors head into the backcountry. Arid climates do not decompose these materials as fast as they are being left behind. It is generally advisable to carry a portable toilet. Otherwise, keep a small shovel handy and bury feces 4 to 6 inches deep, away from trails, campsites and at least 300 feet from any water source, which includes dry washes. The best place is beneath a juniper or pinon pine tree where cryptobiotic crust does not form. Seal toilet paper and feminine hygiene products in a small plastic bag and discard with your trash.

Campfires. Regulations vary across the state and restrictions may apply when fire danger is high. Always use fire rings when they are provided. Try to build fires in spots where others have had a fire. Bring your own firewood whenever possible and know local regulations for firewood gathering. Thoroughly douse all campfires. Carry out fire debris with your trash. Consider using a propane camping stove instead of building a fire. Stoves are very convenient for cooking and are environmentally preferred.

Washing, cleaning, and bathing. If you must use soap, use biodegradable soap but never around lakes or streams. Heat water without using soap to clean utensils whenever possible.

GRAND CANYON NATIONAL PARK

The park is 277 miles long, one mile deep and 18 miles wide at the widest point. The North Rim is only 10 miles from the South Rim but the drive around is 215 miles. This explains why only 10% of the park's annual five million visitors make it to the North Rim. The South Rim is open all year; the North Rim is usually open mid-May to mid-October. Park entry fee is $20 per private vehicle and is good for seven days on both rims.

For general information, call 928-638-7888. Questions about hiking, backpacking and backroads should be directed to the main Backcountry Office in Grand Canyon Village. It is located in the Maswik Transportation Center and is open 8 a.m.-noon and 1-5 p.m. To speak with someone in person on the phone, call (928) 638-7875 between the hours of 1-5 p.m. Day hikers do not need a permit but a permit is required when you camp overnight. It takes time to get a permit, so obtain one by mail well in advance of your trip.

A *Trip Planner* for the Park will answer many of your questions. Write to: Trip Planner, P.O. Box 129, Grand Canyon, AZ 86023. Information is also available online at www.nps.gov/grca. Prices are higher in Tusayan and Grand Canyon Village, so stock up on supplies before you leave.

NATIONAL FOREST SERVICE
& BUREAU OF LAND MANAGEMENT

The National Forest Service and the Bureau of Land Management have offices across the state (see appendix for addresses and phone numbers). Maps and helpful information are available at most locations. You may obtain maps in person or via mail.

Staffs of both agencies work hard to protect our public lands so that all of us can enjoy them for generations to come. One of the most critical challenges facing both agencies is users straying from backcountry roads and trails. This results in ugly scars, spoils the scenery, kills vegetation and accelerates erosion. Please stay on established roads at all times and learn as much as possible about minimum impact practices.

ARIZONA STATE ASSOCIATION OF 4-WHEEL DRIVE CLUBS

This organization works hard to promote responsible four-wheeling and Tread Lightly practices across the state. Most clubs in Arizona belong to the state association. For information write to P.O. Box 23904, Tempe, AZ 85285 or call (602) 258-4294. A complete club listing and other information can be found on their Web site at www.asa4wdc.org.

BACKCOUNTRY DRIVING LESSONS

Trail Etiquette. A little common courtesy goes a long way in making everyone's travel in the backcountry more enjoyable. After all, we're all out to have fun. Take your time and be considerate of others. If you see someone approaching from behind, look for a wide spot on the trail, pull over and let him pass. Conversely, if you get behind a slowpoke, back off or look for a scenic spot to pull over for a while. Stretch your legs and take a few pictures. Slow down when approaching blind curves. Assume someone is coming around the corner. When you're out of your vehicle, pick a wide spot where you can pull over so others can get by. A horn is rarely needed in the backcountry. When one is heard, it's a foreign sound that disturbs people and wildlife. The same is true of a loud radio. When you see bikers, pull over and let them pass. Give them plenty of room. Exchange courtesies. Ask if they have enough water. Share some of yours if you have plenty. Many bikers underestimate their water requirements and are extremely grateful when you offer. Control your pets at all times. Don't let them bark or chase wildlife.

The basics. If you have never shifted into low range, grab your owner's manual now and start practicing. Read the rest of this book, then try some of the easy trails. Gradually you'll become more proficient and eventually you'll be ready to move up in difficulty.

Low and slow. Your vehicle was designed to go over rocky and bumpy terrain but only at slow speed. Get used to driving slowly in first gear low range. This will allow you to idle over obstacles without stalling. You don't need to shift back and forth constantly. Get into a low gear and stay there as much as possible so your engine can operate at high RPM and at maximum power. If you have a standard transmission, your goal should be to use your clutch as little as possible. As you encounter resistance on an obstacle or an uphill grade, just give it a little gas. As you start downhill, allow the engine's resistance to act as a brake. If the engine alone will not stop you from accelerating, then help a little with the brake. When you need more power but not more speed, press on the gas and feather the brake a little at the same time. This takes a little practice, but you will be amazed at the control you have. This technique works equally well with automatic transmissions.

Rocks and other high points. Never attempt to straddle a rock that is large enough to strike your differentials, transfer case or other low-hanging parts of your undercarriage. Instead, drive over the highest point with your tire, which is designed to take the abuse. This will lift your undercarriage over the obstacle. As you enter a rocky area, look ahead to determine where the high points are, then make every effort to cross them with your tires. Learn the low points of your undercarriage.

Using a spotter. Sometimes there are so many rocks you get confused.

In this case, have someone get out and guide you. They should stand at a safe distance in front, watching your tires and undercarriage. With hand signals, they can direct you left or right. If you are alone, don't be embarrassed to spot for yourself by getting in and out of your vehicle several times.

Those clunking sounds. Having made every attempt to avoid dragging bottom, you'll find it's not always possible. It is inevitable that a rock will contact your undercarriage eventually. The sound can be quite unnerving the first time it happens. If you are driving slowly and have proper skid plates, damage is unlikely. Look for a different line, back up and try again. If unsuccessful, see next paragraph.

Crossing large rocks. Sometimes a rock is too large to drive over or at such a steep angle your bumper hits the rock before your tire. Stack rocks on each side to form a ramp. Once over the obstacle, make sure you put the rocks back where you found them. The next driver to come along may prefer the challenge of crossing the rock in its more difficult state.

Getting high centered. You may drive over a large rock or into a rut, causing you to get lodged on the object. If this happens, don't panic. First ask your passengers to get out to see if less weight helps. Try rocking the vehicle. If this doesn't work, jack up your vehicle and place a few rocks under the tires so that when you let the jack down, you take the weight off the high point. Determine whether driving forward or reverse is best and try again. You may have to repeat this procedure several times if you are seriously high centered. Eventually you will learn what you can and cannot drive over.

Look in all directions. Unlike highway driving in which your primary need for attention is straight ahead, backcountry driving requires you to look in all directions. Objects can block your path from above, below, and from the sides. Trees fall, branches droop, and rocks slide, making the trail an ever-changing obstacle course.

Scout ahead. If you are on an unfamiliar trail and are concerned that the trail is becoming too difficult, get out of your vehicle and walk the trail ahead of you. This gives you an opportunity to pick an easy place to turn around before you get into trouble. If you have to turn around, back up or pull ahead until you find a wide flat spot. Don't try to turn in a narrow confined area. This can damage the trail and perhaps tip over your vehicle.

Anticipate. Shift into four-wheel drive or low range before it is needed. If you wait until it is needed, conditions might be too difficult, e.g., halfway up a hillside.

Blind curves. When approaching blind curves, always assume that there is a speeding vehicle coming from the opposite direction. This will prepare you for the worst. Be aware that many people drive on the wrong side of the road to stay away from the outer edge of a trail. Whenever possible, keep your windows open and your radio off so that you can hear an approaching vehicle. You can usually hear motorcycles and ATVs. Quiet

24

SUVs are the biggest problem. Collisions do occur, so be careful.

Driving uphill. Use extreme caution when attempting to climb a hill. The difficulty of hill climbing is often misjudged by the novice four-wheeler. You should have good tires, adequate power, and be shifted into four-wheel drive low. There are four factors that determine difficulty:

Length of the hill. If the hill is very long, it is less likely that momentum will carry you to the top. Short hills are easier.

Traction. Smooth rock is easier to climb than dirt.

Bumpiness. If the road surface undulates to the point where all four tires do not stay on the ground at the same time, you will have great difficulty climbing even a moderately steep hill.

Steepness. This can be difficult to judge, so examine a hill carefully before you attempt it. Walk up the hill if necessary to make sure it is not steeper at the top. If you are not absolutely sure you can climb a hill, don't attempt it. Practice on smaller hills first.

If you attempt a hill, approach it straight on and stay that way all the way to the top. Do not turn sideways or try to drive across the hill. Do not use excessive speed but keep moving at a steady pace. Make sure no one is coming up from the other side. Position a spotter at the top of the hill if necessary. Do not spin your tires because this can turn you sideways to the hill. If you feel you are coming to a stop due to lack of traction, turn your steering wheel back and forth quickly. This will give you additional grip. If you stall, use your brake and restart your engine. You may also have to use your emergency brake. If you start to slide backwards even with your brake on, you may have to ease up on the brake enough to regain steering control. Don't allow your wheels to lock up. If you don't make it to the top of the hill, shift into reverse and back down slowly in a straight line. Try the hill again but only if you think you learned enough to make a difference. As you approach the top of the hill, ease off the gas so you are in control before starting down the other side.

Driving downhill. Make sure you are in four-wheel drive. Examine the hill carefully and determine the best route that will allow you to go straight down the hill. Do not turn sideways. Use the lowest gears possible, allowing the engine's compression to hold you back. Do not ride the clutch. Feather the brakes slightly if additional slowing is needed. Do not allow the wheels to lock up. This will cause loss of steering and possibly cause you to slide sideways. The natural reaction when you begin to slide is to press harder on the brakes. Try to stay off the brakes. If you continue to slide despite these efforts, turn in the direction of the slide as you would on ice or snow and accelerate slightly. This will help maintain steering control.

Parking on a steep hill. Put your vehicle in reverse gear if pointing downhill and in forward gear if pointing uphill. For automatic transmissions, shift to park. Set your emergency brake hard and block your tires.

Tippy situations. No one can tell you how far your vehicle can safely lean. You must learn the limitations through practice. Remember that sport utility vehicles have a higher center of gravity and are less stable than a passenger car. However, don't get paranoid. Your vehicle will likely lean a lot more than you think. Drive slowly to avoid bouncing over. A good way to learn is to watch an experienced driver with a vehicle similar to yours. This is an advantage to traveling with a group. Once you see how far other vehicles can lean, you will become more comfortable in these situations. Remember, too, that you're likely to slide sideways before you tip over. This can be just as dangerous in certain situations. Use extreme caution if the road surface is slippery from loose gravel, mud, or wet clay. Turn around if necessary.

Crossing streams and water holes. You must know the high water point of your vehicle before entering any body of water. Several factors can determine this point, including the height of the air intake and the location of the computer module (newer vehicles). Water sucked into the air intake is a very serious matter. If you don't know where these items are located, check with your dealer or a good four-wheel drive shop. A low fan can throw water on the engine and cause it to stall. You may have to disconnect your fan belt. Water can be sucked into your differentials so check them regularly after crossing deep streams.

After you understand your vehicle's capabilities, you must assess the stream conditions. First determine the depth of the water. If you are with a group, let the most experienced driver cross first. Follow his line if he is successful. If you are alone, you might wait for someone else to come along. Sometimes you can use a long stick to check the depth of small streams or water holes. Check for deep holes, large obstacles, and muddy sections. If you can't determine the water depth, don't cross. A winch line or long tow strap can be used as a safety line to pull someone back if he gets into trouble, but it must be attached before entering the water. It must also be long enough for him to reach shallow water on the other side. Once in the water, drive slowly but steadily. This creates a small wake which helps form an air pocket around the engine. I've seen people put a piece of cardboard or canvas over the front of their vehicle to enhance the wake affect. This only works if you keep moving. After exiting a stream, test your brakes. You may have to ride them lightly for a short distance until they dry out. Always cross streams at designated water crossings. Don't drive in the direction of the stream. Try to minimize disruption of the water habitat.

Mud. Don't make new mud holes or enlarge existing ones. Stay home if you have reason to believe the trail will be too wet. Some trails, however, have permanent mud holes that you must cross. Mud can build up suction around your tires and be very difficult to get through. Always check a mud hole carefully to see how deep it is. Take a stick and poke around. Check the other side. If there are no tracks coming out, don't go in. If you decide to cross, keep moving at a steady pace and, if necessary, turn the steering wheel back and forth quickly for additional traction. If you get stuck, dig around the tires to break the suction and place anything hard under the tires for traction. It may be necessary to back out. If you are with a friend, and you are doubtful if you can get through without help, attach a tow strap before you enter so that you can be pulled back. But beware, sometimes the mud can be so bad, even a friend can't pull you out. Your only protection against this happening is to use your head and not go in the mud in the first place. When I've seen people stuck this badly, it is usually due to a total disregard for the obvious. If you can't get though the mud, search for an alternate route but don't widen the trail. If there is no alternate route, turn around.

Ruts. If you get stuck in a rut and have no one to pull you out, dig a small trench from the rut to the right or left at a 45-degree angle. The dirt you remove from this trench should be used to fill the rut ahead of the turning point. If both tires are in parallel ruts, make sure the trenches are parallel. Drive out following the new rut. Repair any damage after you get out.

Gullies or washouts. If you are running parallel to a washed-out section of the trail, straddle it. If it becomes too large to straddle, drive down the middle. The goal is to center your vehicle so you remain as level as possible. This may require that you drive on the outer edges of your tires, so drive slowly and watch for any sharp objects. If you begin to tilt too far in one direction, turn in the direction of the tilt until you level out again. Sometimes it helps to have a spotter. To cross a gully from one side to the other, approach at a 45-degree angle and let each tire walk over independently.

Ravines. Crossing a ravine is similar to crossing a gully. Approach on an angle and let each tire go through independently. If the ravine is large with steep sides, you may not be able to cross at an angle because it could cause a rollover. If you don't cross at an angle, two things can happen. You will drag the front or rear of your vehicle, or you will high center on the edge of the ravine. If this is the case, ask yourself if you really need to cross the ravine. If you must cross, your only solution is to stack rocks to lift the vehicle at critical points.

Sand. Dry sand is more difficult than wet sand (unless it's quicksand). In either case, keep moving so that your momentum helps carry you through. Stay in a higher gear and use a little extra power but don't use excessive power and spin your tires. If necessary, turn your steering wheel back and forth quickly to give your tires a fresh grip. Airing down your tires is often necessary. Experiment with different tire pressures. Make sure you have a way to air up after you get through the sand. If you do get stuck, wet the sand in front of your tires. Try rocking the vehicle. If necessary, use your floor mats under the tires.

Washboard roads. Washboard roads are a natural part of backcountry travel. Vibration from these roads can be annoying. It is a problem for everybody so don't think there is something wrong with your vehicle. Experiment with different speeds to find the smoothest ride. Slowing down is usually best, but some conditions may be improved by speeding up a little. Be careful around curves where you could lose traction and slide. Check your tires to make sure they are not overinflated.

Airing down. There may be times when you need to let air out of your tires to get more traction or improve your ride, e.g., when driving through sand, going up a steep hill, or driving on washboard roads. It is usually safe to let air out of your tires until they bulge slightly, provided you are not traveling at high speed. If you let out too much air, your tires may come off the rims, or the sidewalls may become vulnerable to damage by sharp objects. Consider how or where you will reinflate. A small air pump that plugs into your cigarette lighter is handy for this purpose. Airing down on hard-core trails is essential. I've seen some wheelers with larger tires air down to as little as 3-5 lbs. A typical SUV can usually be aired down to 18 to 20 lbs. without noticeable handling difficulties at low speeds.

Winching. Next to tow points and skid plates, a winch is one of the best investments you can make. If you drive more difficult trails and you don't have a winch, travel with someone who does. I've known some hard-core wheelers who have gone for years without owning a winch but they always travel with a group. If you never intend to buy a winch, carry a high-lift jack or come-along. Although these tools are slow and inconvenient, when used in place of a winch, they can get you out of difficulty when there is no other way.

If you own a winch, make sure you also have these five basic winch accessories:

1. Heavy-duty work gloves.

2. A tree strap—looks like a tow strap but is shorter. It has a loop on each end.

3. A snatch block—a pulley that opens on the side so you can slip it over your winch cable.

4. A clevis—a heavy U-shaped device with a pin that screws across one end. This enables you to connect straps together and to your vehicle. It has many other uses.

5. A heavy-duty chain with grab hooks to wrap around rocks. It's also handy when trying to pull another vehicle that does not have tow points.

Winching tips:

• Your winch cable should be lined up straight with the pulling vehicle. If you can't pull straight, attach a snatch block to a large tree or rock to form an angle. This technique also works for pulling a fallen tree off the trail.

• If your winch cable bunches up at one end of the spool but there's still room for the cable, let it go and rewind the cable later.

• When winching from trees, attach to the largest tree possible using your tree strap and clevis. If no tree is large enough, wrap several smaller trees. The strap should be put as low as possible on the tree. Finding a decent size tree in the desert may be impossible.

• Keep your engine running while winching to provide maximum electrical power to the battery.

• Help the winch by driving the stuck vehicle slowly (except in quicksand). Be in the lowest gear possible and go as slowly as possible without spinning your tires. Don't allow slack in the winch cable. This can start a jerking motion that could break the cable.

• If there is not enough power to pull the stuck vehicle, attach a snatch block to the stuck vehicle and double the winch cable back to the starting point. This block-and-tackle technique will double your pulling power.

• Set the emergency brake on the anchor vehicle and block the wheels if necessary. In some cases, you may have to connect the anchor vehicle to another vehicle or tree.

• Throw a blanket or heavy coat over the winch cable while pulling. This will slow the end of the winch cable if it breaks and snaps back.

• Make sure there are at least 5 wraps of the winch cable left on the spool.

• Never hook the winch cable to itself. Use a tree strap and clevis. Never allow the winch cable to kink. This creates a weak spot in the cable.

• If tow points are not available on the stuck vehicle, attach to the vehicle's frame not the bumper. Use your large chain to wrap around the frame. If you are helping a stranger, make sure he understands that you are not responsible for damage to his vehicle.

• Never straddle or stand close to the winch cable while it is under stress.

• If you are stuck alone with no place to attach your winch cable, bury your spare tire in the ground as an anchor point. When you are finished, repair any damage to the ground.

• When finished winching, don't let the end of the cable wind into the spool. It can become jammed and damage your winch. Attach the hook to some other part of your vehicle like a tow point.

FINAL COMMENTS

I've made every effort to make this book as accurate and as easy to use as possible. If you have ideas for improvements or find any significant errors, please write to me at FunTreks, Inc., P.O. Box 49187, Colorado Springs, CO 80949-9187. Or, send e-mail to: *funtreks@pcisys.net*. Whether you're a novice or expert, I hope this book makes your backcountry experience safer, easier, and more fun.

Map Legend

Interstate

Paved Road*

Easy Trail*

Moderate Trail*

Difficult Trail*

Other Road*

Described in text

Hiking Trail

Boundaries
& Divides

Cliff, Canyon

Railroad

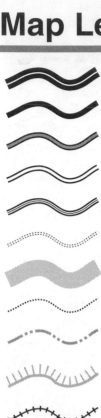 Mountain Peak

MT. PEALE

Lake

Map Orientation

Interstate (25)

U.S. Highway (50)

State & County
Road (35)

Forest Service
Road (586)

Starting point
of trail (Start here)

These items repeated on each map for your convenience. See Mini Key.

 Public Toilet

 Gas

 Parking

 Picnic Area

 Camping Area

 Mine

 Hiking Trailhead

 Mountain Biking

 Cabin

 Water Crossing

 Bridge

 Fishing

 ATVs, Dirt bikes

 Scenic Point

 Windmill

 Ghost town

 Archaeological
Site, Ruin

 Major Obstacle

GPS Waypoint

**Scale indicated
by grid**

**Scale is different
for each map;
check grid size at
bottom of map.**

THE TRAILS

Steep descent into the Bob Miller Extension on Sleeping Princess (Trail #7), rated difficult.

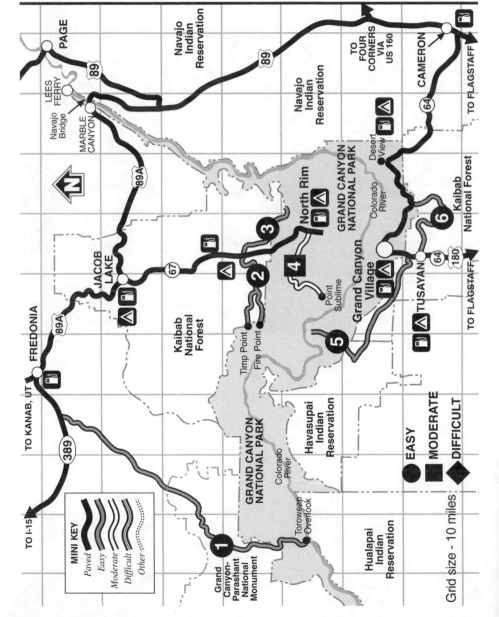

AREA 1

Grand Canyon National Park, Tusayan

1. Toroweap Overlook
2. Fire Point, Timp Point
3. Saddle Mountain Road
4. Point Sublime
5. South Bass Trailhead
6. Grandview Lookout

MINI KEY

Paved
Easy
Moderate
Difficult
Other

● EASY
■ MODERATE
◆ DIFFICULT

Grid size - 10 miles

TO I-15

TO KANAB, UT

FREDONIA

389

89A

JACOB LAKE

67

Kaibab National Forest

GRAND CANYON NATIONAL PARK

Grand Canyon-Parashant National Monument

Toroweap Overlook

Colorado River

Havasupai Indian Reservation

Hualapai Indian Reservation

Timp Point
Fire Point

Point Sublime

North Rim

Grand Canyon Village

TUSAYAN

64   180

TO FLAGSTAFF

64

Kaibab National Forest

6

Desert View

Colorado River

GRAND CANYON NATIONAL PARK

TO FOUR CORNERS VIA US 160

CAMERON

89

Navajo Indian Reservation

Navajo Indian Reservation

89A

N

MARBLE CANYON

Navajo Bridge

LEES FERRY

89

PAGE

Navajo Indian Reservation

TO FLAGSTAFF

1
2
3
4
5

32

Grand Canyon National Park, Tusayan

At first glance, one might assume there are few quiet backroads to explore in and around Grand Canyon National Park; after all, it's one of the world's most popular national parks. With as many as five million visitors a year, could there possibly be anywhere to go without fighting crowds of people? Surprisingly, the answer is yes. Most people visit just a small portion of the park near Grand Canyon Village and ignore the park's massive border that has many more outstanding viewpoints. They don't realize that much of the park is accessible through Kaibab National Forest which shares a common border on both the south and north rims. The forest provides hassle-free camping, quiet picnic areas and, best of all, an opportunity to see the park in solitude. Of course, you'll want to visit the main areas of the park first to see all of its famous viewpoints. After that, you can escape the hustle and bustle by exploring the backroads explained on the following pages. Obviously, this will take a little more time and preparation, especially if you visit what I think is the best of all viewpoints in the park—*Toroweap Overlook*.

Looking west from Toroweap Overlook at Lava Falls and the Colorado River.

Side trip to Lava Falls.

WARNING
PRIMITIVE / UNIMPROVED ROAD
TRAVEL AT OWN RISK
NO SERVICES BEYOND THIS POINT

The Colorado River—3,000 feet below the overlook.

Take heed, you are on your own.

This campsite, on the edge of the overlook, is one of eleven. Use caution next to the edge.

Toroweap Overlook ①

Location: Southwest of Fredonia on the north rim of the Grand Canyon. Toroweap Overlook is located in a broader area called Tuweep. The names Toroweap and Tuweep are often used interchangeably.

Difficulty: Easy. A wide gravel road most of the way, suitable for passenger cars in good weather. The road is susceptible to flash floods and wash-outs. To travel at the posted speed of 45 mph, you may wish to air down your tires for comfort on the washboard surface. Use caution when approaching blind curves. In places, deep arroyos have cut into the edge of the road and are often camouflaged by thick brush. There are sheer vertical walls 10 to 15 feet high right next to the road. Several serious rollover accidents have occurred in an area just south of the turn for Mt. Trumbull. The road gradually narrows and becomes rockier as you approach the camping area. Some campsites can only be reached with high-clearance vehicles. The side road to Lava Falls also requires high clearance and is deeply rutted where it crosses a soft, dry lake bed. Avoid this road when wet.

      SPECIAL CAUTION: This area is extremely remote with no services. Make sure your vehicle is in good shape. Carry plenty of water, food and spare parts. Travel with another vehicle if possible.

      For general questions, call 928-638-7644. For specific questions, you can leave a message for the Tuweep Ranger at 928-638-7805. It may take a while for him to return your call.

Features: The 3,000 feet vertical drop at Toroweap Overlook is breathtaking. You can hike above the rim and camp in designated campsites without a fee or permit. All sites are primitive with picnic tables and pit toilets and are available on a first-come, first-served basis. There are two prime camping spots at the overlook and nine more about a mile inland. You can't go wrong with any of the campsites which are nestled in a beautiful redrock setting. Finding a campsite is easier during the week than weekends. When I was there on Sept. 10, only two of the sites were occupied. It can get crowded on big holiday weekends like Memorial Day.

      The hiking route at Lava Falls goes to the bottom of the Grand Canyon and is suited for experts only. It is hard to find, extremely steep, and very dangerous. Portions of the route are nearly vertical. You'll need a permit if you camp overnight in the backcountry.

Time & Distance: Allow 2 to 3 hours one-way to reach the overlook from Highway 389. RVs and camping trailers are not recommended although some high clearance pop-up campers can make it. You'll want to allow a full day to explore the area.

To Get There: From the intersection of Highways 89A and 389 in Fredonia, drive west 8.4 miles on Highway 389. Watch for a parking area and wide gravel road on the left 0.7 miles past mile post 25. You won't see a sign until after you turn. You can also reach Toroweap Overlook from St. George, UT on BLM Roads #1069 and #5. I did not drive this route myself but G.C.N.P. brochures say it is the most scenic route. It may be impassable in the winter due to snow on Mt. Trumbull.

Trail Description: Reset your odometer when you turn left off 389 [01]. The gravel road is very wide and straight. You'll soon pass a large warning sign pictured on the preceding photo page. Read it carefully and realize you are entering a remote area. Ignore all lesser side roads; the main road is obvious. At 23.0 miles [02] continue straight where Hack Canyon goes left. At 27.6 continue straight again as other roads go right and left. The road from Colorado City joins on the right at 40.3 miles [03]. Bear left at 46.6 miles [04]. A right turn here would take you to Mt. Trumbull.

You'll pass an air strip on the right before entering Grand Canyon National Park at 53.5 miles. The Tuweep Ranger Station is on the left at 54.1 miles [05]. The ranger on duty was very helpful. Pick up a brochure on the area if no one is around.

A side road to Lava Falls goes right at 57.6 miles [06]. You can come back later to explore this road. Continue straight following signs through the area to Toroweap Overlook at 60.3 miles [07]. Here you'll see two campsites and a portable toilet. Backtrack for the other campsites and hiking trails.

Return Trip: Return the way you came or try one of the alternate routes mentioned earlier. One returns to St. George, UT, the other to Colorado City, AZ. Both of these routes are more susceptible to road damage after heavy rains.

Services: Toilets at campground. There is an emergency telephone at the Ranger Station. Otherwise, return to Fredonia.

Historical Highlights: Tuweep became part of the Grand Canyon National Monument in 1932. The monument was declared a national park in 1975. Tuweep ranger John Riffey spent 38 years looking after this area. He became somewhat of a local legend with his airplane "Pogo." He is buried south of the ranger station.

Maps: BLM Arizona Strip Visitor Map and USGS 250,000 scale map of the Grand Canyon, Arizona Atlas & Gazetteer.

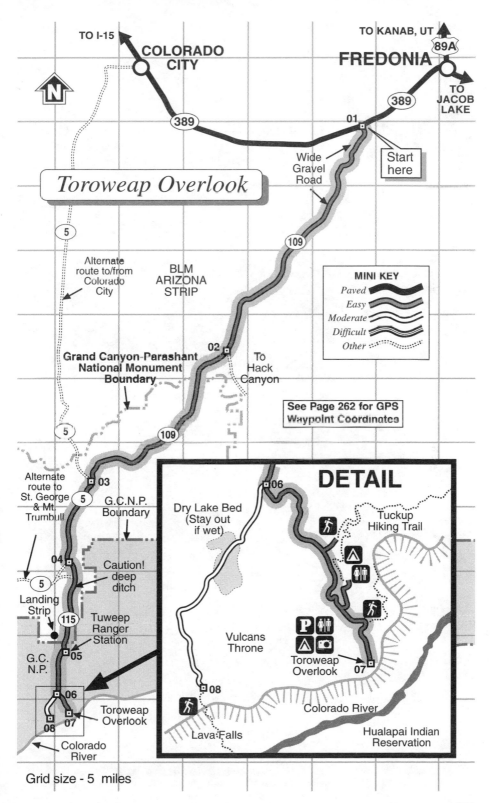

TO I-15

COLORADO CITY

TO KANAB, UT

FREDONIA

89A

TO JACOB LAKE

N

389

389

01

Wide Gravel Road

Start here

Toroweap Overlook

109

5

Alternate route to/from Colorado City

BLM ARIZONA STRIP

MINI KEY
Paved
Easy
Moderate
Difficult
Other

Grand Canyon-Parashant National Monument Boundary

02

To Hack Canyon

See Page 262 for GPS Waypoint Coordinates

109

5

Alternate route to St. George & Mt. Trumbull

03

5

G.C.N.P. Boundary

04

5

Caution! deep ditch

Landing Strip

115

Tuweep Ranger Station

G.C. N.P.

05

06

07

Toroweap Overlook

08

Colorado River

DETAIL

06

Dry Lake Bed (Stay out if wet)

Tuckup Hiking Trail

Vulcans Throne

P

Toroweap Overlook

07

08

Lava Falls

Colorado River

Hualapai Indian Reservation

Grid size - 5 miles

37

Grand Canyon as seen from Fire Point.

The last section to Fire Point looks like this when it's dry. Stay out when wet.

This is a fun area for ATVs. Make sure you stay out of posted areas, meadows and wet areas.

Fire Point, Timp Point ②

Location: In the North Kaibab National Forest north of Grand Canyon National Park. South of Jacob Lake on the west side of Hwy. 67.

Difficulty: Easy. The main forest roads that run east to west, including those to Fire and Timp Points, are well-maintained gravel roads suitable for high-clearance passenger cars. These roads tend to follow ridge lines and are fairly flat. Roads that run north to south like F.S. 609 and F.S. 250 are narrower with steeper grades. The Forest Service recommends four-wheel drive on these roads but I found high ground-clearance two-wheel drive adequate during good weather. The last section of road to Fire Point is in Grand Canyon National Park. This road is not maintained and is deeply rutted. Don't drive this road when the ground is wet.

Features: The Kaibab National Forest offers great views of the Grand Canyon in a quiet, remote setting. Camp anywhere within the forest boundaries without a fee. You're not restricted to developed campgrounds, although those are available too. Just make sure you practice "leave-no-trace" camping ethics. Use great caution when driving at night; deer are virtually everywhere. For more information on the Kaibab Forest, stop in at the Visitor Center in Jacob Lake or the North Kaibab Ranger Station in Fredonia.

Time & Distance: The basic route as decribed here is about 41.7 miles. Allow a relaxing 3 to 4 hours after leaving Highway 67. It's a lot more fun to pack a picnic lunch and spend a full day exploring. Better yet, take your camping gear and spend a weekend or more. That way you can see many more viewpoints and perhaps do some hiking. Remember, if you hike into Grand Canyon National Park, you'll need a permit to camp overnignt in the backcountry.

To Get There: Take Highway 67 south from Jacob Lake about 27 miles. When you reach the De Motte F.S. Campground, continue another 0.7 miles to F.S. Road 22 on the right.

Trail Description: Reset your odometer when you turn right off Hwy. 67 [01]. Follow F.S. 22 up the hill 2.1 miles and bear left onto F.S. 270 (not marked) following signs to Fire Point [02]. Bear left at 3.0 miles at a posted snowmobile area. Continue straight at 3.2 where F.S. 222 goes right [03]. At 4.4 miles [04] bear right on F.S. 223 (not marked). You'll stay on 223 all the way to

Fire Point. Stay left at 5.1 miles where 239 goes right.

At 10.3 miles [05] continue straight past unmarked F.S. 268B on the left. *(Note: This is an alternate way to reach Point Sublime, Trail #4 inside Grand Canyon National Park.)* Continue straight at 11.1 miles [06] where F.S. 609 goes right. You'll come back to this point later. As you continue, the road narrows to one lane and muddy conditions are possible in wet weather. Some very low clearance passenger cars may have a problem. At 16.6 a cattle guard marks the boundary to Grand Canyon National Park. From this point, the road becomes very rutted and high clearance is recommended (see photo). Fire Point is reached in just another mile [07]. Under wet conditions, this portion can be hiked.

After visiting Fire Point, return 6.5 miles to F.S. 609. *Reset your odometer.* Turn left and follow narrower 609 as it drops into a valley and cuts over to F.S. 271. Forest Service maps do not show this road going all the way through, but it does. High clearance is recommended on the road. At 0.7 bear left at a junction with 206. Turn left when you reach F.S. 271 at 3.8 miles [08]. As you begin heading west, you'll immediatlely see F.S. 250 on the right. This is an interesting north/south route that takes you to other viewpoints. As you continue west on 271 stay left at 5.0 miles where 271A goes to North Timp Point. Timp Point is reached at 7.9 miles [09].

Return Trip: *Reset your odometer* at Timp Point [09] and follow 271 back to where you joined it at F.S. 609 [08]. From this point, continue east on 271 until it intersects with F.S. 206 [10] at 8.1 miles. Turn right and follow 222 back to 270 at 13.1 miles [03]. Turn left to F.S. 22 then take a right back to Highway 67.

Services: There is a small general store with gas and a phone on Hwy. 67 just north of De Motte Campground. Otherwise, head north to Jacob Lake or south to Grand Canyon National Park North Rim Visitor Center.

Maps: Kaibab National Forest North Ranger District, USGS 100,000 scale Grand Canyon, AZ #36112-A1-TM-100, Arizona Atlas & Gazetteer.

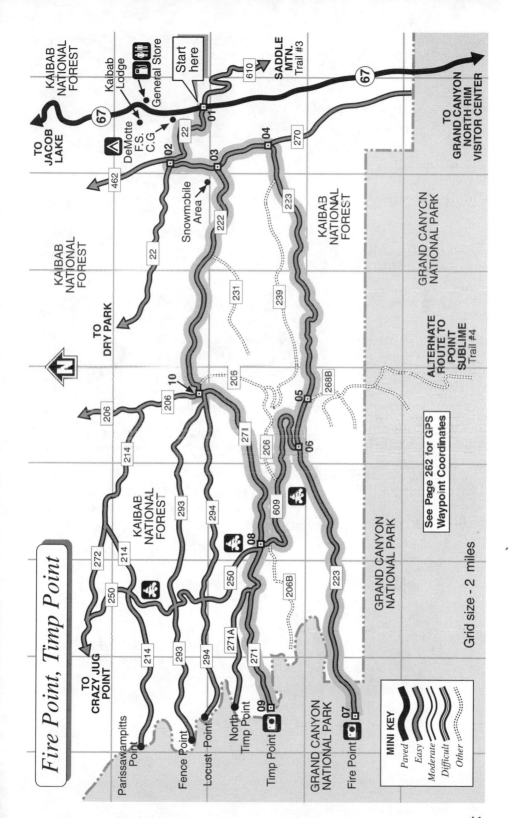

Fire Point, Timp Point

MINI KEY
Paved
Easy
Moderate
Difficult
Other

Grid size - 2 miles

See Page 262 for GPS Waypoint Coordinates

TO JACOB LAKE
TO DRY PARK
TO CRAZY JUG POINT

KAIBAB NATIONAL FOREST

Start here

Kaibab Lodge
DeMotte F.S. C.G.
General Store

SADDLE MTN. Trail #3

TO GRAND CANYON NORTH RIM VISITOR CENTER

GRAND CANYCN NATIONAL PARK

ALTERNATE ROUTE TO POINT SUBLIME Trail #4

Snowmobile Area

Parissawampitts Point
Fence Point
Locust Point
North Timp Point
Timp Point

GRAND CANYON NATIONAL PARK

Fire Point

N

67
610
01
22
02
462
22
03
222
04
270
223
231
239
206
10
206
206
214
271
206
05
268B
06
293
294
609
08
250
271A
271
250
293
294
214
272
214
09
07
223
206B

The road gets narrower than this.

The view at the end of Saddle Mountain Road.

Deer sightings were frequent.

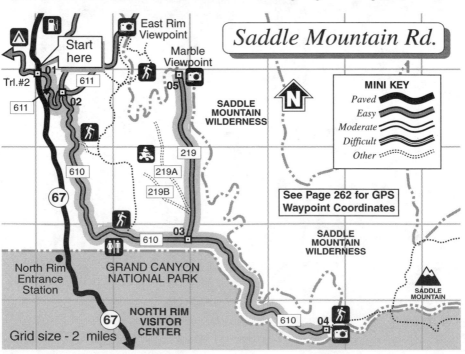

East Rim Viewpoint

Start here

Marble Viewpoint

Trl.#2

611

611

01

02

05

Saddle Mountain Rd.

N

SADDLE MOUNTAIN WILDERNESS

MINI KEY

Paved
Easy
Moderate
Difficult
Other

219

219A

219B

610

See Page 262 for GPS Waypoint Coordinates

610

03

SADDLE MOUNTAIN WILDERNESS

67

North Rim Entrance Station

GRAND CANYON NATIONAL PARK

SADDLE MOUNTAIN

610

04

67

NORTH RIM VISITOR CENTER

Grid size - 2 miles

Saddle Mountain Road ③

Location: In the North Kaibab National Forest north of Grand Canyon National Park. South of Jacob Lake on the east side of Hwy. 67.

Difficulty: Easy. Well-graded gravel suitable for passenger cars.

Features: A short pleasant drive to a great overlook of the Grand Canyon with side trips to other viewpoints of the Saddle Mountain Wilderness. Great hiking trails including Saddle Mountain Trail which connects to Nankoweap Trail into the Grand Canyon. *Note: This area is closed to all vehicles in the winter between December 15 and April 15.*

Time & Distance: 13.6 miles one way. Takes less than an hour. The side trip to Marble Viewpoint adds another eight miles round trip and takes about a half hour. Allow 2 to 3 hours altogether.

To Get There: Take Highway 67 south from Jacob Lake about 27 miles. When you reach the De Motte F.S. Campground, continue another 0.7 miles to F.S. Road 611 on the left.

Trail Description: Reset your odometer at Hwy. 67 [01]. Head southeast on F.S. 611 until it intersects with 610 at 1.4 miles [02]. Turn right. There's a vault toilet on the right at 6.2 miles. At 8.1 miles [03] F.S. 219 goes left to Marble Viewpoint. Continue straight to the end of Saddle Mountain Road reached at 13.6 miles [04]. There's a loop to turn around at the end of the road and a sign for the Nankoweap Hiking Trail. Late in the day, I saw many deer on the side trip to Marble Viewpoint [05].

Return Trip: Return the way you came.

Services: There is a small general store with gas and a phone on Hwy. 67 just north of De Motte Campground. Otherwise, head north to Jacob Lake or south to Grand Canyon National Park North Rim Visitor Center.

Maps: Kaibab National Forest North Ranger District, USGS 100,000 scale map, Grand Canyon, AZ #36112-A1-TM-100, Arizona Atlas & Gazetteer.

Off Highway Vehicle Use: Except where posted, the North Kaibab National Forest allows motorized vehicle use on and off road as long as no damage is done to the land. The corridor along each side of Hwy. 67 is off-limits.

As the sun sets the moon rises over Point Sublime.

Steep & rocky in places.

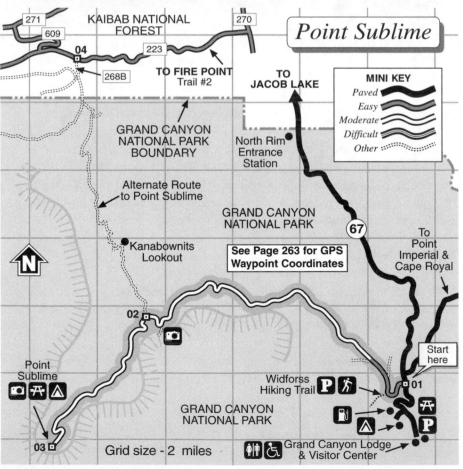

Point Sublime

KAIBAB NATIONAL FOREST

271
609
270
04
223
268B

TO FIRE POINT
Trail #2

TO JACOB LAKE

MINI KEY
Paved
Easy
Moderate
Difficult
Other

GRAND CANYON NATIONAL PARK BOUNDARY

North Rim Entrance Station

Alternate Route to Point Sublime

GRAND CANYON NATIONAL PARK

67

To Point Imperial & Cape Royal

Kanabownits Lookout

See Page 263 for GPS Waypoint Coordinates

02

N

Point Sublime

Start here

01

Widforss Hiking Trail

P

GRAND CANYON NATIONAL PARK

P

03

Grid size - 2 miles

Grand Canyon Lodge & Visitor Center

44

Point Sublime 4

Location: South of Jacob Lake inside Grand Canyon National Park and west of the North Rim Visitor Center.

Difficulty: Moderate. This trail offers a variety of terrain including sand, rock and mud. Several of the rocky places are steep and narrow but stock SUVs with four-wheel drive and high clearance will not have a problem.

Features: Although not well publicized by the park, this is a fun backroad and offers surprising challenge for adventure-seeking SUV owners. The view from Point Sublime is truly outstanding. Picnic tables are provided and overnight camping is allowed with a permit.

Time & Distance: 18 miles one way. Allow 3 to 4 hours for the round trip.

To Get There: Take Highway 67 south from Jacob Lake to Grand Canyon National Park North Rim Area. Enter the park (fee required) and continue south about 11 miles. After you pass the road to Cape Royal on the left, watch for a dirt road on the right to Widforss Hiking Trail.

Trail Description: *Reset your odometer at Hwy. 67* [01]. Continue west past a parking area for the Widforss Hiking Trail then turn left at a large fork at 0.9 miles. At 2.1 miles bear right at another fork. Bear right again at a small side road to an overlook at 11.3. Bear left at a T at 11.9 miles [02]. (*Note: This is where the alternate route from Kaibab National Forest joins the trail. It is possible that the first part of the route described here may be closed in the future but vehicles would still be allowed to reach Point Sublime via the alternate route. See directions to Fire Point & Timp Point Trail #2 to find the start of the alternate route.*) After turning left at the T, continue until reaching Point Sublime at 17.9 miles [03].

Return Trip: Return the way you came or try the alternate route. (I did not drive the alternate route. Although unlikely, it could be more difficult than the route described here. Travel at your own risk.)

Services: There's a store and gas station on the right if you continue south on Hwy. 67 to the Visitor Center.

Maps: Kaibab National Forest North Ranger District, USGS 100,000 scale Grand Canyon, AZ #36112-A1-TM-100, Arizona Atlas & Gazetteer.

View from South Bass Trailhead. This hiking trail is for serious hikers only.

Mud can be a problem after a rainy period.

The last part of the trip is very rutted.

Historic Pasture Wash Ranger Station is unmanned. Located 3.6 miles before the trailhead.

South Bass Trailhead ⑤

Location: Northwest of Grand Canyon Village and Tusayan.

Difficulty: Easy. When dry, this road is fairly easy to negotiate with a high-clearance, two-wheel-drive vehicle. After heavy rains, the road may be impassable even with four-wheel drive. The worst section is across Pasture Wash before and after the ranger station. Help is a long way away so don't take any chances.

Features: This trip probably isn't practical if you just want to sightsee for an afternoon. People who come here are usually serious backpackers who plan to spend a while in the Grand Canyon. It's a long drive through remote country. In addition, the Havasupai Indian Reservation charges a not-so-insignificant $25 per vehicle to cross its land. Be prepared to pay cash either at the entry gate or anywhere along the route inside the reservation. Someday a route may be established that does not require crossing the reservation. Check with the Grand Canyon Backcountry Office for changes in the status of this trail. If you plan to camp overnight inside Grand Canyon National Park, you'll need a permit from the Backcountry Office. Fortunately, the majority of this trip is in Kaibab National Forest where dispersed camping is allowed and no permit is required. You cannot camp within 1/4 mile of major highways or watering tanks. **ATVs are allowed in Kaibab National Forest but not in Grand Canyon National Park**.

Time & Distance: It's almost 30 miles one way from Tusayan to South Bass Trailhead. Allow at least 4 hours driving time for the round trip.

To Get There: Take U.S. Hwy. 180 north from Flagstaff or State Hwy. 64 north from Williams to the town of Tusayan just south of the entrance to Grand Canyon National Park's South Rim. On the north side of Tusayan, turn left at the Moqui Lodge. This turn is almost across the street from the Kaibab National Forest Tusayan Ranger Station. You can also reach F.S. 328 from the Backcountry Office in Grand Canyon Village.

Trail Description: *Reset your odometer when you turn west off Hwy. 64* [01]. Drive along the south end of the Moqui Lodge and make an immediate left onto F.S. 328. This road heads south briefly before turning west. There are many side roads but the main route is obvious. At 4.9 miles, the alternate entry point from the Grand Canyon Backcountry Office joins on the right [02]. Continue west on 328 but immediately bear right at the next fork before crossing a set of railroad tracks. F.S. 328 is well-marked as many side roads branch off.

You'll stay in the forest for a while, but eventually it opens up. Bear left at a fork at 14.9 miles [03]. You'll pass several tanks including Homestead Tank and Sheep Tank. Watch for mudholes along the way. At 20.4 miles bear slightly left through Cecil Dodd Tank. Vehicles often get stuck here in the mud. You enter the Havasupai Indian Reservation when you cross a cattle guard at 20.8 miles. F.S. 838 goes right at this point. (It does not go all the way through to G.C.N.P.). As you continue west on 328, you'll soon come to a closed, unlocked gate. A Havasu Ranger may charge you the $25 entry fee at this point or he may stop you later. If no one is present, pass through and close the gate. You are not allowed to picnic or camp inside the reservation.

At 22.6 miles bear right at a fork in an open area before reaching a 4-way intersection marked by a couple of large posts at 22.7 [04]. Turn right and head north through Pasture Wash. This is the worst part of the trip. It could be impassable if wet. You'll pass through the National Forest again before entering G.C.N.P. Read and follow all posted regulations. At 26.1 miles swing right past the Pasture Wash Ranger Station. The road eventually narrows through tight brush before reaching the trailhead at 29.7 miles [05].

To reach F.S.328 from the Backcountry Office in Grand Canyon Village: *Reset your odometer in the Backcountry Office parking lot.* Bear left out of the parking lot. Turn left at the 4-way stop, cross the railroad tracks and follow signs to the kennels. You'll end up heading south on Rowe Well Road. After passing the kennels on the left, the pavement ends. Bear left at 2.9 miles before leaving the park. At 4.3 miles turn left uphill and cross the railroad tracks again. Turn right when you reach 328 at 4.9 miles [02] and follow the original directions.

Return Trip: Return the way you came.

Services: None anywhere along the trail. Return to Tusayan or Grand Canyon Village.

Maps: Kaibab National Forest, Tusayan, Williams and Chalender Ranger Districts, USGS 100,000 scale Grand Canyon, AZ #36112-A1-TM-100, Arizona Atlas & Gazetteer.

South Bass Trailhead

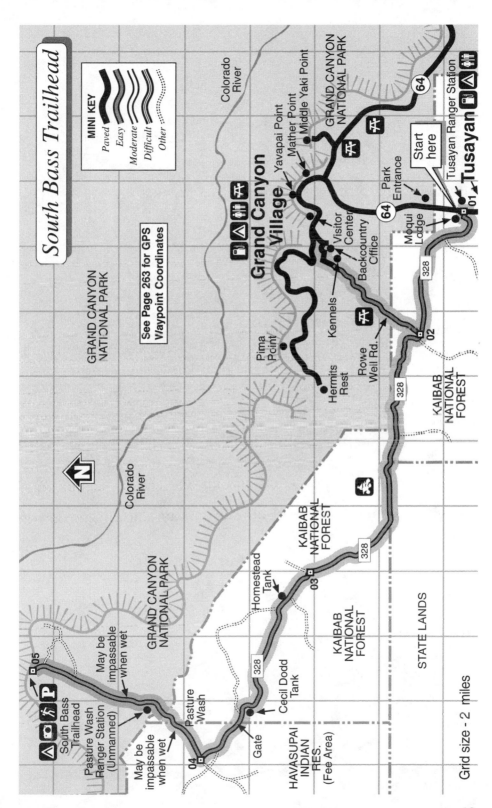

MINI KEY

- Paved
- Easy
- Moderate
- Difficult
- Other

See Page 263 for GPS Waypoint Coordinates

GRAND CANYON NATIONAL PARK

Colorado River

GRAND CANYON NATIONAL PARK

Grand Canyon Village

Yavapai Point
Mather Point
Middle Yaki Point

Visitor Center

Backcountry Office

Kennels

Pima Point

Hermits Rest

Rowe Well Rd.

Moqui Lodge

Park Entrance

64

328

Start here

01

Tusayan Ranger Station

Tusayan

02

KAIBAB NATIONAL FOREST

328

KAIBAB NATIONAL FOREST

328

03

Homestead Tank

KAIBAB NATIONAL FOREST

STATE LANDS

328

Cecil Dodd Tank

Gate

04

Pasture Wash

HAVASUPAI INDIAN RES. (Fee Area)

May be impassable when wet

South Bass Trailhead

Pasture Wash Ranger Station (Unmanned)

May be impassable when wet

P

05

N

Colorado River

GRAND CANYON NATIONAL PARK

Grid size - 2 miles

49

Grandview Lookout Tower.

View of Grand Canyon from top of tower.

Entrance to Grand Canyon National Park.

Hull Cabin was built in 1889.

Watch for elk on F.S. Road 303.

50

Grandview Lookout 6

Location: East of Tusayan and south of Grand Canyon National Park.

Difficulty: Easy. Washboard gravel road except for F.S. 303 which narrows to a single lane. This road has a few ruts and muddy spots that require high clearance and perhaps four-wheel drive when wet.

Features: Beautiful, uncrowded forest immediately adjacent to Grand Canyon National Park. Free camping is allowed almost anywhere in the forest except within 1/4 mile of highways and surface water. Also, you can't camp within 1 mile of Hull Cabin. If dispersed camping is not your thing, try the Ten-X Forest Service Campground 2 miles south of Tusayan on Highway 64. This is a fee area but it's a great campground and is seldom crowded.

There are many other roads to explore in the area. The forest is teeming with wildlife. I saw an entire herd of elk while on F.S. 303. You are permitted to climb the stairs of the Grandview Tower which has a distant view of the Grand Canyon. I found the side trip to historical Hull Cabin interesting. You might want to stop at the Forest Service Ranger Station just north of Tusayan to find out more about the area.

Locals tell me the best time to make this trip is late in the afternoon. That way you can swing through the park on the return trip and catch the sun setting over Grand Canyon National Park.

There are mountain biking and hiking trails, including the Arizona Trail, in the vicinity of Grandview Tower. One hiking trail loops through the park to viewpoints along the rim then returns via a connection with the Arizona Trail.

The small town of Tusayan has motels, fast food restaurants, ATMs, service stations, an IMAX Theatre and a full-hook-up campground. Expect heavy traffic during peak summer months and tourist prices.

Time & Distance: The trip as described here is 21.5 miles plus 3.6 miles round trip to Hull Cabin. Allow 1 1/2 to 2 hours to reach the entrance to the park. Add another 1/2 hour for the side trip to Hull Cabin.

To Get There: Take U.S. Hwy. 180 north from Flagstaff or State Hwy. 64 north from Williams. Before reaching Tusayan, you'll pass the Grand Canyon Airport on the left. As you enter town watch for F.S. 302 on the right. It is marked with a sign displaying a giant set of binoculars.*(Note: To reach Grandview Tower without the long forest drive, head south from*

Highway 64 from inside Grand Canyon National Park. The turn is half way between mile posts 252 and 253.)

Trail Description: *Reset your odometer when you turn east off Hwy. 64* [01]. Follow this wide gravel road 2.7 miles and make a left on F.S. 303 [02]. *(You can continue straight on 302 but you'll miss the best part of the trip.)* Continue straight on 303 ignoring side roads. For a while, follow bike trail signs. Make a right at 6.3. The bike trail heads left at 6.9 miles [03]. Bear right at this point staying on 303. *(You can continue to follow the bike route for a distance, but all roads for motorized vehicles eventually are blocked.)* When you get back to F.S. 302 at 9.9 miles [04], turn left.

Continue east on 302 passing several side roads that head south. Turn left when you reach a T with F.S. 310 at 18.8 miles [05]. The side trip to Hull Cabin can be made by turning right at 20.1 miles on F.S. 307 [06]. *(See directions below.)* If you continue on 310, you'll reach the Grandview Lookout Tower at 20.2. There's a modern vault toilet at this location. The entrance to Grand Canyon National Park is reached at 20.9 miles. Park fees can be paid when you exit the park. Connect with paved Hwy. 64 at 21.5 miles [07].

Directions to Hull Cabin: *Reset your odometer at the intersection of F.S. 310 and 307* [06]. Follow 307, an old stagecoach route, northeast. You'll drop down a hill on several switchbacks. Turn left on F.S. 851 at 1.5 miles. Open and close a gate to get on this single lane road. Hull Cabin is reached at 1.8 miles [08]. Hull Cabin was a sheep camp when it was built in 1889. Today it's owned by the Forest Service and serves as a summer work center.

Return Trip: Return to Grand Canyon Village or Tusayan by turning left when you reach Highway 64 inside the park.

Services: Full services in Tusayan and Grand Canyon Village.

Maps: Kaibab National Forest, Tusayan, Williams and Chalender Ranger Districts, USGS 100,000 scale Grand Canyon, AZ #36112-A1-TM-100, Arizona Atlas & Gazetteer.

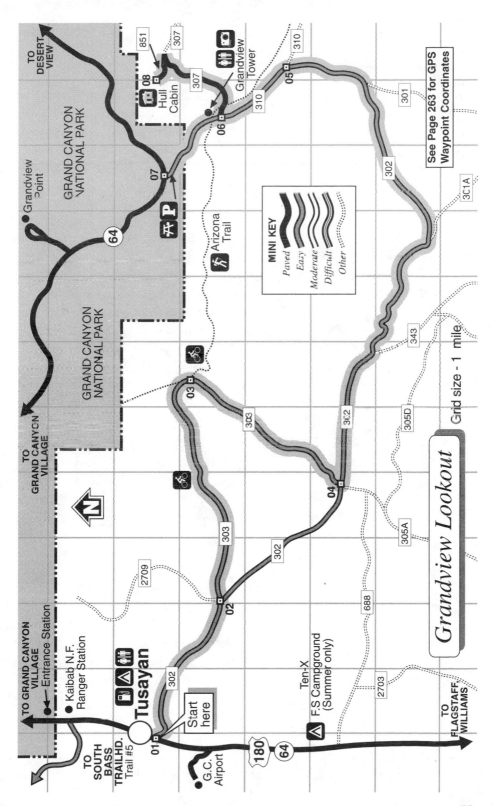

Grandview Lookout

Grid size - 1 mile

AREA 2

Bullhead City,
Kingman

7. Sleeping Princess
8. Chloride Mines
9. Pass Canyon
10. Secret Pass
11. Backway to Oatman
12. Moss Wash
13. Hualapai Mountains

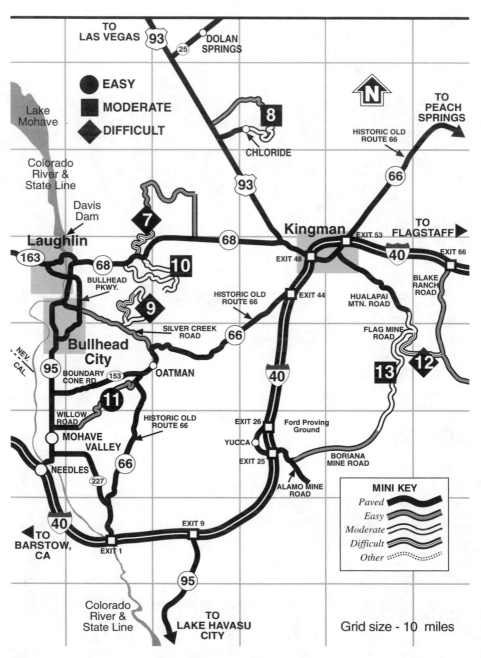

Bullhead City, Kingman

Whether it's cruising easy and moderate routes in your new SUV or tackling insane obstacles in your modified rock crawler, you won't be bored with any of the routes in this area. Take your pick of old mining roads stretching across hot desert lowlands along the Colorado River to cooler, high-elevation mountain roads above Kingman. Visit historic ghost towns like Oatman, where donkeys wander freely on Main Street outside the old Oatman Hotel. Inside, you can see the room where Clark Gable and Carole Lombard spent their wedding night. Drive some of the most scenic stretches of old Route 66 on your way to the trails. Head north to Chloride, Arizona's oldest silver mining camp. Behind Chloride, you'll discover one of the best mining roads in Arizona accessible by high-clearance, four-wheel-drive vehicles. Spend all day wandering in bliss through the heavily forested, mining-rich Hualapai Mountains. For those seeking extreme adventure, you must drive one of the scariest, best kept secrets in Arizona—*Sleeping Princess*. A recently added extension is sure to leave gonzo-wheelers smiling. Northerners, with wintertime cabin fever, fill your tank and hit the road—these trails are waiting for you now.

Summit of Coal Slurry Line Road on Secret Pass (Trail #10), Moderate.

Start is clearly marked. Near the top it is extremely steep and narrow with loose rock.

The only way into the "Bob Miller Extension" is down this steep embankment. Use a spotter.

This tight spot is called "The Rock Fall." Note tight turn of second Jeep.

Sleeping Princess ◆7◆

Location: Between Bullhead City and Kingman. North of State Hwy. 68.

Difficulty: Difficult. This is a nasty, dangerous trail that should be driven with at least two other vehicles. Besides an array of challenging rock obstacles, the road climbs over 2,000 feet through the heart of the Black Mountains. Much of the road is loose, steep gravel. One spot, along the edge of a narrow shelf, requires a sharp inside turn. As your vehicle rounds the bend, your rear outside tire drops into a gravelly low spot. Power must be applied at just the right time to reduce the possibility of going over the edge. Recently a new loop, dubbed the *Bob Miller Extension*, has been added to the trail. To start the route, you must get around a 15-ft. vertical wall then drop down a very steep embankment. The descent down the northeast side is relatively easy albeit somewhat long and dusty. Stock, high-clearance vehicles can drive up to the top from this side with little difficulty.

Features: Rock challenges and thrills will delight the most ardent four-wheeler. There's a great place to stop for lunch just below the summit. The northeast-side descent includes a functioning windmill, ruins of an old homestead complete with a hard-to-find waterfall, and the Wayfarer's Inn. Watch carefully for bighorn sheep. **If you stack rocks to get over obstacles, make sure to remove them when you are done.**

Time & Distance: This trip can be completed in 4 to 5 hours under ideal circumstances. Better to allow a full day. Our group of 6 vehicles took 7 hours. Several vehicles turned back because of mechanical problems. From Hwy. 68, it's 7.2 miles to the top of Sleeping Princess and an additional 19.8 back down. If you return down the difficult side, overall trip time will likely be longer.

To Get There: Turn northwest off Hwy. 68 about a tenth of a mile northeast of mile marker 8.

Trail Description: *Reset your odometer when you turn off Hwy. 68* [01]. Head north on a potholed macadam road and turn left at 0.4 miles [02]. Continue heading north, ignoring lesser spurs. Bear right at 0.5 and continue straight at 2.0, following a shallow wash. Turn right at a large sign that marks the official start of the trail at 2.3 miles [03]. Bear left at 2.6 miles. You'll see a rocky canyon on the left at 3.8 miles [04]. This is the exit point of the *Bob Miller Extension*. Those who would rather not drive this part of the trail can wait here or walk down and watch the action. You will return to this point later.

To drive the *Bob Miller Extension*, turn left uphill and backtrack on a defined road. Continue straight as a road joins on the right at 4.2 miles. At 4.6 miles [05] make a hard left into a narrow canyon. Before you come face to face with a 15-ft. vertical wall, turn left and drive uphill around it. Swing right across a tippy spot and drop steeply down to a spot above the vertical wall (see photo). Use a spotter to come down the embankment. Once at the bottom, turn left and continue through the narrow canyon. You'll return to the start of the *Bob Miller Extension* at 5.5 miles [04]. From here, continue uphill northeast on a narrow road. *(Note: You can exit the trail from the west end of the Bob Miller Extension. Instead of turning left into the canyon, continue straight. After passing through a fence, turn left. You'll return to the starting sign for Sleeping Princess in about one mile.)*

At 5.6 miles there's a tight right turn at a narrow, tippy spot. Your rear tire will try to slide down the hill on loose gravel. This is a dangerous spot so be extremely careful. A tight spot at 5.9 is called *The Rock Fall*. It tips you into a large rock on the right (see photo). This is followed by a tight left turn that requires backing up. You enter a steep area called *Boulder Alley* at 6.0 miles [06]. This section is the last of the rock obstacles. You'll climb very steeply up a loose gravel road. After winding around the back side of the mountain and returning to the front, bear right uphill at 6.8 miles at a large area of light-colored rock. This is a great lunch spot. *(Caution: A left turn here dead ends at a 100-ft. cliff with little space to turn around.)* You reach the top at 7.2 miles [07].

Reset your odometer and start down the other side (or go down the way you came up). Make a left at 1.2 and 1.8 miles [08]. Bear right at 2.1. Make a hard right over a cattle guard to avoid a gate at 5.5.

There's an optional 1/2-mile side trip to Burn's Spring on the left at 6.5 miles [09]. It winds down a hill and turns to the right at the botton. It ends at a small turnaround area. You'll have to hike downhill to a couple of collapsed cabins. Hiding deep in dense overgrowth is a small spring and waterfall. Legend has it that a homesteader lived here with several wives. They built the cabins and rock walls seen on the hillsides.

To continue down the mountain, bear right. Watch for the Wayfarer's Inn on the right at 8.1 miles [10]. (Don't count mileage for the side trip.) Cross cattle guard at 9.5. Join a wider road bearing left at 9.7. At 14.7 miles [11] turn right on Egar Road. You'll reach Hwy. 68 at 19.8 miles [12].

Return Trip: Turn left for Kingman or right for Bullhead City.

Services: In Kingman or Bullhead City.

Maps: USGS 100,000 scale Davis Dam, AZ-Nevada-California N3500-W11400/30x60, Arizona Atlas & Gazetteer.

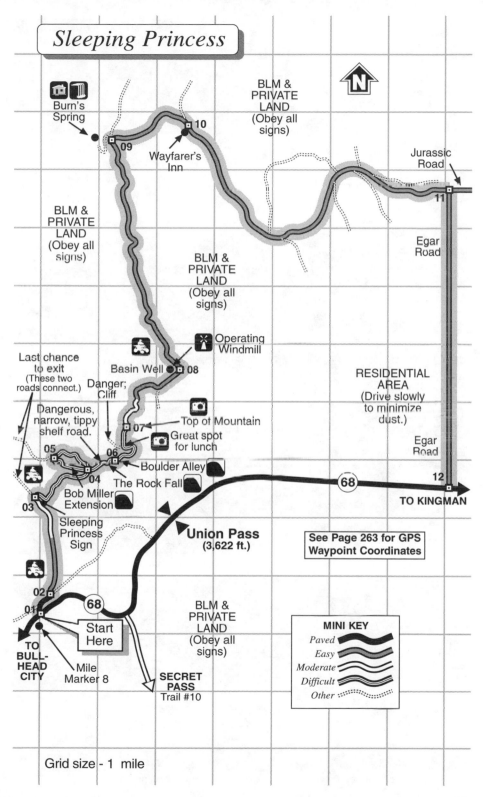

Sleeping Princess

N

Burn's Spring

BLM & PRIVATE LAND (Obey all signs)

Jurassic Road

09

10

Wayfarer's Inn

11

Egar Road

BLM & PRIVATE LAND (Obey all signs)

BLM & PRIVATE LAND (Obey all signs)

Operating Windmill

Basin Well   08

RESIDENTIAL AREA (Drive slowly to minimize dust.)

Last chance to exit (These two roads connect.)

Danger; Cliff

Top of Mountain

Egar Road

Dangerous, narrow, tippy shelf road.

07

Great spot for lunch

05

06

Boulder Alley

12

04

The Rock Fall

68

TO KINGMAN

03

Bob Miller Extension

Sleeping Princess Sign

Union Pass (3,622 ft.)

See Page 263 for GPS Waypoint Coordinates

02

68

01

Start Here

BLM & PRIVATE LAND (Obey all signs)

MINI KEY

Paved
Easy
Moderate
Difficult
Other

TO BULL-HEAD CITY

Mile Marker 8

SECRET PASS Trail #10

Grid size - 1 mile

59

A few rough spots going up.

Be careful—mines can be dangerous.

The view from Windy Point.

Painted murals outside Chloride.

Chloride Post Office on left in business since 1893.

The winding road coming down from Windy Point is easy and scenic.

Chloride Mines 8

Location: Northwest of Kingman, East of Highway 93.

Difficulty: Moderate. The uphill side requires high-clearance two-wheel drive and occasional four-wheel drive on a few steep, rough spots. Wet conditions increase difficulty. The downhill side is an easy graded road suitable for passenger cars. If you explore any of the side roads, use extra caution and expect more difficult conditions.

Features: Explore a once-bustling mining area. Watch for wild mustangs that still roam the hillsides. Walk through Chloride's historic buildings, including a post office that has been in operation since 1893. Learn about the town's history viewing exhibits in the Visitor Center. See Native American petroglyphs and colorful painted rock murals. Enjoy full-hookup camping in Chloride or rough it high above the town in two scenic BLM campgrounds with picnic tables and modern vault toilets. Hike several great trails in the Cerbat Mountains.

Time & Distance: The complete loop is almost 19 miles as described here. Allow about 2 hours driving time plus stops. You can easily spend a full day or weekend exploring the area.

To Get There: Take Highway 93 north from Kingman about 18 miles. Turn right 0.3 miles north of mile marker 53, following signs to Chloride. Drive east about 4 miles to Chloride.

Trail Description: Reset your odometer at the Visitor Center in Chloride [01]. Continue east, crossing a cattle guard where the pavement ends. Bear right at 0.6 and 0.9 miles and left at 1.6. At 1.9 miles [02] you arrive at the painted murals seen on the right. Harder to find are the Native American petroglyphs which are scattered about the area. Most are on the left side of the road. The petroglyphs are less dramatic but more important from a historical perspective.

Continue east from the murals on a much rougher road. Bear left at 2.9 and 3.4 miles [03]. From here, parts of the road are washed out and four-wheel drive is sometimes needed. At one point, Cherum Peak, the highest point in the Cerbats, can be seen straight ahead. At 4.4 miles [04] you can't miss an ore bin next to the road (see photo). Part of an ore car trestle also remains. If you climb up the steep bank, you can see where the ore cars rolled out of the mine shaft and over to the large tailings pile. Pass through a gate at 4.8 before making a sharp right at 5.1. Going straight here would run into the Rainbow Mine. As you reach the top of the Cerbat Mountains, the road is maintained starting at 6.0 miles [05]. The road to the right of the Cherum Hiking Trailhead dead ends past the Lucky Boy Mine.

Turn left at 7.8 miles [06] into the Windy Point Campground. This is a great place to catch your breath and enjoy some outstanding views. You'll also find campsites, picnic tables and modern pit toilets. There's a small fee to camp. When you return to the main road, your odometer should read 8.4 miles. Turn left and continue. The Packsaddle Campground is on the left at 9.8 [07]. This site is mainly for tents and no fee is charged. Beautiful switch-backs follow as you begin to descend the mountain. Watch for wild mustang hoof prints in the sand along trails near the road. See if you can spot any wild horses. Continue straight past a corral at 15.1 miles [08] before reaching Highway 93 at 18.6 miles [09].

Return Trip: Turn left on Highway 93 to get back to Kingman. Remember this is a divided highway, so cross the median before turning left. Right would take you to Dolan Springs and eventually Las Vegas, Nevada.

Services: Besides the Visitor Center, Chloride has gift shops, a post office, a grocery store, a few small cafes and two full-hook-up campgrounds. The gas station in town is mainly for show and dispenses no gas. You can get gas in Kingman or Dolan Springs.

Historical Highlights: Mining started in Chloride in 1840 but the boom years were from 1900 to 1920. A variety of ores were mined, including sil-ver, gold, lead, zinc, molybdenum, vanadium and turquoise. At one point, 2,000 people lived in town, unearthing about 75 mines on the surrounding hillsides. Mining continued until 1944. Despite the loss of mining, the town survived and today is a popular tourist attraction due in part to Chloride's high elevation and cooler temperatures. The murals were painted by Roy Purcell in 1966. The town has a variety of popular events including gun-fights and vaudeville shows. Contact the Chloride Chamber of Commerce for information. (See appendix.)

Maps: USGS 100,000 scale Davis Dam, AZ-Nevada-California N3500-W11400/30x60, Arizona Atlas & Gazetteer.

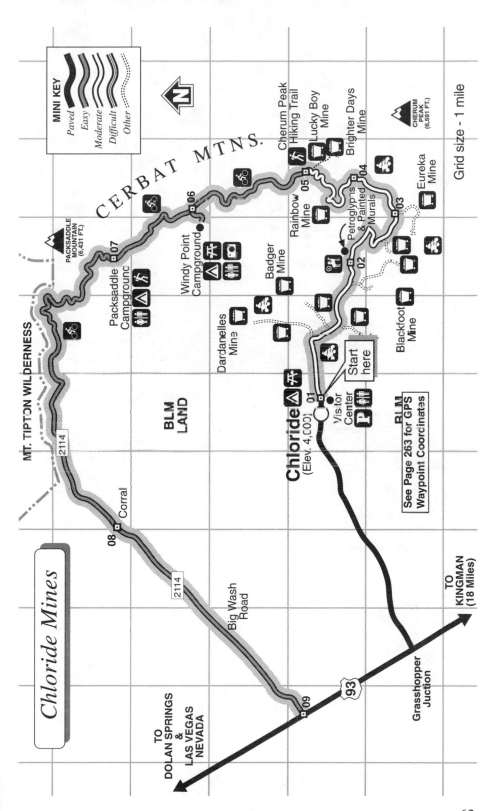

Chloride Mines

MINI KEY
Paved
Easy
Moderate
Difficult
Other

N

CERBAT MTNS.

MT. TIPTON WILDERNESS

PACKSADDLE MOUNTAIN (6,431 FT.)

CHERUM PEAK (6,591 FT.)

Grid size - 1 mile

Cherum Peak Hiking Trail
Lucky Boy Mine
Brighter Days Mine

Rainbow Mine

Eureka Mine

05

04

03

Petroglyphs & Painted Murals

02

06

07

Packsaddle Campground

Windy Point Campground

Badger Mine

Dardanelles Mine

Blackfoot Mine

Corral

08

2114

BLM LAND

Chloride (Elev. 4,000)

01

Visitor Center

Start here

P

BLM

See Page 263 for GPS Waypoint Coordinates

2114

Big Wash Road

09

93

Grasshopper Juction

TO KINGMAN (18 Miles)

TO DOLAN SPRINGS & LAS VEGAS NEVADA

Much of the trail is undulating sandy wash bottom. Mount Nutt Wilderness in distance.

Pass Canyon

TO SECRET PASS
Trail #10

Knoll

MINI KEY
Paved
Easy
Moderate
Difficult
Other

N

MOUNT NUTT WILDERNESS (Stay out)

05

04

Pass Canyon

07

06

Water tank on hill

Toughest Spot

See Page 264 for GPS Waypoint Coordinates

Moss Mine
(First discovery of gold in Mohave County)

08

09

Finger Butte

03

Orange Truck

Mossback Mine

Start here

Mossback Wash

SILVER CREEK ROAD

02

TO BULL-HEAD CITY

01

TO OATMAN

Silver Creek Spring

Grid size - 1 mile

Toughest spot in Pass Canyon.

Pass Canyon 9

Location: Between Bullhead City and Oatman. North of Silver Creek Road.

Difficulty: Difficult. A bad spot at the start of Pass Canyon requires this trail be rated difficult. Most of the trail is just rutted sandy wash. Experienced SUV drivers with a good spotter can make it. Route-finding is difficult.

Features: Rugged desert and mining country bordering closed wilderness.

Time & Distance: About 14 miles as described here. Allow 3 to 4 hours.

To Get There: From Bullhead City: From the Bullhead Parkway 95 Bypass, head east on Silver Creek Road 6.3 miles and turn left on a nondescript dirt road. There are many roads in the area so watch your mileage carefully. *From Oatman:* Head north from Oatman on Route 66 about a mile. Turn left on Silver Creek Road. Go 4.7 miles and turn right.

Trail Description: Reset your odometer as you turn north off Silver Creek Road [01]. Almost immediately, make a right at a fork. Generally, stay in a wide wash heading northeast. Bear left at 0.2 miles. At 0.3 [02] bear right following Mossback Wash. At 1.7 note a rusty orange truck. Make a left at 2.9 and a right at 3.0. Go straight at 3.1 through scattered mines. At 3.2 [03] make a right. *(There's an interesting cave to the left called the "Dugout," once used by miners as living quarters.)* The trail is well defined now as it follows the wilderness boundary on the right. Obey all signs. Make a left at 3.3 and a right at 5.8 miles [04]. At 7.1 miles [05] the road climbs to the top of a knoll. Turn left towards Pass Canyon. *Reset your odometer at this point.*

Bear right into a wash at 2.1 miles. This starts your descent into Pass Canyon. The roughest spot on the trail is reached at 2.3 miles [06]. At 4.0 [07] make a hard left out of the wash on a very steep, rutted road. Bear left at a T at 5.2 [08]. Ignore side roads. Bear left at a triangular intersection at 5.9 [09]. Bear right around a knoll with many roads. Go sraight across a wash at 6.2. You're back to an earlier intersection at 7.0 miles [02]. Head southwest opposite the way you came in. Silver Creek Rd. is reached at 7.3 miles [01].

Return Trip: Turn right for Bullhead City and left for Oatman.

Services: In Bullhead City and Oatman.

Maps: USGS 100,000 scale Davis Dam, AZ-NV-CA N3500-W11400/30x60.

The road is wide at the start but soon narrows. Black Mountains in distance.

Some hills are steep with loose gravel.

Hiker heads into Secret Pass Canyon.

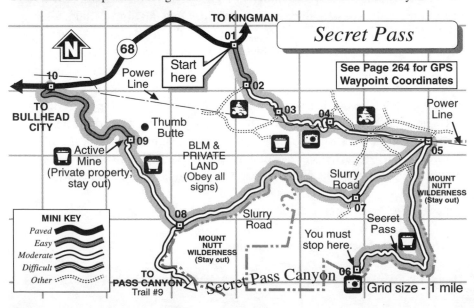

TO KINGMAN

68

N

Secret Pass

01

Start here

Power Line

See Page 264 for GPS Waypoint Coordinates

10

02

Power Line

TO BULLHEAD CITY

Thumb Butte

03

04

05

Active Mine (Private property; stay out)

09

BLM & PRIVATE LAND (Obey all signs)

Slurry Road

MOUNT NUTT WILDERNESS (Stay out)

MINI KEY
Paved
Easy
Moderate
Difficult
Other

08

Slurry Road

07

Secret Pass

You must stop here.

MOUNT NUTT WILDERNESS (Stay out)

TO PASS CANYON Trail #9

Secret Pass Canyon

06

Grid size - 1 mile

Secret Pass 10

Location: Between Bullhead City and Kingman. South of Highway 68.

Difficulty: Moderate. A few steep hills with occasional rocky spots. Many side roads make route-finding challenging.

Features: Rugged desert and rolling foothills. Explore many side roads. Part of trail follows liquefied coal pipeline (Slurry Road).

Time & Distance: About 16 miles as described here. Allow 3 to 4 hours.

To Get There: Turn south off Hwy. 68 after a guard rail ends at curve near mile marker 10.

Trail Description: Reset your odometer as you turn off Hwy. 68 [01]. Generally head south/southeast towards the power line. Turn right on a single lane road at 0.6 miles. Go straight at 0.7 then make an immediate left [02]. Maneuver up and down several steep hills and turn left at T at 1.5 miles [03]. Follow a narrow shelf road under power line. Tight squeeze around base of one tower. Stay right at 2.8 miles [04] as road joins on left. At 4.3 miles [05] take second right at complex intersection. Don't turn too soon or you'll end up on Slurry Road. Follow wilderness boundary. Go left at 4.7 and straight at 5.6. Important right at 6.3; watch for cairns. Ignore many side roads. Road soon swings to left and drops downhill to wilderness boundary at 7.6 miles [06]. Hike from here. Backtrack to complex intersection [05].

 Reset odometer at complex intersection [05] and make sharp left reversing direction to get on Slurry Road. Continue straight at 0.7 and 1.3 miles [07]. Left at 4.2. At 4.5 miles [08] bear right at a large rock formation. A left here would take you to Pass Canyon (Trail #9).

 Reset odometer [08]. Make a right at 0.1 and a left onto ledge road at 0.8. Tall pointed rock is Thumb Butte. Pass around the right side of an active mine at 1.7 miles [09]. After mine, bear left onto wide gravel road. Watch for speeding trucks. Continue straight as major road joins on left at 2.7. Follow wide road to Highway 68 at 3.7 miles [10].

Return Trip: Turn left for Bullhead City or right for Kingman.

Services: In Bullhead City and Kingman.

Maps: USGS 100,000 scale Davis Dam, AZ-NV-CA N3500-W11400/30x60.

Make a left off this road to start the trail. Boundary Cone stands tall in the distance.

Information kiosk at the east end of the trail.

4WD trail crosses railroad bed.   The burros in Oatman are very well fed.

Heavy rains created this high bank along the edge of a wash. It took some effort to get over.

Backway to Oatman ⑪

Location: Located between the town of Mohave Valley on Hwy. 95 and Oatman.

Difficulty: Easy. Most of this road is fairly flat and can be driven in a high-clearance two-wheel-drive vehicle. Four-wheel drive may be needed occasionally after heavy rains when ruts and washouts occur. The road is sometimes faint and difficult to find, especially at the west end. Use Boundary Cone as a directional landmark. The trail can also be driven in the opposite direction.

Features: This route roughly follows the original bed of the old Mohave and Milltown Railroad. A hiking trail follows the railroad route, while the four-wheel-drive route weaves back and forth across it. Look at the trail markers carefully to see whether they are for hikers or Jeeps. To fully appreciate your drive, please read *Historical Highlights* section that follows.

Time & Distance: About 18 miles from Hwy. 95 in Mohave Valley to Oatman. Allow 2-3 hours.

To Get There: From Mohave Valley on Hwy. 95, turn east on Willow Road at a traffic light halfway between mile markers 232 and 233. *Reset your odometer when you turn off Hwy. 95.* Continue east after the pavement ends until the road forks. Bear left, cross a wash, then continue straight uphill through a 4-way intersection. An information kiosk at 5.3 miles [01] marks the start of the trail and is the general location of the Milltown Site.

Trail Description: Reset your odometer at the information kiosk [01]. Continue northeast 0.7 miles and turn left at sign post [02]. The road is barely visible when you turn. Continue straight across a wash at 1.1. At 1.2 miles [03] the hiking trail goes left; you go right. Cross a deep wash at 1.2. Swing left at 1.9 miles [04]. (The trail appears to go straight here, but it soon disappears.) Bear left out of a wash at 2.4 miles [05]. Bear right and cross a wash at 3.0. You begin to cross back and forth over the railroad bed. Continue straight over a road for the power line at 4.8 miles [06]. At 6.5 [07] turn right out of a deep wash. The lip of the wash can be high after heavy rains. You may have to knock down the edge by driving up on it a few times or use a shovel. At this point the trail is well marked with cairns and signs. At 7.0 the trail makes a sharp right then back left. Bear right following sign posts at 7.7. You reach a larger dirt road at 7.9 miles [08]. Another information kiosk here marks the end of the trail. Turn left to reach paved Route 66 at 8.5 miles at mile marker 21. Another left on Route 66 takes you into Oatman at 11.9 miles. As you head towards Oatman, Boundary Cone Road joins on the left.

Return Trip: From Oatman, return to Mohave Valley via Boundary Cone Road. North on Route 66 takes you to Kingman. South on Route 66 takes you to Topock at Interstate 40.

Services: Oatman is a bustling little tourist town with restaurants, hotels and gift shops. Oatman does not have a gas station. Closest gas is in Mohave Valley via Boundary Cone Road.

Other Activities: Allow plenty of time to see Oatman. Most of the buildings in town remain much as they did when they were built in the early 1900s. Many people feed the wild burros that roam the streets. Visit the Old Oatman Hotel where Clark Gable and Carole Lombard spent their wedding night. See authentic gold mines, both old and new, in the surrounding area. Call the Oatman Chamber of Commerce for a list of scheduled activities that take place all year. (See appendix for phone number.)

Historical Highlights: The Mohave and Milltown Railroad was built in 1903. Its sole purpose was to carry ore from the mountains around Oatman closer to the Colorado River where a plentiful water supply was used to process gold ore. Water was needed to run steam engines that powered a 40-stamp mill in Milltown. At the start of the trail, near the information kiosk, you can still see a concrete reservoir for the water. After the ore was processed and condensed in Milltown, it was hauled by train to the river. Ferries carried the ore across the river where it was hauled to a smelter in Needles, California. After spending $250,000 to build the narrow gauge railroad, the project was abandoned a year later when only $40,000 in gold was produced.

The town of Oatman started as a tent camp at the turn of the century. It flourished as a major mining town until 1942 when Congress declared gold mining unnecessary for the war effort. An estimated 36 million dollars in gold (at 1930s prices) was mined in the area. Today, Oatman is one of the most popular tourist attractions in Arizona and entertains over 500,000 visitors each year.

Maps: USGS 100,000 scale Needles, California-Arizona 34114-E1-TM-100, Arizona Atlas & Gazetteer.

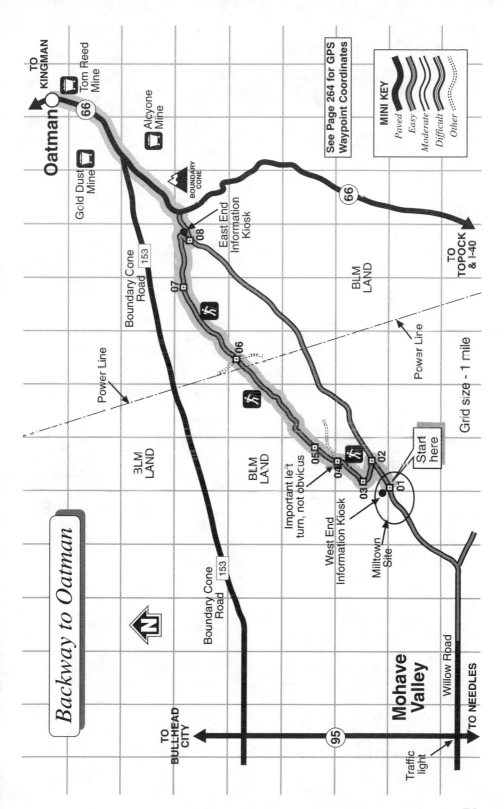

Backway to Oatman

TO KINGMAN

Oatman

Tom Reed Mine

Alcyone Mine

Gold Dust Mine

66

BOUNDARY CONE

East End Information Kiosk

08

07

06

05

04

03

02

01

Boundary Cone Road 153

Power Line

Power Line

BLM LAND

BLM LAND

BLM LAND

66

TO TOPOCK & I-40

Important left turn, not obvious

West End Information Kiosk

Milltown Site

Start here

Grid size - 1 mile

N

Boundary Cone Road 153

Mohave Valley

Willow Road

TO BULLHEAD CITY

95

Traffic light

TO NEEDLES

MINI KEY
Paved
Easy
Moderate
Difficult
Other

See Page 264 for GPS Waypoint Coordinates

71

Volunteers from the Walapai 4-Wheelers clean up Gold King Mansion

This spot is not bad. It gets much tougher.

Last part of trail has several steep climbs.

Moss Wash is the adopted trail of the Walapai 4-Wheelers Club.

Location: Southeast of Kingman in the Hualapai Mountains.

Difficulty: Difficult. Deep washouts, challenging rock obstacles and steep climbs. Frequently narrow road with tight brush. Excellent articulation or lockers required. High ground clearance a must. Not suitable for stock sport utility vehicles. Avoid this trail when heavy rains are forecast because dangerous flash flooding is possible.

Features: BLM road climbs through forested mining country. Visit historic Gold King Mansion a few feet from trail. Camp in Wild Cow Spring Campground (fee area).

Time & Distance: The trail, as described here, is about 14 miles. Allow 3 to 4 hours. This does not include Blake Ranch Road or Hualapai Mountain Road.

To Get There: From Kingman, head east on Interstate 40 to Exit 66 at a large truck stop. *Reset your odometer* and head south on Blake Ranch Road. Stay on the Blake Ranch Road as side roads join and branch off. A stop sign a 6.9 miles marks a small landing strip. Continue straight with caution. After that, the road narrows briefly then widens again. The start of the trail is on the right at 11.3 miles [01].

Trail Description: Reset your odometer at the start [01]. Head west on a sandy road that soon narrows. Bear left at 0.4 as a road joins on the right. Deep ruts test articulation. A challenging rocky section at 1.3 has a bypass on the right. The trail swings left around the back of the Gold King Mansion at 1.8 miles [02] (See *Historical Highlights*). More challenges follow through a narrow valley. Bear left at 3.0 as the trail widens a bit. At 3.6 miles [03] pass a corral and turn right. A collapsing structure, part of the Merlo Mine, can be see on the hillside to the right at 4.5 miles. Soon after the mine, the trail begins to follow a scenic wash through black walnut trees. At 5.7 miles bear left at a large tree which hides another trail to the right.

      Bear right out of the main wash at 6.3 miles [04]. (Turn left if you are looking for a quick way out.) Soon the trail becomes a narrow, deep trench. In places, it is barely wide enough to get a vehicle through. This section can change drastically after heavy rains. You may need a shovel to dig through in places if damage is too bad. After the trench, you begin to climb a narrow, tippy shelf road. There's a very steep, loose spot at 7.7 miles. Bear left uphill at 7.8 where a steep road comes up the hill on the right. Bear left at 8.2 miles [05]. The road to the right goes back to Blake Ranch Road. Pass through a gate at 8.4 miles. The road climbs and descends for quite a while with some challenging washed-out sections. Turn left at 9.1 miles. At 9.7 [06] you meet Antelope Wash Road. A sign here identifies Moss Wash as the adopted trail of the Walapai 4-Wheelers. Turn left and continue uphill. After a tough washed-out spot, cross a cattle guard and turn right uphill at 9.9. Straight would take you into the Wild Cow Spring Campground. Turn right on Flag Mine Road at 10.3 miles [07]. This road passes through a residential area and joins Hualapai Mountain Road at 13.5 miles [08].

Return Trip: Turn left on paved Hualapai Mountain Road to reach Kingman (about 15 miles).

Services: Vault toilets at Wild Cow Spring Campground and Ponderosa Recreation Area just after you turn left on Hualapai Mountain Road. Other services in Kingman.

Historical Highlights: In 1929 it was rare to see a building constructed of poured concrete. But this was the method used by the Gold King Corporation to build the Gold King Mansion. Because of this sturdy construction, much of the structure remains today. At one time, this was an ornate building used to entertain wealthy clients. It also housed the mine foreman, who directed the mining operations of the Gold King Mine located across the trail north of the mansion.

You are allowed to walk through the structure provided you leave it the way you find it. The day I was there it was getting cleaned up and painted by volunteers of the Walapai 4-Wheelers Club in cooperation with the BLM. Vandals had sprayed graffiti on the walls and had left piles of trash throughout the building. The archaeological site is monitored by the *Arizona Site Stewards* for vandalism and theft. If you see vandalism in progress, call 1-800-VANDALS immediately.

Maps: USGS 100,000 scale Valentine, Arizona 35113-A1-TM-100, Arizona Atlas & Gazetteer.

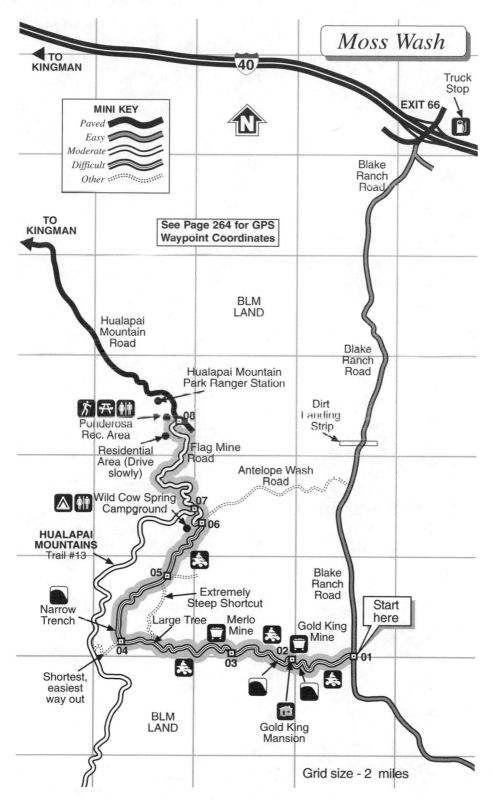

Moss Wash

TO KINGMAN

40

Truck Stop

EXIT 66

MINI KEY
Paved
Easy
Moderate
Difficult
Other

N

Blake Ranch Road

TO KINGMAN

See Page 264 for GPS Waypoint Coordinates

BLM LAND

Hualapai Mountain Road

Blake Ranch Road

Dirt Landing Strip

Hualapai Mountain Park Ranger Station

Ponderosa Rec. Area

08

Residential Area (Drive slowly)

Flag Mine Road

Antelope Wash Road

Wild Cow Spring Campground

07

06

HUALAPAI MOUNTAINS Trail #13

05

Blake Ranch Road

Extremely Steep Shortcut

Narrow Trench

Large Tree

Merlo Mine

Gold King Mine

Start here

04

Shortest, easiest way out

03

02

01

BLM LAND

Gold King Mansion

Grid size - 2 miles

A great way to escape the heat of summer. Not too tough for SUVs.

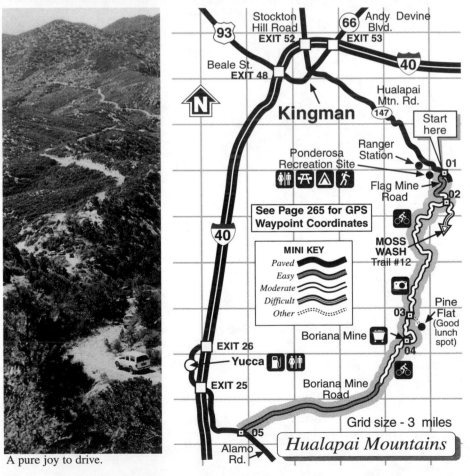

A pure joy to drive.

Stockton Hill Road — EXIT 52
93
Andy Devine Blvd. — **66** — EXIT 53
Beale St. — EXIT 48
40
Hualapai Mtn. Rd. — **147**
Kingman
N
Ranger Station
Ponderosa Recreation Site
Flag Mine Road
Start here
01
02

See Page 265 for GPS Waypoint Coordinates

MOSS WASH Trail #12

MINI KEY
Paved
Easy
Moderate
Difficult
Other

40

Pine Flat (Good lunch spot)
03
Boriana Mine
04

EXIT 26
Yucca
EXIT 25
Boriana Mine Road

Grid size - 3 miles

05
Alamo Rd.

Hualapai Mountains

Hualapai Mountains 13

Location: Southeast of Kingman.

Difficulty: Moderate. A narrow, rocky shelf road with switchbacks and steep climbs. Vertical drop-offs may be intimidating to novice drivers. Suitable for stock SUVs.

Features: A gorgeous drive on a classic mountain mining road. Just enough challenge to make the drive fun but not overwhelming for stock vehicles. Cool in summer with elevations over 6,000 feet. Picnic and hike at the Ponderosa Recreation Site on Hualapai Mountain Road before the turn for Flag Mine Road.

Time & Distance: About 37 miles as described here. Allow 4 to 6 hours.

To Get There: Take Stockton Hill Road, Exit 52, south from Interstate 40 in Kingman. Stockton Hill Road soon changes to Hualapai Mountain Road. Continue south past mile marker 12 and turn right on Flag Mine Road.

Trail Description: Reset your odometer as you turn right off Hualapai Mountain Road [01]. Follow Flag Mine Road as it climbs rapidly through a residential area. Bear right at 3.3 miles [02]. Spectacular views unfold as the road serpentines for many miles along a series of high ridges. Bear right at 16.4 miles [03]. A lesser road to the left goes downhill to a nice shady spot for lunch. There's a side road into the giant Boriana Mine on the right at 19.9 [04]. This was the largest tungsten mine in Arizona but closed in 1957 after a major fire. Bear right at 20.2 and 25.0. When the road reaches the valley floor, it becomes wide, straight and dusty. Turn right at paved Alamo Road at 34.1 miles [05]. Alamo Road goes south of the Ford Proving Ground before swinging right along Interstate 40. You reach Exit 25 at 37.2 miles.

Return Trip: Left on I-40 takes you in the direction of Bullhead City and Lake Havasu City; right goes to Kingman.

Services: Vault toilets at the Ponderosa Recreation Site. Convenience store with gas in Yucca on west side of I-40 at Exit 25. Truck stop and fast food restaurant at Exit 9 west on I-40. Full services in Kingman.

Maps: This trail covers four USGS 250,000 scale maps: Kingman, Williams, Prescott and Needles; or use Arizona Atlas and Gazetteer.

AREA 3

Flagstaff, Sedona,
Cottonwood,
Jerome

14. Lockett Meadow
15. Schultz Pass
16. Elden Mountain
17. Cinder Hills OHV Area
18. Soldier Pass
19. Van Deren Cabin
20. Schnebly Hill Road

21. Greasy Spoon
22. Oak Creek Homestead
23. Broken Arrow
24. Hutch Mountain
25. Smiley Rock
26. Mingus Mountain

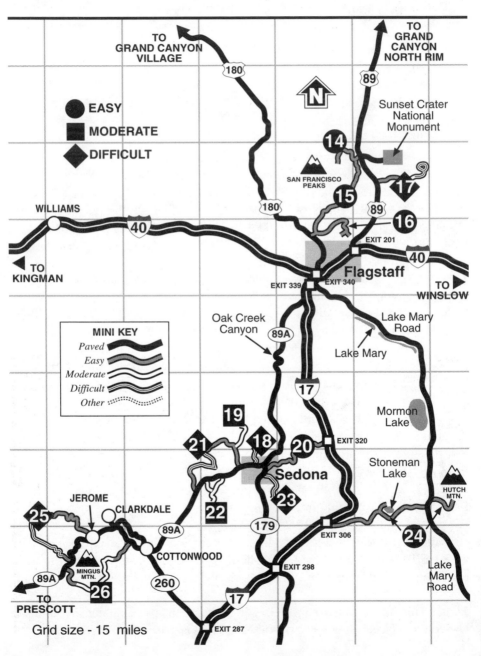

Flagstaff, Sedona, Cottonwood, Jerome

Flagstaff is located at the foot of Arizona's highest mountain range—the San Francisco Peaks. Scenic drives and cool temperatures are just a short drive away from town. Most of the roads are well-maintained and rated easy. One exception is the *Cinder Hills OHV Area* northeast of Flagstaff. Here you can find trails as difficult as you like in a 13,000-acre play area set aside for 4-wheelers, ATVs and dirt bikes. A deep layer of volcanic ash makes a perfect, and surprisingly clean, surface for off-roading. South of Flagstaff, you'll find Sedona, an area of unsurpassed red rock beauty. Visitors worldwide come here to enjoy Sedona's famous Jeep tours, most of which are on public roads and are described in this book. A spectacular way to reach Sedona is via *Schnebly Hill Road*, an easy 4-wheel-drive road directly west of Interstate 17 from Exit 320. No trip to Sedona would be complete without driving Sedona's best known Jeep trail—*Broken Arrow*. Further west, visit Jerome, once a booming mining town, now a thriving artists' community. Like Sedona and Flagstaff, Jerome is working hard to preserve the beauty of its backcountry. When visiting these areas, make sure to leave no trace of your visit.

Broken Arrow, Trail #23, rated difficult. Many stock high-clearance SUVs can get through.

Lockett Meadow and Humphrey's Peak.

Great views along the way.

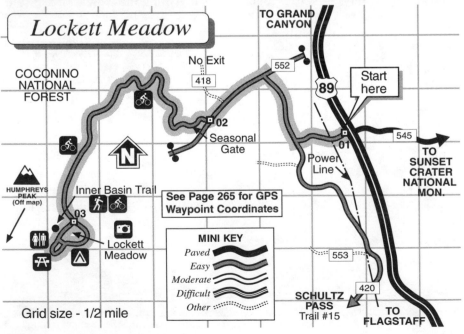

Lockett Meadow

TO GRAND
CANYON

COCONINO
NATIONAL
FOREST

No Exit
418

552

US 89

Start
here

545

TO
SUNSET
CRATER
NATIONAL
MON.

02

Seasonal
Gate

Power
Line

01

N

HUMPHREYS
PEAK
(Off map)

Inner Basin Trail

See Page 265 for GPS
Waypoint Coordinates

03

Lockett
Meadow

553

MINI KEY

Paved

Easy

Moderate

Difficult

Other

420

SCHULTZ
PASS
Trail #15

TO
FLAGSTAFF

Grid size - 1/2 mile

Lockett Meadow ⑭

Location: North of Flagstaff, west of Highway 89 and the Sunset Crater National Monument.

Difficulty: Easy. A dusty gravel road with minor steep sections. The road climbs over 1,300 feet to an elevation over 8,600 feet. Low-slung passenger cars and long RVs should avoid this road.

Features: A great place to escape for an afternoon picnic or weekend camp-out. Hike and mountain bike on the Inner Basin Trail. This is a favorite spot for artists and photographers, especially in the spring when flowers are blooming or fall when the leaves are changing. Contact the Peaks Ranger Station in Flagstaff for information. *(See appendix.)*

Time & Distance: Round trip from Highway 89 and back is about 10 miles. Allow about two hours.

To Get There: From east side of Flagstaff, take Hwy. 89 north about 12 miles. Turn left on a gravel Forest Service road across from entrance to Sunset Crater National Monument (Note: this is a new entry point since Highway 89 was changed to a four-lane, divided highway.)

Trail Description: Reset your odometer as you turn left off Highway 89 [01]. Head west and turn right at T at 0.5 miles. Turn left at 1.1 miles following signs to Lockett Meadow. Turn right at 1.7 miles [02] and head uphill. Seasonal gate will be closed during the winter. The road climbs up the mountain with some nice views along the way. Watch for ATVs and dune buggies around blind curves. I came very close to a collision with a dune buggy as he came down the hill at high speed. A one-way loop goes around Lockett Meadow at 4.5 miles [03]. The trailhead for the Inner Basin Trail is on the right at 4.8 miles. The road reconnects to the original road at 5.4 miles.

Return Trip: Return the way you came or via Shultz Pass Road Trail #15.

Services: Vault toilet near the Inner Basin Trailhead. Return to Flagstaff for all other services.

Maps: USGS 100,000 scale map Flagstaff, AZ, N3500-W11100/30x60, Arizona Atlas and Gazetteer.

An easy drive all the way.

Camp anywhere except where posted.

Schultz Creek Multi-Use Trail.

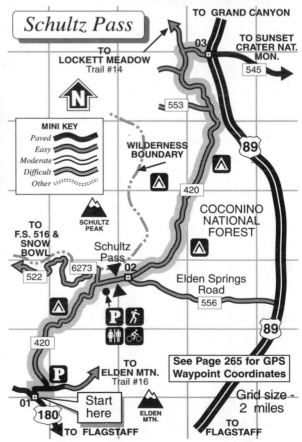

Schultz Pass

TO GRAND CANYON

TO
LOCKETT MEADOW
Trail #14

03

TO SUNSET
CRATER NAT.
MON.

545

N

553

MINI KEY
Paved
Easy
Moderate
Difficult
Other

**WILDERNESS
BOUNDARY**

89

420

COCONINO
NATIONAL
FOREST

SCHULTZ
PEAK

TO
F.S. 516 &
SNOW
BOWL

Schultz
Pass

522

6273

02

Elden Springs
Road

556

89

420

P

See Page 265 for GPS
Waypoint Coordinates

P

TO
ELDEN MTN.
Trail #16

Grid size -
2 miles

01

180

Start
here

ELDEN
MTN.

TO FLAGSTAFF

TO
FLAGSTAFF

Schultz Pass ⑮

Location: Immediately north of Flagstaff between Highways 89 and 180.

Difficulty: Easy. Mostly smooth gravel road with typical washboard stretches. Fairly flat and suitable for passenger cars.

Features: A beautiful mountain drive just a few miles out of Flagstaff. Many marked side roads in the area can be explored—some offer considerable challenge. Dispersed camping allowed almost anywhere along main and side roads except where posted. Numerous multi-use trails in the area are open to hikers, mountain bikers, horseback riders and dirt bikers. You must stay on marked trails only. Contact the Peaks Ranger Station in Flagstaff for more information. *(See appendix.)*

Time & Distance: The entire 14.6-mile trip can be driven in about an hour one-way. You'll likely want to spend much longer exploring the area.

To Get There: Take Highway 180 northwest about 2 miles out of Flagstaff in the direction of Grand Canyon National Park. (See map of Flagstaff on next page.) Turn right on Schultz Pass Road F.S. 420 where marked.

Trail Description: Reset your odometer as you turn right off Highway 180 [01]. Follow a paved road as it swings right then left into the forest. You'll see a parking lot on the right for the Schultz Creek Multi-Use Trail. Two side roads deserve special mention: The first is at 5.1 miles on the left. It is marked as F.S. 6273 but later changes to 522. This road is narrow and rocky and requires high clearance. Just after another parking area at 6.0 miles [02], Elden Springs Road goes right to Hwy. 89. Shultz Pass Road is uneventful from here; however, there are numerous side roads to explore. I tried one on the left at 7.7 miles marked #14. It had some difficult sections and some great camping spots. Stay out of the wilderness. Bear left at 12.1 miles then stay right at 12.3 where F.S. 553 goes left. Turn right at 14.1 miles. (Straight goes to Lockett Meadow, Trail #14.) Hwy. 89 is reached at 14.6 miles [03].

Return Trip: Turn right and take Hwy. 89 back to Flagstaff.

Services: Vault toilet is noted on map. Full services in Flagstaff.

Maps: USGS 100,000 scale map Flagstaff, AZ, N3500-W11100/30x60, Arizona Atlas and Gazetteer.

View of Flagstaff from south side of Elden Mountain (Elevation 9,299 ft.).

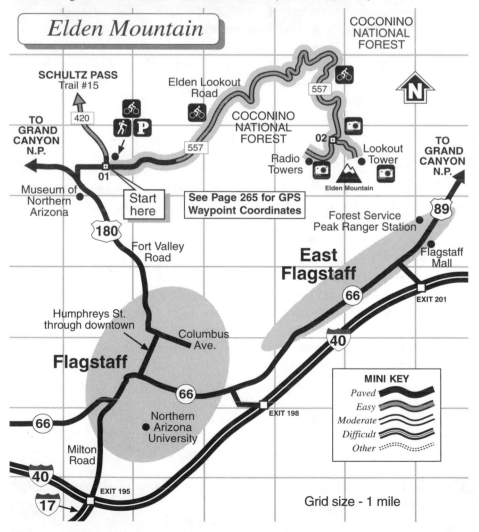

Elden Mountain

COCONINO
NATIONAL
FOREST

SCHULTZ PASS
Trail #15

Elden Lookout
Road

557

420

**TO
GRAND
CANYON
N.P.**

557

COCONINO
NATIONAL
FOREST

02

Radio
Towers

Lookout
Tower

Elden Mountain

**TO
GRAND
CANYON
N.P.**

P

01

Museum of
Northern
Arizona

Start
here

**See Page 265 for GPS
Waypoint Coordinates**

Forest Service
Peak Ranger Station

89

180

Fort Valley
Road

**East
Flagstaff**

Flagstaff
Mall

Humphreys St.
through downtown

Columbus
Ave.

66

EXIT 201

Flagstaff

66

40

66

EXIT 198

Northern
Arizona
University

Milton
Road

MINI KEY

Paved
Easy
Moderate
Difficult
Other

40

EXIT 195

17

Grid size - 1 mile

84

Elden Mountain 16

Location: Immediately north of Flagstaff, east of Highway 180.

Difficulty: Easy. Bumpy gravel road with washboard stretches. After a flat section, the road climbs over 2,100 feet to an elevation of 9,299 ft. Passenger cars can get to the top but they may find the trip a little rough.

Features: Views from the top are outstanding. If the gate is open, you can drive to the lookout tower. Rangers on duty may allow you to climb the tower for a great 360-degree view. If the weather is clear, you can see Oak Creek Canyon, Mormon Lake, Humphreys Peak, Sunset Crater National Monument and the Painted Desert. A network of hiking trails surrounds the mountain. This is a popular road for mountain bikers, so drive carefully. Contact the Peaks Ranger Station in Flagstaff for more information. *(See appendix.)*

Time & Distance: From the start to the point where the road splits at the top is 6.3 miles. Add another 1/2 to 3/4 mile for each of the spur roads. It takes about 30 minutes to drive to the top.

To Get There: Take Highway 180 northwest about 2 miles out of Flagstaff in the direction of Grand Canyon National Park. Turn right at a sign for Schultz Pass Road. After the paved road turns east, go straight on Elden Lookout Road when the road forks.

Trail Description: Reset your odometer at the fork of Schultz Pass Road and Elden Lookout Road [01]. The road stays paved for about a mile as it passes through a residential area. Potholes abound once the road changes to dirt. The climb to the top intersects hiking trails. At 6.3 miles [02] the road forks. Left takes you to the lookout tower provided the gate is open. If not, park at the gate and enjoy the views. Right goes to a cluster of radio towers—a pretty drive but not much to see at the end.

Return Trip: Return the way you came.

Services: Full services in Flagstaff. Parking at start for Schultz Creek Multi-Use Trail.

Maps: USGS 100,000 scale map Flagstaff, AZ, N3500-W11100/30x60, Arizona Atlas and Gazetteer.

Looking into largest of craters.

Descent from crater rim is steep and loose.

Stay on established trails and obey all signs.

Dune buggy meets 4-wheeler.

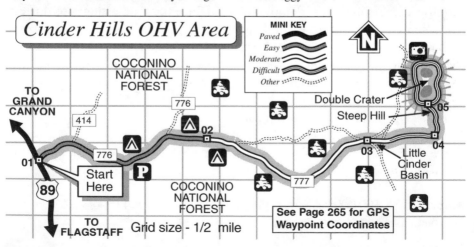

86

Cinder Hills OHV Area 17

Location: Northeast of Flagstaff, east of Highway 89.

Difficulty: Easy to difficult. Easy rolling hills to steep climbs. Loose, gravelly ash is soft like sand and can quickly overheat engines.

Features: Route described here is just a small sample of this 13,500-acre area of volcanic cinder cones, craters and pine forest. Open to off-highway vehicle users with certain restrictions. Only licensed vehicles allowed on Forest Service roads leading into the area. Helmets and spark arresters required. Dispersed camping permitted in posted areas along F.S. 776. No glass containers allowed. Trails go almost everywhere throughout the area; do not create new ones. Stay off the steepest slopes to minimize impact. Obey all signs and stay within the area boundary at all times. Obtain full map of the area with complete list of restrictions from Peaks Ranger Station across from Flagstaff Mall on Highway 89. *(See appendix.)*

Time & Distance: The route described here is about 8 miles one way. Allow about 3 hours to get in and back out. Camp and explore up to 14 days.

To Get There: Take Highway 89 northeast from the Flagstaff Mall 7.7 miles and turn right. The road is marked for the Cinder Hills OHV Area but you don't see the sign until after you turn.

Trail Description: Reset your odometer as you turn right off Hwy. 89 [01]. Turn right on F.S. 776 at 0.5 miles. Camping is allowed after 1.2 miles. Parking area at 1.3 miles where ramps are provided to help unload vehicles. Turn right at 2.1 on F.S. 777. Sign at 2.6 miles [02] describes area, routes and restrictions. Gravel road ends at 2.9; bear slightly right. Follow trail marked with red stakes as best as you can. Reach Little Cinder Basin at 5.2 miles [03]. Continue east through a swale as the road climbs quickly. Reach top of hill at 6.3 miles [04]. Head north up extremely steep hill to top of Double Crater at 6.6 [05]. Loop goes all the way around another 1.7 miles.

Return Trip: Return the way you came.

Services: Dispersed camping, no toilets (yet). Full services in Flagstaff.

Maps: Coconino National Forest, USGS 100,000 scale map Flagstaff, AZ, N3500-W11100/30x60, Arizona Atlas and Gazetteer.

Side road stops at Devil's Kitchen

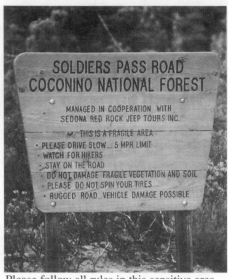

Please follow all rules in this sensitive area.

The trail is steep in spots but manageable.

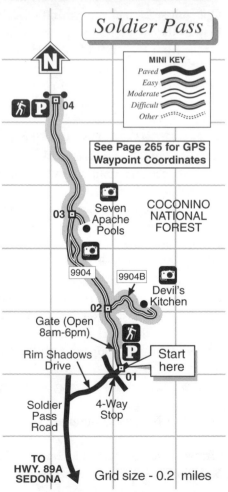

Soldier Pass

MINI KEY

Paved
Easy
Moderate
Difficult
Other

See Page 265 for GPS Waypoint Coordinates

COCONINO NATIONAL FOREST

Seven Apache Pools

Devil's Kitchen

9904

9904B

04

03

02

01

Gate (Open 8am-6pm)

Rim Shadows Drive

Soldier Pass Road

4-Way Stop

Start here

TO HWY. 89A SEDONA

Grid size - 0.2 miles

Soldier Pass ◆18

Location: Immediately north of Sedona.

Difficulty: Difficult. Many steep, rocky steps; however, articulation demands are minimal. Many stock high-clearance vehicles can make it.

Features: If you are looking for a great drive but don't have much time, try this short route. The red rock beauty of the area is quite stunning and includes two interesting features: the stair-stepped Seven Apache Pools and the unusual Devil's Kitchen. Challenges are exciting without being over-whelming. If you've been itching to try a difficult trail, this may be your best opportunity. The trail is on the edge of Sedona immediately adjacent to a beautiful residential area. It's also a very popular hiking area, so drive slowly and don't spin your tires. In short, be a good neighbor. If you park, hike, or stop along the route, you'll need a Red Rocks Pass (see page 15).

Time & Distance: The trail is less than one mile long. Add a little mileage for the two side trips. It can be driven comfortably in less than an hour.

To Get There: From the intersection of Highways 89A and 179 in the middle of Sedona, drive west on 89A about 1.3 miles and turn right on Soldier Pass Road. This is a major intersection with a traffic light. Go north 1.4 miles and turn right on Rim Shadows Drive. Pass through a 4-way intersection in another 0.2 miles and turn left into a parking area. A gate is open between the hours of 8 a.m. and 6 p.m.

Trail Description: Reset your odometer as you turn into the parking area [01]. Proceed through the gate heading north. You are now on Coconino National Forest Road 9904. The turn for Devil's Kitchen is on the right at about 0.2 miles [02]. It's a tight, steep turn between two close trees and easier done on the way out. As you continue, the road splits. Either way is okay, but right is more fun. The turn for Seven Apache Pools is on the right about 0.5 miles [03]. The trail ends at a wilderness boundary at 0.9 [04].

Return Trip: Return the way you came.

Services: None. Return to Sedona.

Maps: Coconino National Forest, USGS 7.5 minute map Wilson Mountain, AZ, N3452.5-W11145/7.5.

Watch for rattlesnakes in Van Deren Cabin.

A few rocky ledges along the route.

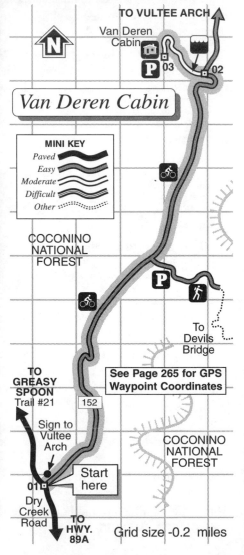

TO VULTEE ARCH

Van Deren Cabin

03   02

Van Deren Cabin

MINI KEY

Paved
Easy
Moderate
Difficult
Other

COCONINO
NATIONAL
FOREST

P

To
Devils
Bridge

TO
GREASY
SPOON
Trail #21

152

See Page 265 for GPS
Waypoint Coordinates

COCONINO
NATIONAL
FOREST

Sign to
Vultee
Arch

Start
here

01

Dry
Creek
Road

TO
HWY.
89A

Grid size -0.2 miles

Flash flooding possible at Dry Creek.

Van Deren Cabin 19

Location: North of Sedona.

Difficulty: Moderate. Several rock ledges require careful tire placement. Tight brush in a few places. Stock SUVs with high ground clearance can make it.

Features: Another short but interesting drive close to Sedona. Only the last part of the trip is challenging. See remains of a well-preserved homesteader's cabin. A metal roof has been added to the cabin to help preserve it. Watch for rattlesnakes inside the cabin. Side trip to Devils Bridge makes a great hike. If you park, hike, or stop along the route, you'll need a Red Rocks Pass (see page 15).

Time & Distance: This trip is 2.7 miles one way and takes less than a hour to drive. Allow more time to explore, hike and enjoy the area.

To Get There: From the intersection of Highways 89A and 179 in the middle of Sedona, drive west on 89A about 3.1 miles and turn right on paved Dry Creek Road. This is a major intersection with a traffic light. Go north 2 miles and turn right on F.S. 152(C). Follow sign to Vultee Arch.

Trail Description: Reset your odometer as you turn right onto F.S. 152(C) [01]. Continue straight at 1.3 miles. The road on the right goes to a small parking area for the Devils Bridge Hiking Trail.This is a great hike if you have the time. Turn left off the main road onto a much narrower road at 2.3 miles [02]. You'll pass through some tight brush and cross over rocky Dry Creek. This area can flood during a heavy downpour so check for dark clouds before crossing. Immediately after climbing out of the creek, make a sharp left. The road appears to go straight so pay attention. The road has a few large ledges to get over. The road ends at a small parking area at 2.7 miles [03]. Van Deren Cabin is a short hike to the right. Remember, if you walk to the cabin, you'll need a Red Rocks Pass.

Return Trip: Return the way you came. You can also turn left when you get back to the main road and continue to Vultee Arch.

Services: None. Return to Sedona.

Maps: Coconino National Forest, USGS 7.5 minute map Wilson Mountain, AZ, N3452.5-W11145/7.5, Arizona Atlas & Gazetteer.

Breathtaking views around every turn.

Merry-Go-Round (Carousel) Rock.

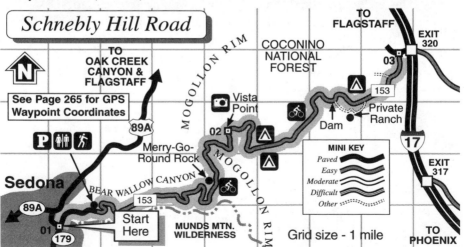
Schnebly Hill Road

TO FLAGSTAFF

EXIT 320

MOGOLLON RIM

COCONINO NATIONAL FOREST

03

N

TO OAK CREEK CANYON & FLAGSTAFF

See Page 265 for GPS Waypoint Coordinates

153

Vista Point

Private Ranch

89A

02

Dam

I 17

Merry-Go-Round Rock

MOGOLLON

MINI KEY

EXIT 317

Sedona

BEAR WALLOW CANYON

Paved
Easy
Moderate
Difficult
Other

89A

153

01

179

Start Here

MUNDS MTN. WILDERNESS

R I M

Grid size - 1 mile

TO PHOENIX

92

Schnebly Hill Road 20

Location: East of Sedona between Highways 89A and Interstate 17.

Difficulty: Easy. Signs recommend only trucks or off-highway vehicles, but cars (not low-slung) can make it in good weather. Although the road is wide and well-maintained, expect a bumpy ride. Much of the lower portion is a shelf road. This road is closed during the winter.

Features: Towering red rock buttes set against a backdrop of deep-green forest and clear blue sky make this road one of Arizona's most photogenic. The road climbs over 2,200 feet from Sedona to the top of massive Mogollon Rim. Memorable hiking trails depart from several places along the road, and dispersed camping is allowed above Vista Point. The drive is impressive in either direction. Elk may be seen before sunset. Mountain bikers looking for an easy day will enjoy the ride down. If you park, hike, or stop along the route, you'll need a Red Rocks Pass (see page 15).

Time & Distance: About 12 miles one way. The road can be driven in an hour but allow much more time; you'll want to stop many times.

To Get There: From the bottom: From the intersection of Highways 89A and 179 in Sedona, drive south 0.4 miles on Hwy. 179. Turn left immediately after crossing the Oak Creek Bridge on a well marked paved road. *From the top:* Get off I-17 at exit 320 and head west on a short paved road. Bear left on a well-marked dirt road at the first turn.

Trail Description: From the bottom: Reset your odometer at the start [01]. Parking lot with modern vault toilet on the left where pavement ends at 0.9. Climb through Bear Wallow Canyon to Merry-Go-Round Rock. The road is wide with several pull-outs. Vista Point on the left at 6.3 miles [02]. Typical forest drive above Vista Point on well-marked F.S. 153. Turn right at pavement at 11.9 [03]. Interstate 17 is directly ahead. *From the top: Reset your odometer where the dirt road starts* [03]. Follow well marked F.S 153 through forest to Vista Point at 5.6 miles [02]. Pass Merry-Go-Round rock and descend into Bear Wallow Canyon. Road ends at 11.9 miles at Hwy. 179 [01]. Right for Sedona; left for Interstate 17 exit 298.

Services: Toilet at Sedona end. Otherwise, return to Sedona or Flagstaff.

Maps: Coconino National Forest, USGS 100,000 scale map Sedona, Arizona 34111-E1-TM-100, Arizona Atlas & Gazetteer.

You'll go by this corral and cattle loading ramp on the first part of the trip.

First canyon descent is steep.

At the bottom of one of the canyons.

Yet another canyon.

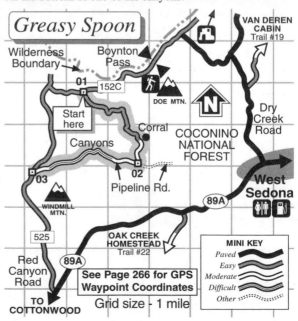

Greasy Spoon

Wilderness Boundary
Boynton Pass
VAN DEREN CABIN
Trail #19
01   152C
DOE MTN.
Start here
Canyons
Corral
COCONINO NATIONAL FOREST
N
Dry Creek Road
03   02
Pipeline Rd.
WINDMILL MTN.
89A
West Sedona
525
OAK CREEK HOMESTEAD
Trail #22
Red Canyon Road
89A

See Page 266 for GPS Waypoint Coordinates

TO COTTONWOOD
Grid size - 1 mile

MINI KEY
Paved
Easy
Moderate
Difficult
Other

94

Greasy Spoon 21

Location: West of Sedona, north of Hwy. 89A. (Note: Locals refer to this trail by two other names: *Diamond Back* and the *Pipeline Road*.)

Difficulty: Difficult. Steep descents and climbs over rocky terrain. The first part of the trail is easy when dry, but slippery and difficult when wet. Don't drive on a rainy day. Route finding can be confusing at times because of numerous side roads. Suitable for many stock high-clearance SUVs when dry.

Features: More remote and less traveled than the other Sedona trails. Park and hike to two mountain peaks near Boynton Pass. One trail goes to Bear Mountain in the Secret Mountain Wilderness. If you park, hike, or stop along the route, you'll need a Red Rocks Pass (see page 15).

Time & Distance: The trail measures 5.8 miles as shown here. Add another 11 miles to get there and return. Allow 2 to 3 hours for the whole trip.

To Get There: From the intersection of Highways 89A and 179 in the middle of Sedona, drive west on 89A about 3.1 miles and turn right on paved Dry Creek Road. *Reset your odometer.* Go north 2.8 miles and turn left at a T, then left again at another T at 4.5 miles. (Right at second T takes you to Indian ruins.) A well-traveled dirt road heads southwest. Ignore numerous side roads. Finally, turn left at 7.6 miles. This begins the trail.

Trail Description: Reset your odometer at the start [01]. Cross a cattle guard at 0.3 and bear left. Again many side roads branch off, so follow the best traveled route. Bear right then left around a corral at 2.4 miles. The road gradually gets more rutted. Continue straight at 2.6 where a road branches to the left. Turn right at 2.8 miles [02]. You are now on the pipeline road. The first canyon descent comes at 3.8 miles. Bear left at 4.2 where a lesser road goes right. Cross another cattle guard at 5.1 and bear left where four roads come together. The trail ends at Red Canyon Road at 5.8 miles [03]. Turn left to reach Hwy. 89A in 3.1 miles.

Return Trip: Turn left at 89A for Sedona; right for Cottonwood.

Services: None. Full services in Sedona and Cottonwood.

Maps: Coconino National Forest, USGS 100,000 scale map Sedona, Arizona 34111-E1-TM-100, Arizona Atlas & Gazetteer.

Great scenery.

Relaxing in the shade by Oak Creek.

Steep shelf road.

A great day to soak up some sunshine.

Another climb.

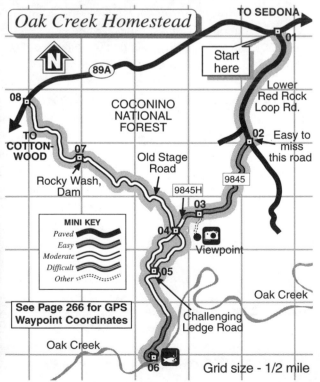

Oak Creek Homestead

TO SEDONA

Start here

01

89A

N

08

COCONINO
NATIONAL
FOREST

Lower
Red Rock
Loop Rd.

02 Easy to
miss
this road

TO
COTTON-
WOOD

07

Old Stage
Road

9845

Rocky Wash,
Dam

9845H

03

MINI KEY
Paved
Easy
Moderate
Difficult
Other

04

Viewpoint

05

**See Page 266 for GPS
Waypoint Coordinates**

Challenging
Ledge Road

Oak Creek

Oak Creek

06

Grid size - 1/2 mile

96

Oak Creek Homestead 22

Location: Southwest of Sedona, south of Highway 89A.

Difficulty: Moderate. Mostly easy except for a couple of rocky stretches. One short section of ledge road is crossed in both directions and requires careful tire placement coming back up. Stock SUVs should have high ground clearance, good articulation and skid plates. Route-finding can be confusing at times.

Features: A short, beautiful drive across classic desert terrain. Stop for lunch beside the cool waters of Oak Creek. This is a popular horseback riding area. Pull over and shut off your engine. If you park, hike, or stop along the route, you'll need a Red Rocks Pass (see page 15).

Time & Distance: A total of 8 miles as described here. Allow about 2 hours.

To Get There: Head southwest from Sedona on Highway 89A. Turn left between mile markers 369 and 368 on Lower Red Rock Loop Road.

Trail Description: Reset your odometer at the start [01]. Follow Lower Red Rock Loop Road south about 1.1 miles [02] and turn right on easy-to-miss F.S. 9845. Go straight at 1.3, right at 2.0 [03] then left at 2.1. You end up on F.S. 9845H. Go either way at 2.3 to reach a 4-way intersection at 2.4 miles [04], then turn left. Climb a steep knoll to the right at 2.8. You can go several ways here; straight up is very difficult. Make a left on a slightly wider road at 3.0 [05]. You'll come back to this spot later. The trail swings to the right down a steep shelf road. This is the toughest spot on the trail. Take your time and use a spotter if necessary. Bear left at a loop at 3.9. There's a shady spot for lunch next to Oak Creek at 4.0 [06]. Continue on around the loop to the right and return the way you came. When you reach the intersection above the narrow shelf road at 5.2 miles [05], go straight, taking a different route than before. Turn left at the 4-way intersection at 5.7 [04]. Bear left at 6.1 onto an old stagecoach road. Cross a rocky wash at 7.1 [07] by a dam. Go left at a T at 7.8. Go straight through the next two intersections to reach Hwy. 89A at 8.0 miles [08].

Return Trip: Right at 89A for Sedona; left for Cottonwood.

Services: None. Full services in Sedona and Cottonwood.

Maps: USGS 100,000 scale map Sedona, Arizona 34111-E1-TM-100.

"Chicken Point" is popular with mountain bikers.

"The Steps" can be bypassed.

Obstacles are fun without being overwhelming.

Popular trail for aggressive, high-clearance, stock SUVs.

"Devil's Dining Room"

Broken Arrow ◆23◆

Location: South of Sedona, east of Highway 179.

Difficulty: Difficult. Several large rock ledges require high ground clearance but the obstacles are not overwhelming because little articulation is required. The hardest obstacle is called "The Steps," which is driven downhill. This obstacle is very steep and will be intimidating to an inexperienced driver; however, stock SUVs with high ground clearance should be able get down just fine. You may scrape bottom so skid plates are recommended. This trail is very well marked and easy to follow.

Features: Although fairly short, this trail has to be considered one of the best in Arizona. It is extremely fun to drive and the red rock scenery is knock-out beautiful. This is an extremely popular route and traffic can be very heavy at times. Pull-outs are provided. Do not widen the trail by trying to pull over anywhere other than the pull-outs. You may have to back up. This is also a very popular hiking and mountain biking area, so be alert and courteous at all times. If you park, hike, or stop along the route, you'll need a Red Rocks Pass (see pg. 15).

Time & Distance: If you take all the side trips, the entire drive is slightly more than 4 miles. Allow 1-1/2 to 2 hours. It could take longer on a busy weekend.

To Get There: Drive 1.3 miles south on Highway 179 from the intersection of 89A and 179 in the center of Sedona (this is called the "Y"). Turn left on Morgan Road at a sign for Broken Arrow Estates. Follow Morgan Road through a residential area about a half mile. Continue straight at a "No Outlet" sign onto Forest Service Road 179F.

Trail Description: Reset your odometer at the "No Outlet" sign [01]. You'll quickly come to a parking lot on the left. Bear right at a large sign outlining regulations for the area. A large bump has been constructed to keep out unsuitable vehicles. If you don't have enough ground clearance to get over this bump, park in the parking lot and hike (fee required). At 0.4 miles bear right over the first obstacle. At 0.5 [02] bear left at a turn for the Devil's Dining Room on the right. (I drove this side trip on the way out.) The road splits into two one-way sections then merges again before a hiking trail to Submarine Rock. You must stay left at 1.0 [03]. The road on the right is one-way coming out. Bear left at 1.1 miles [04] on a challenging side trip to

Submarine Rock, then return to this point and turn left. Continue straight at 1.7 miles [05]. You arrive at Chicken Point at 2.0 [06]. This is a great place to soak up some sun and take in the views.

Turn around at Chicken Point and return the way you came. Turn left on a one-way stretch when you reach the fork at 2.3 miles [05]. (To avoid "The Steps," you can also go out the way you came in but you'll miss the best part of the trail.) This part of the trip winds around unusual rock formations and has some fantastic views. Tire marks clearly indicate the route so make sure you stay on it. Watch for a spot on the left where you can loop around and take some dramatic pictures coming down a steep rock. "The Steps" are encountered at 2.9 miles. Look over the obstacle first then take your time going down. Use a spotter if necessary. Swing right at the bottom of "The Steps," then turn left on the original trail and go out the way you came in. Don't forget to make the side trip to the Devil's Dining Room on the left at 3.5 miles [02].

Return Trip: At Highway 179, right takes you back to the center of Sedona; left takes you to Interstate 17.

Services: Return to Sedona.

Maps: This trail is shown as a faint Jeep road on USGS 7.5 minute maps Sedona, Arizona N3445-W11145/7.5 and Munds Mountain, Arizona N3443-W11137.5/7.5.

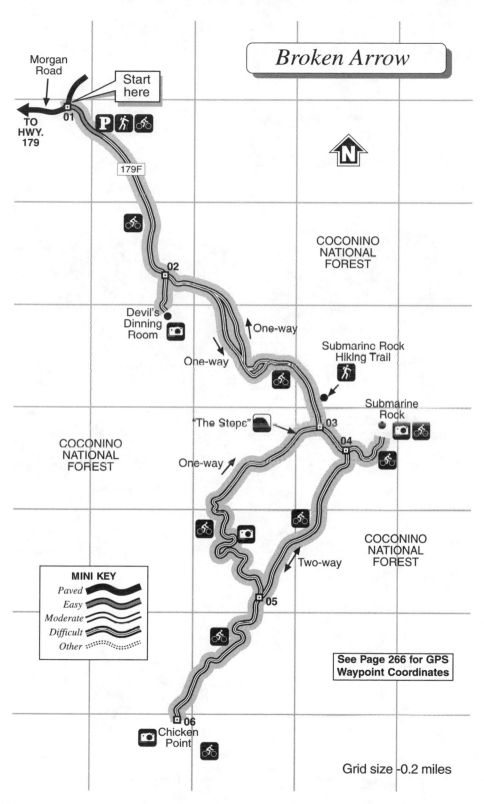

Morgan Road

Start here

TO HWY. 179

01

179F

Broken Arrow

N

COCONINO NATIONAL FOREST

02

Devil's Dinning Room

One-way

One-way

Submarine Rock Hiking Trail

Submarine Rock

"The Steps"

03

04

One-way

COCONINO NATIONAL FOREST

COCONINO NATIONAL FOREST

Two-way

MINI KEY
Paved
Easy
Moderate
Difficult
Other

05

See Page 266 for GPS Waypoint Coordinates

06
Chicken Point

Grid size -0.2 miles

One of many side roads.

Hutch Mountain Lookout Tower.

Picnic area next to Stoneman Lake.

A popular area for ATVs.

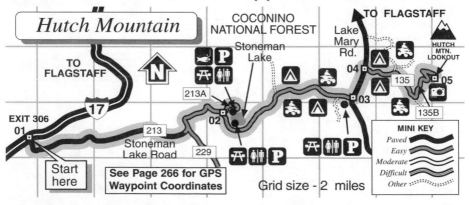

Hutch Mountain

COCONINO NATIONAL FOREST

TO FLAGSTAFF

Stoneman Lake

Lake Mary Rd.

HUTCH MTN. LOOKOUT

TO FLAGSTAFF

N

213A

04

135

05

135B

EXIT 306
01

17

02

03

213

Stoneman Lake Road

229

Start here

See Page 266 for GPS Waypoint Coordinates

Grid size - 2 miles

MINI KEY
Paved
Easy
Moderate
Difficult
Other

102

Hutch Mountain ㉔

Location: South of Flagstaff, east of Interstate 17.

Difficulty: Easy. Gravel road with intermittent washboard surface. Four-wheel drive not necessary except if muddy or snow covered. Side roads in the area are more challenging. Camping near main roads suitable for motor homes.

Features: Mile after mile of quiet, secluded forest. Camp far away from others in the shade of tall ponderosa pines. Many side roads and ATV trails to explore. Enjoy picnic areas overlooking Stoneman Lake.

Time & Distance: About 20 miles one-way as described here. Allow 2 to 3 hours. Add more time to explore numerous side roads.

To Get There: Get off I-17 at Stoneman Lake Road, exit 306, and head east.

Trail Description: *Reset your odometer when you exit Interstate 17* [01]. Head east on Stoneman Lake Road F.S. 213 following signs to Stoneman Lake. The pavement ends after 5.7 miles. Turn left at 7.9 miles [02] on F.S. 213A to visit a picnic area below Stoneman Lake. *(Deduct 1.2 miles if you don't take this side trip)* Continue east on 213 to another picnic area on the left that overlooks Stoneman Lake. Go straight at 12.3 where F.S 765 goes left. Continue straight at 14.9 miles where F.S. 230 joins on the right. Pass another picnic area on the right just before reaching paved Lake Mary Road at 15.3 miles [03]. Sign says Flagstaff is 38 miles from this point.

Turn left on Lake Mary Road heading north. Drive 1.3 miles and turn right on F.S. 135. *Reset your odometer as you turn off Lake Mary Road* [04]. Turn left at 2.6 miles on F.S. 135B. Immediately turn left again and head north to stay on 135B. This road ends at the peak of Hutch Mountain at 4.4 miles [05]. You'll find an old lookout tower, a small picnic area and a primitive outhouse at the top. There's also a smaller trail for ATVs that converges at the top.

Return Trip: Return the way you came or try one of the many side roads that eventually goes back to Lake Mary Road.

Services: Vault toilets at picnic areas. Full services in Flagstaff.

Maps: Coconino National Forest, USGS 250,000 scale map Holbrook, Arizona , Arizona Atlas and Gazetteer.

Smiley Rock.

Last open area before Martin Canyon.

Signs for the Great Western Trail.

Gold King Mine and Ghost Town.

Martin Canyon is narrow and rocky.

Smiley Rock 25

Location: West of Jerome and Cottonwood, northeast of Prescott.

Difficulty: Difficult. This rating applies to the portion of the trip through Martin Canyon which is narrow and rocky. Skid plates and good articulation are recommended. Brush is tight in several places. Much of the route is an easy gravel road.

Features: Allow plenty of time to see historic Jerome. The town is a major tourist attraction offering an array of quaint gift shops, art galleries, museums and restaurants. If you're into mining history, plan a stop at the Gold King Mine and Ghost Town along the route or take a short side trip to Jerome State Historic Park. Both of these attractions require a small fee. Once in the backcountry, you'll enjoy your secluded adventure through Martin Canyon, which follows the southern border of the Woodchute Wilderness. Hike and camp at various points along the way. Some of this trail is officially part of the Great Western Trail. The section described here is adopted and maintained by the Prescott Mountain Goats 4-Wheel-Drive Club.

Time & Distance: Approximately 23 miles of off pavement driving. Allow about 4 hours driving time.

To Get There: Follow Highway 89A through Jerome and turn north at the fire station. The fire station is located at a tight turn along a switchback that winds through the center of town. You can't miss the fire station if you stay on 89A.

Trail Description: *Reset your odometer at the fire station* [01]. Head northwest on a paved road that soon changes to gravel. At 0.9 miles [02] turn right at a fence and head uphill on a road marked as primitive. You'll see the Gold King Mine and Ghost Town below you on the left. As you climb, great views of Verde Valley can be seen on the right. Stay left on the main road at 1.7 miles. Bear left on a lesser road at 7.7 miles [03] on F.S. 318A. The road remains mostly flat as it follows an old railroad route. This road is part of the Great Western Trail and is marked with signs. At 9.0 miles pass a trailhead for the Woodchute Hiking Trail #102. Stay on the best-traveled road as spurs branch off.

At 14.3 miles pass under major power lines, then at 14.4 [04] bear left on an equal size road. Follow signs for the Great Western Trail. You'll cross a cattle guard while still under the power lines. Bear left at 14.9.

Continue straight uphill at 15.2 [05] where F.S. 9002G goes to the left. The road deteriorates quickly from here, so shift into 4-wheel drive. Bear left at a T at 16.1 miles [06] onto F.S. 103. You'll cross a series of rocky washes as Martin Canyon narrows. Don't continue if heavy rains are forecast because of the danger of flash floods. Brush is very tight through this section. Watch for Smiley Rock on the left at 17.7 miles [07]. Make a hard left at 18.0 miles, staying in the wash. The trail gets tougher with several boulder fields before you begin to climb out of Martin Canyon.

Bear left at a T at 20.4 [08] and left again at 21.0 miles. Take another left at 21.2 where F.S.106 goes right. There are some good camping spots through this area. Pass through a gate then turn right at a parking area for the Woodchute Hiking Trail at 22.2 miles [09]. Pass through another gate at 22.8 [10] to a parking area and vault toilet. Follow a paved road to the left. You'll reach a T at 23.0 miles. Potato Patch Campground is to the left. Highway 89A is to the right at 23.3 miles [11].

Return Trip: Left on Highway 89A takes you back to Jerome and Cottonwood; right goes to Prescott.

Services: Vault toilet at the end of the trail. Some services in Jerome. Full services in Cottonwood and Prescott.

Historical Highlights: Miners began staking claims in the Jerome area way back in the 1870s. By the 1920s Jerome had grown to a massive copper mining town of over 15,000 people. Despite numerous fires and other disasters, the town always managed to survive. By 1953, however, mining was all but dead. Only 50 people remained in town. By the '60s and '70s artists and craftsmen began moving into town, renovating homes and fixing-up shops to sell their work. Today Jerome is a thriving tourist attraction and National Historic Landmark.

Maps: Prescott National Forest, USGS 250,000 scale map Prescott, Arizona, Arizona Atlas and Gazetteer.

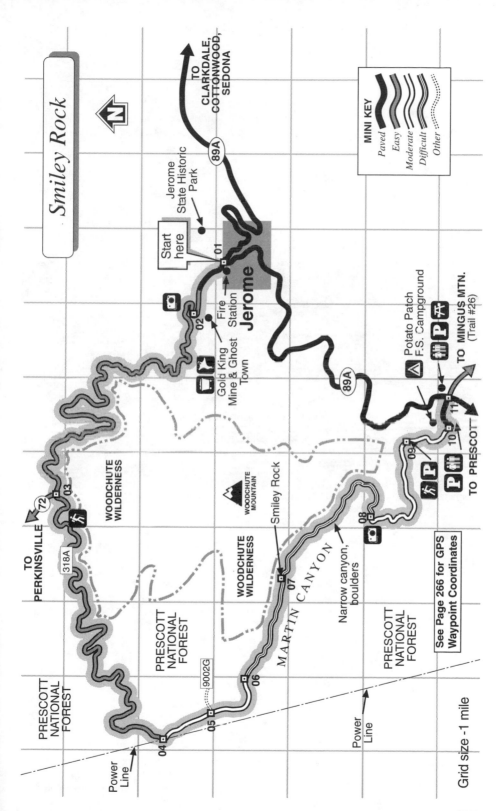

Smiley Rock

N

TO CLARKDALE, COTTONWOOD, SEDONA

89A

Jerome State Historic Park

Start here

01

Jerome

Fire Station

02

Gold King Mine & Ghost Town

89A

Potato Patch F.S. Campground

TO MINGUS MTN. (Trail #26)

11

10

09

P

TO PRESCOTT

WOODCHUTE WILDERNESS

03

72

TO PERKINSVILLE

318A

WOODCHUTE MOUNTAIN

Smiley Rock

WOODCHUTE WILDERNESS

08

MARTIN CANYON

07

Narrow canyon, boulders

PRESCOTT NATIONAL FOREST

PRESCOTT NATIONAL FOREST

9002G

06

05

04

PRESCOTT NATIONAL FOREST

Power Line

Power Line

See Page 266 for GPS Waypoint Coordinates

Grid size - 1 mile

MINI KEY
Paved
Easy
Moderate
Difficult
Other

107

The east side climb looks down on Verde Valley and Sedona.

Dispersed camping is popular in the Prescott National Forest on the west side.

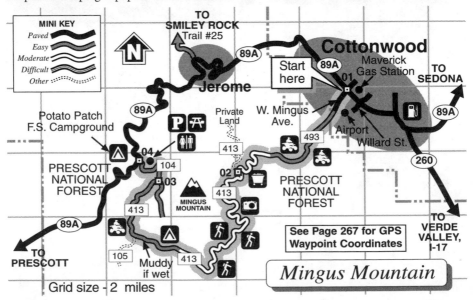

MINI KEY
Paved
Easy
Moderate
Difficult
Other

N

TO
SMILEY ROCK
Trail #25

89A

Cottonwood

Maverick
Gas Station

89A

Start
here

01

TO
SEDONA

Jerome

W. Mingus
Ave.

89A

89A

Private
Land

Airport

Willard St.

Potato Patch
F.S. Campground

P

413

493

260

04

PRESCOTT
NATIONAL
FOREST

104

02

PRESCOTT
NATIONAL
FOREST

03

413

MINGUS
MOUNTAIN

413

See Page 267 for GPS
Waypoint Coordinates

89A

105

413

TO
PRESCOTT

Muddy
if wet

TO
VERDE
VALLEY,
I-17

Mingus Mountain

Grid size - 2 miles

108

Mingus Mountain 26

Location: West of Cottonwood, southwest of Jerome.

Difficulty: Moderate. Most of the trail is easy except for a few rocky places. Narrow shelf road on east side of Mingus Mountain. Stay off this trail during rainy periods; the last part can get very muddy. Suitable for stock SUVs.

Features: After passing through an unimpressive lower section, the road climbs quickly up the side of scenic Mingus Mountain. Great views of Verde Valley and Sedona looking east. An enjoyable forest drive. ATVs are restricted to main Forest Service roads only.

Time & Distance: About 19 miles. Allow 2 to 3 hours.

To Get There: Follow Hwy. 89A northwest through Cottonwood towards Jerome. Turn left (west) 0.6 miles north of Willard Street onto West Mingus Avenue (not marked).

Trail Description: Reset your odometer as you get off Hwy. 89A [01]. Follow paved W. Mingus Avenue west. It becomes F.S. 493 as it narrows and changes to dirt. Continue straight as numerous side roads branch off. Bear right at 3.0 and 4.8 miles. Note foundations of Copper Chief Mine on left at 5.3. Shift into low range as trail gets steeper and rockier. Continue straight at 6.2 miles [02]. You are now on F.S. 413. Pass through seasonal gate at 9.4. The road gradually swings around to southwest side of Mingus Mountain. Hiking trail #512 on left at 10.2. Continue through cattle guard at 10.8 and pass by Coleman Hiking Trail #108. Pass Black Canyon Hiking Trail #114 at 10.9 miles. Popular dispersed camping begins about 14.0 miles. Continue straight at 14.7. Continue straight where road joins F.S. 105 (Great Western Trail) at 15.1 miles. Bear left at T at 17.4 miles [03] and follow F.S. 104 to Hwy. 89A, reached at 18.8 miles [04]. Parking, toilets and covered picnic tables on right at Hwy. 89A. This point is across from entrance to Potato Patch Campground.

Return Trip: Turn right at 89A for Jerome and Cottonwood. Prescott is left.

Services: Vault toilet at end of trail. Full services in Jerome and Cottonwood.

Maps: Prescott National Forest, USGS 100,000 scale map Prescott, Arizona N3430-W11200/30x60, Arizona Atlas and Gazetteer.

AREA 4

Lake Havasu City,
Parker

27. Crossman Peak
28. Mohave Wash
29. Vampire Mine
30. Swansea Townsite
31. Buckskin Mountains
32. Cattail Cove
33. President's Choice

TO KINGMAN

FRANCONIA
EXIT 13

40

EXIT 9

TO TOPOCK, AZ & CALIFORNIA

95

MINI KEY

Paved
Easy
Moderate
Difficult
Other

● EASY
■ MODERATE
◆ DIFFICULT

27

CROSSMAN PEAK

Lake Havasu City

Lake Havasu

Standard Wash

28

Arizona

N

Colorado River & State Boundary

95

California

32

Bill Williams River National Wildlife Refuge

Parker Dam

Colorado River & State Boundary

95

31

Desert Bar

29

Swansea Townsite

Parker

62

33

30

95

TO QUARTZSITE

Grid size - 10 miles

110

Lake Havasu City, Parker

Most of us recognize Lake Havasu City for its famous London Bridge. Few people realize it's a great place to go four-wheeling. The town is surrounded by remote, rugged desert and low mountain ranges. The local four-wheel-drive club, the Havasu 4-Wheelers, is one of the largest and most active clubs I've seen anywhere. Although summers are dangerously hot, winter months are glorious with daytime temperatures commonly above sixty degrees. At anytime you can take a break from the heat to camp, fish, and boat along the Colorado River with its many dams, reservoirs and state parks. The area offers a full range of trails including two easy desert drives: one through *Mohave Wash,* the other to historic *Swansea Townsite.* One exciting four-wheeling adventure leads to a unique and popular bar located in the remote desert. This trip, through the *Buckskin Mountains*, offers an easy front-door approach or a moderate back way. Other moderate trails include *Cattail Cove* and *Crossman Peak.* A notch tougher than these trails is exciting *Vampire Mine.* If it's extreme rock terror you're looking for, you won't want to miss *President's Choice* near Parker. The town is known for its hard-core trails and their local club sponsors the popular *Desert Splash* four-wheel-drive event in November.

Rugged descent in search of the *Vampire Mine*, Trail #29, Difficult.

Toughest, narrowest section.

Several steep hills with loose gravel.

Great views from this high ridge. A good point to stop for lunch.

Steep spot coming down from the high ridge.

Location: East of Lake Havasu City, south of Interstate 40.

Difficulty: Moderate. Most of this trail is easy but there is one hilly section that is fairly challenging. The road is narrow in places and brush rubs against your vehicle. A couple of rocky sections require careful tire placement. One steep descent on a narrow shelf road may be intimidating to a novice driver. High ground clearance and skid plates are required. Route-finding is complex and confusing at times. Be careful when exploring mines. Some have exposed vertical shafts hundreds of feet deep. ATVs and dirt bikes need to be especially careful.

Features: This route crosses remote desert around the south and east sides of Crossman Peak. It does not go to the top of the peak. Drivers should be self-reliant and prepared for emergencies. Do not drive alone, especially in the heat of summer.

Time & Distance: This fairly long trip covers over 36 miles off-pavement. Allow 4 to 5 hours.

To Get There: Head south from Lake Havasu City on Hwy. 95. Turn left into Standard Wash 0.6 miles past mile marker 173. Make sure you go past the kiosk for Standard Wash before you turn left. Stop and review rules and regulations on the kiosk. Always stay on existing trails. Standard Wash is very wide and has several entry points but all eventually funnel together.

Trail Description: Reset your odometer as you get off Hwy. 95 [01]. Try to follow the most traveled path up Standard Wash. The trail splits frequently, but you'll stay on course if you stay in the main wash. Bear left at 5.2 miles [02] following a sign for Dutch Flat. Bear right at 7.0, then at 8.0 continue straight climbing out of the wash up a steep hill. Turn left at 9.3 miles [03].

You'll pass remnants of a corral on the left at 11.1 miles before reaching a fork at 12.0. Turn left at this fork as the trail gets tougher. The roughest stretch is reached at 13 miles where it gets narrow, rocky and steep. Take your time through this section and use a spotter if you don't feel comfortable. You'll climb several steep hills with loose rock. A high ridge is reached at 14.1 miles [04]. As you start down the other side, a shelf road narrows and drops very steeply. Bear left at 15.2. Continue straight past a water tank and corral at 15.8 miles.

The road widens at 16.2 miles. You're actually on an old landing strip used for military training during World War II. Turn left off this landing strip almost immediately onto a rough single lane road. Make two quick left turns at a Y then a T at 18.4 miles [05]. You should be heading southwest. A better-traveled road weaves back and forth across an old washed-out road. At 19.7 the road makes a big sweeping curve to the right. Continue straight at 21.0 as a road joins on the left. Pass through a fence and bear right around a corral at 21.7 miles. Make a soft right turn at a K shaped intersection at 23.7. The road begins to smooth out. Continue straight across a narrow wash at 24.5.

Make a hard right at a T at 25.2 miles [06]. At 27.4 miles the road is blocked by a fenced-in area of private property. Drive around the left perimeter of the property; the road continues on the other side. Go by a water tank and dilapidated windmill before reaching a fork at 29.6 miles [07]. Bear right downhill then immediately turn left. Continue straight when a road joins on the left at 33.0. Go straight again at 34.3 before reaching Interstate 40 (Exit 13) at 36.3 miles [08].

Return Trip: Left on I-40 takes you back to the Hwy. 95 (Exit 9), which goes south to Lake Havasu City. Right on I-40 goes to Kingman.

Services: None on the trail. Closest gas and food are west on I-40 at Exit 9. There's a convenience store with gas in Yucca, which is located north on I-40 between Exits 25 and 26. Full services in Lake Havasu City and Kingman.

Maps: This entire network of roads is shown clearly on USGS 100,000 scale maps Needles, California-Arizona 34114-E1-TM-100 and Parker, Arizona-California 34114-A1-TM-100. Parts of this route are shown on the Arizona Atlas & Gazetteer.

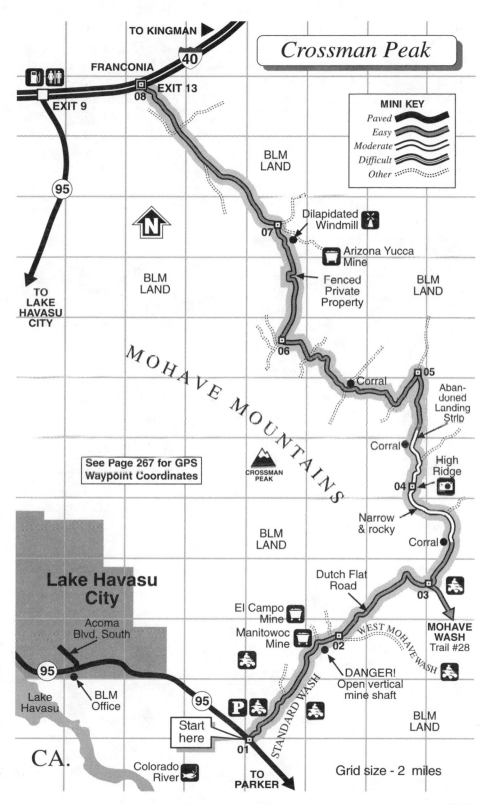

Crossman Peak

TO KINGMAN

FRANCONIA

I-40

EXIT 13
08

EXIT 9

95

TO LAKE HAVASU CITY

MINI KEY
Paved
Easy
Moderate
Difficult
Other

N

BLM LAND

Dilapidated Windmill

07

Arizona Yucca Mine

BLM LAND

Fenced Private Property

BLM LAND

06

MOHAVE MOUNTAINS

Corral

05

Abandoned Landing Strip

Corral

High Ridge

See Page 267 for GPS Waypoint Coordinates

CROSSMAN PEAK

04

BLM LAND

Narrow & rocky

Corral

Dutch Flat Road

03

MOHAVE WASH
Trail #28

Lake Havasu City

Acoma Blvd. South

El Campo Mine

Manitowoc Mine

02

WEST MOHAVE WASH

DANGER! Open vertical mine shaft

95

BLM Office

Lake Havasu

95

P

Start here

01

STANDARD WASH

BLM LAND

CA.

Colorado River

TO PARKER

Grid size - 2 miles

115

Climbing out of wash on Dutch Flat Road.

Dodging a few rocks along the way.

McCracken Mountains in distance.

This old water pump still works.

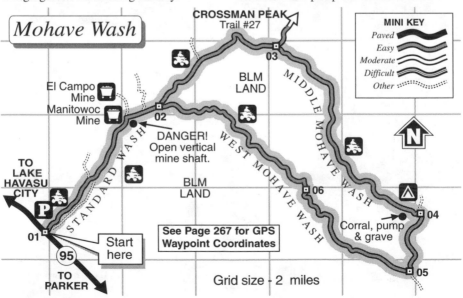

Mohave Wash

CROSSMAN PEAK
Trail #27

03

BLM LAND

MIDDLE MOHAVE WASH

MINI KEY
Paved
Easy
Moderate
Difficult
Other

El Campo Mine
Manitowoc Mine

02

DANGER!
Open vertical
mine shaft.

STANDARD WASH

WEST MOHAVE WASH

TO LAKE HAVASU CITY

P

BLM LAND

06

N

Corral, pump & grave

04

01

Start here

See Page 267 for GPS
Waypoint Coordinates

95

TO PARKER

Grid size - 2 miles

05

Mohave Wash ㉘

Location: Southeast of Lake Havasu City.

Difficulty: Easy. Soft sand, minor hill climbs and a few rocky places. Route-finding is confusing at times. Vehicles overheat quickly in soft sand. Use caution around mines. Some have exposed vertical shafts hundreds of feet deep. Don't let children stray. ATVs and dirt bikes need to be especially careful.

Features: A remote desert drive with a few small challenges to make it interesting. Best to avoid during the extreme heat of summer. Read and follow all regulations posted on the information kiosk at the start of the trail. Most important is to always stay on existing trails.

Time & Distance: About 34 miles for the entire loop. Allow 3 to 4 hours.

To Get There: Head south from Lake Havasu City on Hwy. 95. Turn left into Standard Wash 0.6 miles past mile marker 173. Make sure you go past the brown BLM kiosk for Standard Wash before you turn left.

Trail Description: Reset your odometer as you get off Hwy. 95 [01]. Try to follow the most traveled path up Standard Wash. The trail splits frequently, but you'll stay on course if you stay in the main wash. Bear left at 5.2 miles [02] following a sign for Dutch Flat. Bear right at 7.0, then at 8.0 continue straight climbing out of the wash up a steep hill. Turn right at 9.3 miles [03] and follow Middle Mohave Wash southeast.

The trail is defined by the wash; stay in it. Turn right at 15.4 miles. At 16.8 miles either way is OK. Bear right at 17.0 [04] at a corral and abandoned water pump (which still works). There's also a curious grave marker nearby. Some people like to camp here. Bear right into West Mohave Wash at 18.9 miles [05]. Choose your best line through a rocky spot at 23.4 [06]. We manuevered a stock Grand Cherokee through this spot with little problem. You return to Standard Wash at 29.0 [02]. Turn left and go out the way you came in. Hwy. 95 is reached at 34.1 miles.

Return Trip: Right on Hwy. 95 returns to Lake Havasu City. Parker is left.

Services: None. Return to Lake Havasu City.

Maps: USGS 100,000 scale map Parker, Arizona-California 34114-A1-TM-100, Arizona Atlas and Gazetteer.

This spot can be bypassed.

Water crossing in Bill Williams River Wildlife Refuge.

Articulation needed here.

Stock SUVs can drive this trail but experience is needed.

At the switchback by the Vampire Mine.

One shaft at Vampire Mine.

The trail is very narrow towards the top.

Vampire Mine 29

Location: Between Lake Havasu City and Parker just southeast of the Parker Dam.

Difficulty: Difficult. Mostly easy to moderate with several tough spots. The worst rock obstacle has a bypass, making it possible for stock SUVs to consider this trail. Good articulation, high ground clearance and skid plates are recommended. Inexperienced drivers may find this trail intimidating. The final climb as you approach Vampire Mine is steep, narrow and rocky. The descent after the mine is badly washed out. The drive through Bill Williams River National Wildlife Refuge has several water crossings which are usually shallow. However, water can be deep after an extended period of heavy rain. This part of the drive has some dense vegetation, but it's not too abrasive. Route-finding can be confusing at times. Do not drive this trail by yourself or in the heat of summer.

Features: The trail begins with a drive through Bill Williams River National Wildlife Refuge, a low, sandy area that is densely overgrown and ideal for birds and small animals. Brochures explaining the importance of the area are available at an information kiosk at the start of the trail. Do not leave the road at any time as you pass through. Once through the refuge, you enter BLM land. Learn more about the area by visiting the BLM office in Lake Havasu City on the south side of town at the intersection of Highway 95 and Acoma Boulevard South.

Time & Distance: It's about 12 miles to the difficult part of the trail and about 4 miles around the difficult loop. The quickest way out is the way you came in. The total trip is about 28 miles. Allow 4 to 5 hours.

To Get There: Head south about 19 miles on Hwy. 95 from Lake Havasu City. Turn left onto a wide gravel road (Bill Williams Hwy.) just after the Bill Williams Bridge near mile marker 162. From Parker, turn right about a half mile past the Central Arizona Project Pumping Station.

Trail Description: Reset your odometer as you get off Hwy. 95 [01]. Head uphill on a wide washboard gravel road. The first 3 miles are suitable for passenger cars. The "Road Closed" sign at the start is not accurate. I called the refuge office and they had no explanation for the sign. They just said the road is open. Only 4-wheel-drive vehicles should proceed past the gate at 3.3 miles [02]. At 6.8 miles [03] you exit dense vegetation and run into

Mineral Wash Road. Bear slightly right and follow the sandy wash bottom. Stay left in the wash at 8.7 miles past a road that goes right to Mineral Hill Mine (private property). At 9.5 miles continue straight past Slot Canyon on the left. (See Swansea Townsite, Trail #30, to learn about this fun drive.) Bear right staying in Mineral Wash at 9.8 miles [04]. At 10.5 miles [05] make an important right turn out of Mineral Wash onto a somewhat narrower road.

You must decide how to cross a wide rocky area at 10.6 miles. Stock vehicles can get around the right side with no problem. Modified vehicles usually go left. More rock ledges follow. At 11.0 miles climb a large rock on the right to get around a small concrete dam. At 11.3 miles [06] make another important right turn onto a narrow side road. Turn left at 11.8 miles after crossing a deep trench. There's a steep rocky climb across a ledge at 12.1 miles [07]. Without good articulation, you may have to fill in holes with rocks in order to get up this section. Bear right at a fork at 12.4 and cross a narrow ledge. After that, you'll cross over a ridge and start down. A tight switchback to the right at 12.8 [08] marks the start of Vampire Mine, which has several shafts scattered around the area. After the switch-back and a short descent, look for a mine on the right (see photo). Bear right at a fork at 13.0 as you descend. The road is steep with several washed-out sections. There's a challenging spot to get around at 13.8. At 14.2 miles [09] drop steeply back into Mineral Wash. Turn left and go out the way you came in. (If you turn right, Mineral Wash runs into Shea Road on a long trip into Parker.)

Return Trip: Right at Hwy. 95 returns to Lake Havasu City. Parker is left.

Services: None along the trail. There's a convenience store and gas station about 6 miles to the left on Hwy. 95 in the direction of Parker. Otherwise, return to Lake Havasu City.

Maps: USGS 100,000 scale map Parker, Arizona-California 34114-A1-TM-100, Arizona Atlas and Gazetteer.

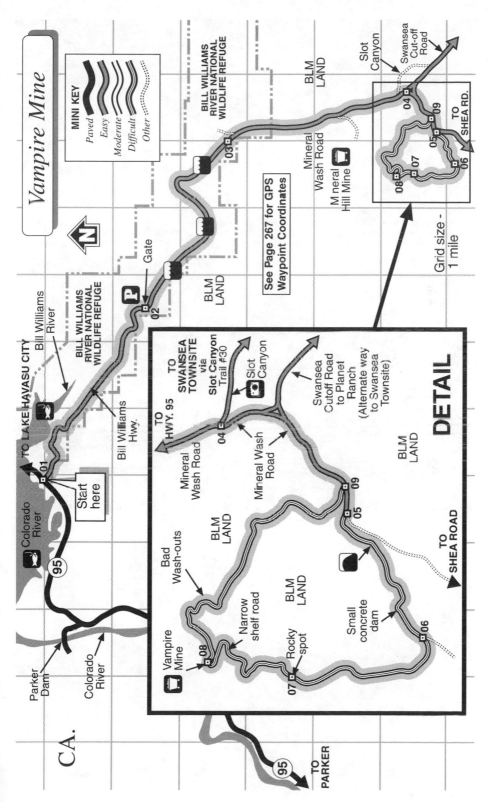

Vampire Mine

MINI KEY
- Paved
- Easy
- Moderate
- Difficult
- Other

N

CA.

TO LAKE HAVASU CITY

Bill Williams River

BILL WILLIAMS RIVER NATIONAL WILDLIFE REFUGE

Bill Williams Hwy.

Start here

01

Colorado River

95

Parker Dam

Colorado River

P

Gate

02

BLM LAND

03

BILL WILLIAMS RIVER NATIONAL WILDLIFE REFUGE

BLM LAND

Mineral Wash Road

Mineral Hill Mine

See Page 267 for GPS Waypoint Coordinates

Slot Canyon

Swansea Cut-off Road

04

09

05

07

08

06

TO SHEA RD.

Grid size - 1 mile

TO PARKER

95

DETAIL

TO HWY. 95

TO SWANSEA TOWNSITE via Slot Canyon Trail #30

Slot Canyon

Mineral Wash Road

04

Mineral Wash Road

Swansea Cutoff Road to Planet Ranch (Alternate way to Swansea Townsite)

BLM LAND

09

05

BLM LAND

Bad Wash-outs

Narrow shelf road

Rocky spot

BLM LAND

Small concrete dam

06

TO SHEA ROAD

Vampire Mine

08

07

One of several water crossings through the Bill Williams River National Wildlife Refuge.

Slot Canyon. Stay out if heavy rains are eminent.

Remains of one of the larger processing plants at the Swansea Townsite.

122

Swansea Townsite ③⓪

Location: Southeast of Lake Havasu City, east of Parker.

Difficulty: Easy. Mostly sandy wash bottoms and gravel roads except for a 3-mile stretch through the Bill Williams River National Wildlife Refuge. This section has short sandy climbs and several water crossings. Water crossings are not a concern except after an extended period of heavy rain. Brush is dense but not abrasive. Slot Canyon is narrow, but easily passable. The trail is suitable for stock SUVs with moderate ground clearance. Route-finding is fairly easy. Flash flooding is possible in the wash bottoms and especially through Slot Canyon. Don't enter if heavy rains are forecast. This trip is not recommended during the heat of summer. Always carry plenty of water.

Features: Drive through Bill Williams River National Wildlife Refuge at the start of this trip. Enjoy over 275 species of birds as you pass through a jungle-like setting. Squeeze through dramatic Slot Canyon. Finish the trip with a visit to Swansea Townsite, once a booming copper mining town. The BLM provides brochures that enable you to understand and appreciate the area. Although brochures are often available at the site, it is best to get one in advance at the BLM Field Office in Lake Havasu City. Swansea Townsite is larger than it first appears once you learn about the area. It has designated trails for 4-wheel-drive vehicles, ATVs and dirt bikes. You'll need a brochure to find the landmarks in the area. Make sure you stay on designated trails at all times. Choose from 5 different camping spots at the site. No water is available. Pack out your trash and don't disturb any of the building remains.

Time & Distance: More than 55 miles as described here. Allow 4 to 5 hours plus extra time to explore Swansea.

To Get There: Head south about 19 miles on Hwy. 95 from Lake Havasu City. Turn left onto a wide gravel road just after the Bill Williams Bridge near mile marker 162. From Parker, turn right about a half mile past the Central Arizona Project Pumping Station.

Trail Description: Reset your odometer as you get off Hwy. 95 [01]. Head uphill on a wide washboard gravel road. The "Road Closed" sign at the start is not accurate. I called the BW Refuge Office and they had no explanation for the sign. They just said the road is open. Only 4-wheel-drive vehicles should proceed past the gate at 3.3 miles [02]. The road surface includes soft sand, short climbs and several water crossings. At 6.8 miles [03] swing right on Mineral Wash Road. Stay left in the wash at 8.7 miles past a road that goes right to Mineral Hill Mine (private property). Turn left into Slot Canyon at 9.5 miles [04]. The canyon is short but dramatic. It takes only a few minutes to drive through. (You can bypass the canyon by continuing to Swansea Cutoff Road just ahead. Follow the sign left to Planet Ranch.) Bear left at a fork inside the canyon. As you exit the canyon, straddle a rocky trench into a wide, sandy wash. Stay in the wash bottom. When the wash forks at 10.3, bear right. Follow the best-worn path south before reaching Swansea Cutoff Road at 10.7 miles [05], then turn left.

Bear right at 12.2 miles [06] then go straight at the stop sign. Planet Ranch Road goes left here. The road gradually gets wider and faster. Turn left at a major 4-way intersection at 17.4 miles [07]. At 24.4 [08] bear right into the Swansea Townsite. Continue past various building remains to an information kiosk and parking area. Many features at the site are not obvious. You'll need the BLM brochure mentioned earlier.

Reset your odometer at the townsite and return 7 miles back to the 4-way intersection [07]. Continue straight through the intersection. Follow this wide gravel road back to Parker. On the way, you'll go under power lines at 10.1 and over a bridge for Central Arizona Project at 13.4. Bear left on paved Shea Road at 17.4 miles [09], which connects to Hwy. 95 at 30.7 miles.

Return Trip: Right on Hwy. 95 goes to Parker and Lake Havasu City. Left goes south to Quartzsite.

Services: None along the trail. Full services in Parker.

Historical Highlights: Although the town of Swansea grew quite large, mining never fulfilled investors' expectations. Silver mining started here as early as 1862 with copper treated as a worthless by-product. Later when the importance of copper was realized, major investments were made to build a smelting plant, power plant and water system. Soon a railroad was built and by 1909 over 500 people lived and worked here. Buildings included saloons, stores, a post office, a manager's house and many residences. The town was revived in 1918 but finally died after the Great Depression.

A favorite place to visit is the water pumping plant on the Bill Williams River north of town, which can only be reached by 4-wheel drive. You must walk the last 150 feet because the station is inside the Swansea Wilderness.

Maps: USGS 100,000 scale maps Parker, Arizona-California 34114-A1-TM-100 and Alamo Lake Arizona, Arizona Atlas and Gazetteer.

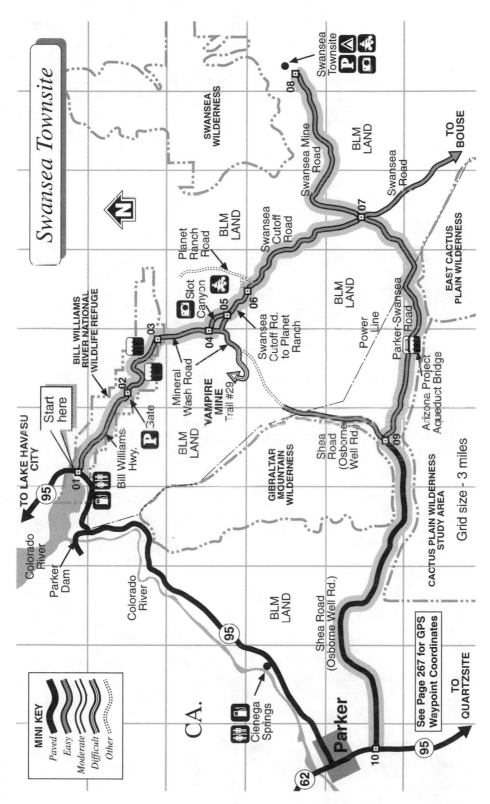

Swansea Townsite

MINI KEY
Paved
Easy
Moderate
Difficult
Other

N

TO LAKE HAVASU CITY

95

Colorado River

Parker Dam

Colorado River

CA.

Cienega Springs

95

Parker

95

62

TO QUARTZSITE

10

Start here

01

Bill Williams Hwy.

Gate

02

03

BILL WILLIAMS RIVER NATIONAL WILDLIFE REFUGE

BLM LAND

Mineral Wash Road

VAMPIRE MINE
Trail #29

04

Slot Canyon

05

06

Planet Ranch Road

BLM LAND

Swansea Cutoff Road

Swansea Cutoff Rd. to Planet Ranch

SWANSEA WILDERNESS

Swansea Mine Road

08

Swansea Townsite

07

Swansea Road

BLM LAND

TO BOUSE

BLM LAND

Power Line

Parker-Swansea Road

Arizona Project Aqueduct Bridge

EAST CACTUS PLAIN WILDERNESS

09

GIBRALTAR MOUNTAIN WILDERNESS

Shea Road (Osborne Well Rd.)

BLM LAND

Shea Road (Osborne Well Rd.)

CACTUS PLAIN WILDERNESS STUDY AREA

See Page 267 for GPS Waypoint Coordinates

Grid size - 3 miles

125

A fun drive with plenty of challenge.

The roughest spot on the trail.

Plenty of wash outs along the route.

Don't go alone in this remote backcountry.

Nellie E. Saloon is open on weekends only. It's closed during the summer.

126

Buckskin Mountains

Location: Northeast of Parker.

Difficulty: Moderate. Stock vehicles will find this trail quite challenging. Several rocky sections require careful tire placement and the help of a good spotter. Other parts of the trail are soft and susceptible to water erosion. Conditions will worsen over time. An experienced member of our group managed to maneuver his stock Cherokee through without a scratch. Stock vehicles should have high ground clearance and skid plates. The trail passes through a remote and desolate area which sees little traffic. Don't drive the road under wet conditions. Route-finding is confusing at the start but gets easier as you proceed. Do not drive this trail by yourself. Avoid during the heat of summer.

Features: This wonderfully challenging backroad culminates at the Nellie E. Saloon, or as the locals call it, the "Desert Bar." People come from all over to visit this most unusual attraction located in the middle of nowhere. It's not necessary to take the 4-wheel-drive route. You can reach the bar on the easy gravel road described here as the exit route. (To learn more about the Nellie E. Saloon, read *Historical Highlights* on the next page.)

Time & Distance: It's 5.5 miles to the bar going in the back way. This part takes about 1-1/2 hours. The exit route is 4.8 miles and takes about 20 minutes.

To Get There: On Hwy. 95, head north from Parker or south from Lake Havasu City to River Island Market and gas station located between mile markers 155 and 156 on the south side of the road. The start of the trail is just west of a fenced-in RV storage area next to the market.

      To reach Nellie E. Saloon the easy way, turn east off Hwy. 95 on an unmarked gravel road between mile markers 149 and 150. This road is about a mile north of the traffic light at Cienega Springs, which is about 5 miles north of Parker.

Trail Description: *Reset your odometer as you get off Hwy. 95 next to the RV storage area* [01]. Follow a gravel road around the back of the storage area and bear left. The road weaves through a narrow canyon and forks immediately at 0.3 miles. Turn left at this fork. When I drove through here, this section was badly washed out and the road was not obvious. At 0.8 miles stay low as the road swings right then forks. Bear right at this fork. Bear left at 0.9 when the road forks again. Go straight at 1.0 miles [02] when

127

a road joins on the left. It is important to keep heading south. There is a wilderness on the east side of the trail which you cannot enter.

Finally, the road becomes more distinct as it weaves up and down through the starkly beautiful Buckskin Mountains. At 3.3 miles [03] pass remnants of an old mining camp on the left. The worst spot on the trail is encountered at 3.6 miles. It's very rocky but, fortunately, downhill. You may need a spotter to get through this section. Bear left at 4.0 miles [04] past a stone cabin on the left. An exit road goes right. At 4.1 bear right at a fork. Before making this turn, you may want to stop here and look at the Gray Eagle Mine just ahead on the left.

After the mine, you'll climb a small ledge road over the crest of a hill. Continue straight at 4.8 as a road joins on the left, then bear right at a fork at 5.0. When you reach a T at 5.2, turn right. At 5.3 miles [05] turn left on a gravel road. Follow this east to the bar at 5.5 miles [06]. Look for the church steeple.

Reset your odometer at the bar. After visiting the bar, go out the way you came in but continue west on the gravel road. Bear left at 4.2 miles as a large road joins on the right. You reach Highway 95 at 4.8 miles [07].

Return Trip: Left on Hwy. 95 takes you to Cienega Springs and Parker. Right goes north to Lake Havasu City.

Services: Gas station and general store at the start of the trail. Drinks, food, and toilets at the bar when it is open. Some services in Cienega Springs (turn west at the light). Full services in Parker and Lake Havasu City.

Historical Highlights: The Nellie E. Saloon is built on an old mining claim by the same name. The saloon is the dream of a local resident known simply as "Ken." He'll likely be there when you stop in. He started his business with a small structure in 1983 and has been expanding it ever since. It's a "jumpin" place on weekends with frequent live music and an outdoor bar and grill. Ken's church is a popular place for couples seeking an unusual wedding. To tell you more would spoil the fun. The bar is open Saturday and Sunday only, Labor Day weekend through Memorial Day weekend. Hours are from noon to sunset. It's closed during the summer.

Maps: USGS 100,000 scale map Parker, Arizona-California 34114-A1-TM-100.

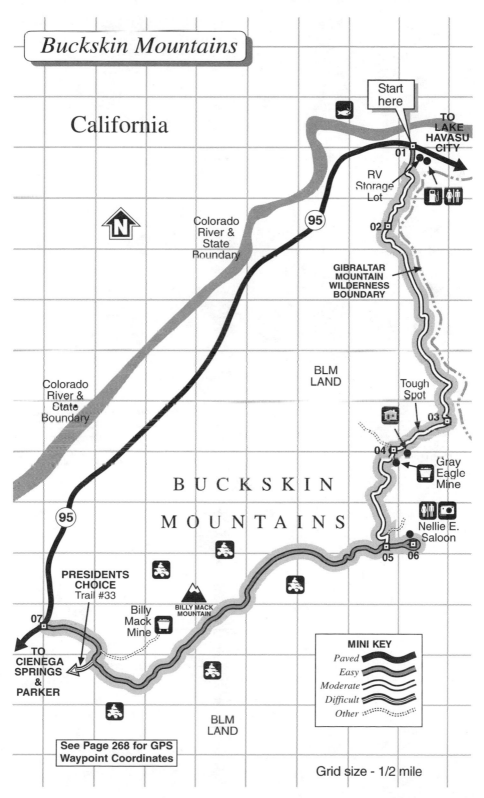

Buckskin Mountains

California

Start here

TO LAKE HAVASU CITY

01

RV Storage Lot

02

GIBRALTAR MOUNTAIN WILDERNESS BOUNDARY

95

Colorado River & State Boundary

N

Colorado River & State Boundary

BLM LAND

Tough Spot

03

04

Gray Eagle Mine

Nellie E. Saloon

05   06

B U C K S K I N

M O U N T A I N S

95

PRESIDENTS CHOICE Trail #33

Billy Mack Mine

BILLY MACK MOUNTAIN

07

TO CIENEGA SPRINGS & PARKER

MINI KEY
Paved
Easy
Moderate
Difficult
Other

See Page 268 for GPS Waypoint Coordinates

BLM LAND

Grid size - 1/2 mile

Easy on the left side, hard on the right.

Crawling through the eye of Rovey's Needle.

Plenty of challenge if that's what you want.

Cattail Cove, a great place for lunch.

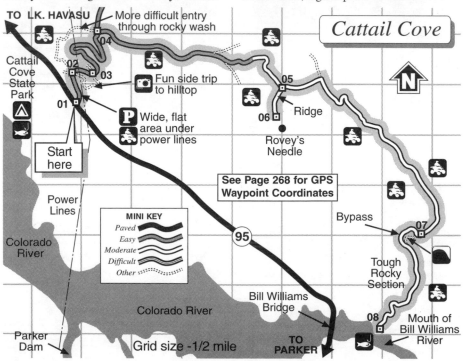

TO LK. HAVASU

More difficult entry through rocky wash

Cattail Cove

04

Cattail Cove State Park

02
03

01

Fun side trip to hilltop

05

06   Ridge

N

P   Wide, flat area under power lines

Start here

Rovey's Needle

See Page 268 for GPS Waypoint Coordinates

Power Lines

MINI KEY
Paved
Easy
Moderate
Difficult
Other

95

Bypass

07

Colorado River

Tough Rocky Section

Bill Williams Bridge

Colorado River

08   Mouth of Bill Williams River

Parker Dam

Grid size -1/2 mile

TO PARKER

Cattail Cove

32

Location: About half way between Lake Havasu City and Parker on Hwy. 95.

Difficulty: Moderate. Mainly follows sandy wash bottoms with intermittent rocky sections. There are several difficult rock obstacles if you are looking for more challenge, but the worst places have bypasses. Tight, scratchy brush just before you get to Cattail Cove. Route-finding is confusing at times.

Features: Visit Rovey's Needle, an interesting rock formation. Lunch at Cattail Cove next to the Bill Williams River.

Time & Distance: It's 8.8 miles to Cattail Cove counting the side trip to Rovey's Needle and 8.2 miles back out. Allow about 4 hours.

To Get There: Turn east off Hwy. 95 just north of mile marker 165. The area looks like a gravel pit under major power lines. It's located adjacent to Cattail Cove State Park which is on the opposite side of Hwy. 95.

Trail Description: Reset your odometer as you get off Hwy. 95 [01]. Follow a wide gravel road north. At 0.3 miles [02] follow the road around to the right behind a hill. Don't turn hard right. Continue straight at 0.5 miles [03] as the road curves left downhill. At 1.6 [04] turn right into a sandy wash. Turn either way at 2.1 miles; left is easier. The wash splits at 2.9; bear right. Bear left when the wash splits again at 3.1. At 3.9 miles [05], bear right at a T at the top of ridge to take a side trip to Rovey's Needle. When you reach the needle at 4.2 miles [06], walk around the left side to find needle hole. Return to T on ridge [05] and continue straight.

Turn right at another T at 4.9 miles. Turn left out of wash at 5.2. Continue straight across another wash at 5.5. Drop down into a wash at 5.6 and bear left. A tough rock obstacle at 7.2 miles [07] has a bypass on the right. It returns to the wash at 7.4. There's no bypass for rocks at 8.3 but it's a moderate drop if you stay right. Continue straight through tight brush at 8.7 before reaching Cattail Cove at 8.8 miles [08]. Relax and enjoy the view, then return the way you came.

Return Trip: Right on Hwy. 95 returns to Lake Havasu City. Parker is left.

Services: None. Return to Lake Havasu City or Parker.

Maps: USGS 100,000 scale map Parker, Arizona-California 34114-A1-TM-100.

Stay right of these rock projections.

Articulation test.

Easiest part of the Launch Pad.

Approaching the end.

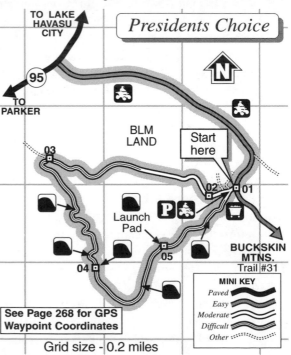

Presidents Choice

TO LAKE HAVASU CITY

95

TO PARKER

BLM LAND

Start here

03

02

01

P

Launch Pad

05

04

BUCKSKIN MTNS.
Trail #31

See Page 268 for GPS Waypoint Coordinates

MINI KEY
Paved
Easy
Moderate
Difficult
Other

Grid size - 0.2 miles

President's Choice ◆33◆

Location: Northeast of Parker, east of Cienega Springs.

Difficulty: Difficult. A real test of the best modified equipment. A lot of tall, jagged rocks with very little room to maneuver. Without a good spotter, expect body damage. Route-finding is confusing at the start.

Features: Best enjoyed with a group of very experienced wheelers.

Time & Distance: Very short. The hard-core part is only about a mile. If all goes well, it can be done in about an hour. However, the chances of that happening are slim. Allow 2 to 5 hours, especially if you have a large group.

To Get There: Turn east off Hwy. 95 on an unmarked wide gravel road between mile markers 149 and 150. Bear right when the road forks at 0.6 then immediately turn right again off the gravel road into a broad area at 0.7 miles [01]. Roads fan out in many directions.

Trail Description: Reset your odometer as you pull off the gravel road [01]. Head west-southwest to the back of the broad area. Follow a single lane road that does not climb any hillsides. Before the first tenth of a mile, the road turns right [02]. Ignore small side roads as the road twists back and forth then begins to climb. At 0.5 miles [03] turn left. Straight takes you back out to Hwy. 95. Drop into a narrow wash heading south. Stay right of jagged rocks that split the wash. At 0.7 turn right out of the wash over a big hump and zigzag through a series of tough obstacles. Go either way at 0.9; right is easier. There's a very bad spot just before 1.0 miles [04]. After that the trail widens a bit and curves to the left heading northeast. Driver's choice through a stretch at 1.1 staying in the wash. Climb left over the Launch Pad, a near vertical wall, at 1.3 miles [05]. Blackened wall is where previous vehicles caught fire in a climbing attempt. One more tight spot remains by a tree at 1.5 miles. After that, continue straight through a cluster of roads back to the start of the trail at 1.6 miles [01]. Take the gravel road north to Hwy. 95.

Return Trip: Left on Hwy. 95 returns to Parker. Lake Havasu City is right.

Services: None. Closest services in Cienega Springs. Turn west at the light.

Maps: This road is not shown on any map that I know. For GPS purposes use USGS 7.5 minute map Cross Roads, Calif.-Ariz. N3407.5-W11407.5/7.5.

AREA 5

North Phoenix, Prescott, Crown King, Wickenburg

34. Bradshaw Mountains
35. Desoto Mine
36. Wickenburg Mountains
37. Castle Hot Springs Road
38. Backway to Crown King
39. New River Canyon
40. Harquahala Peak
41. Belmont Mountain

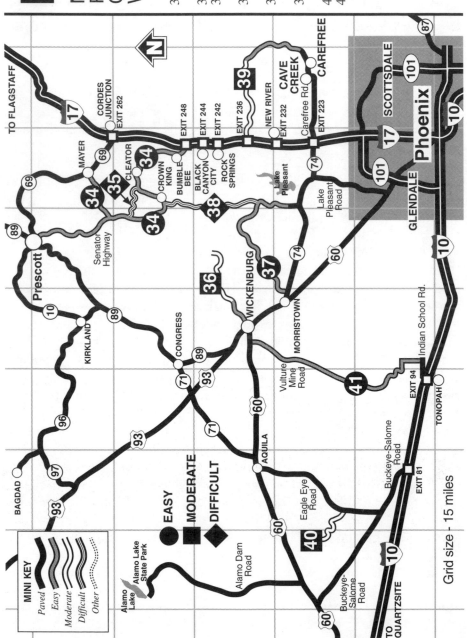

MINI KEY
Paved
Easy
Moderate
Difficult
Other

● EASY
■ MODERATE
◆ DIFFICULT

Grid size - 15 miles

North Phoenix, Prescott, Crown King, Wickenburg

The Bradshaw Mountains, north of Phoenix, include some of the most historically interesting mining country in Arizona. The area is accessed by two major back roads—the Senator Highway from Prescott and Crown King Road from Interstate 17. Both are exceptional scenic drives far from major population centers. A taste of adventure makes them perfect for SUV exploration. The centerpiece of the area is the town of Crown King, a once booming mining center, now a thriving tourist community. Located in gorgeous wooded mountain country, it is pleasantly cool in the summer and a great place to camp and hike. The *Backway to Crown King*, which connects from scenic Lake Pleasant, may be one of the most popular back roads in the state despite its difficult rating. West of Lake Pleasant, enjoy an easy drive to *Castle Hot Springs Resort*. Although no longer open for business, it's an interesting photo opportunity and is a great excuse to hit the road. Farther west, you'll find the *Wickenburg Mountains*. This area is also rich in mining history but is more rugged and remote.

The town of Cleator on the Crown King Highway heading into the Bradshaw Mountains.

Bumble Bee Store is no longer open.

The road to Horsethief Basin Recreation Area.

Road follows railroad cut.

Horsethief Lake. Bring your fishing pole.

General Store in Crown King has one gas pump.

Crown King Road.

136

Bradshaw Mountains ㉞

Location: South of Prescott, west of Interstate 17.

Difficulty: Easy. Crown King Road is a wide gravel road suitable for passenger cars when dry. The road climbs rapidly as it nears the town of Crown King. A high-clearance vehicle is recommended for Senator Highway beyond Crown King where the road is rough and narrow.

Features: This drive passes through historic mining country dating back over 140 years. Drivers enjoy a beautiful mountain drive and many important obvious historic stops along the way, including Bumble Bee, Cleator and Crown King. Unfortunately, many subtle but important features can be missed simply due to ignorance. To fully appreciate your drive, I recommend you read *Crown King and the Southern Bradshaws: A Complete History* by former Crown King resident Bruce M. Wilson. The book is a quick read and is full of wonderful photographs from the past.

Time & Distance: This is a full-day adventure especially if driven from Phoenix or Flagstaff. The dirt road portion of the trip is over 70 miles as described here. You'll want to stop frequently, so start early and allow plenty of time.

To Get There: Get off Interstate 17 at Exit 248 and head northwest to Bumble Bee. If you are coming from the north, you might elect to get off at Exit 259. Head west, then south to connect to Crown King Road north of Bumble Bee. Those coming from Prescott would likely head south on the Senator Highway and drive the trail in the reverse direction.

Trail Description: Reset your odometer as you get off Interstate 17 at Exit 248 [01]. Follow a paved road northwest. The pavement ends after a couple of miles before reaching Bumble Bee near the 5-mile marker. There are a few active businesses in town but the historic Bumble Bee Store is no longer open (see photo). Continue straight at 10.5 miles [02] and 11.2 miles where roads go right to Mayer. Turn left at a Y at 12.2. Continue straight at 13.0 before arriving at Cleator at 14.9 miles [03]. The only active business in town is the Cleator Bar (open weekends only). Many people drive this far just to see this unique tourist attraction.

     Starting at Cleator, the road follows much of the old Bradshaw Mountain Railway bed completed to Crown King in 1904 but dismantled in 1926. On the north side of the road at mile marker 17 is the Middleton

Townsite. There's nothing left now but a pile of tailings and few remnants of towers of an aerial tramway on the hills above the town. The town serviced the Desoto Mine and was an important work center during the construction of the railroad.

Scenic views follow as you climb to the town of Crown King on the right at 28.2 miles. Stop in at the General Store which is open everyday except major winter holidays. They also sell gas. The Crown King Saloon is another popular attraction. There's also a nice restaurant for dinner or a smaller cafe/bar. When not too busy, most residents are happy to tell you about the town.

After Crown King, continue uphill to an intersection at 28.8 miles [04]. Left takes you to the Horsethief Basin Recreation Area [05]. If you have time, it's a great round-trip drive of 13 or 15 miles depending on how far you go. The area offers camping, hiking, and fishing. Whether you take this side trip or not, *reset your odometer* at this point [04] before proceeding.

As you continue northwest on the Senator Highway, marked as F.S. 52, the exit point to *Backway to Crown King (Trail #38)* forks to the left at 1.1 miles. It's marked as F.S. 192. At 1.3 miles, pass the Bradshaw Townsite on the left. At one time, 5,000 people lived here. Continue straight at 3.6 miles where F.S. 52C goes right. This road goes back to most of the famous mines in the area, including the Crown King Mine. At 6.0 continue straight where F.S. 362 joins on the left. Bear left at 13.5 miles. At 14.1 miles [06] *Desoto Mine (Trail #35)* goes right. It's marked as F.S. 89 and is a much lesser road.

At 17.1 miles [07] turn right at the Goodwin Townsite to reach Mayer. Maps show this as County Road 177 but I didn't see any signs. Left would continue on the Senator Highway to Prescott. Bear right at 20.4 where Watson Springs goes left. Continue straight at 25.5 and 27.2. You should see the Mayer Cemetery on the right. Just before you reach Mayer, the road is paved and becomes Jefferson Street. Follow the map detail to find your way to Highway 69 reached at 29.0 miles [08].

Return Trip: From Mayer, take Highway 69 left to Prescott and right to Interstate 17. The Interstate is about 8 miles.

Services: There's a single gas pump at the General Store in Crown King. Mayer has a convenience store and full gas services. Prescott has full services. Before starting the trail, the last chance to get gas heading north on Interstate 17 is at Rock Springs or Black Canyon City. The Rock Springs Cafe at Exit 242 has great food and homemade pies.

Maps: Prescott National Forest, USGS 100,000 scale map Bradshaw Mountains, Arizona 34112-A1-TM-100, Arizona Atlas and Gazetteer.

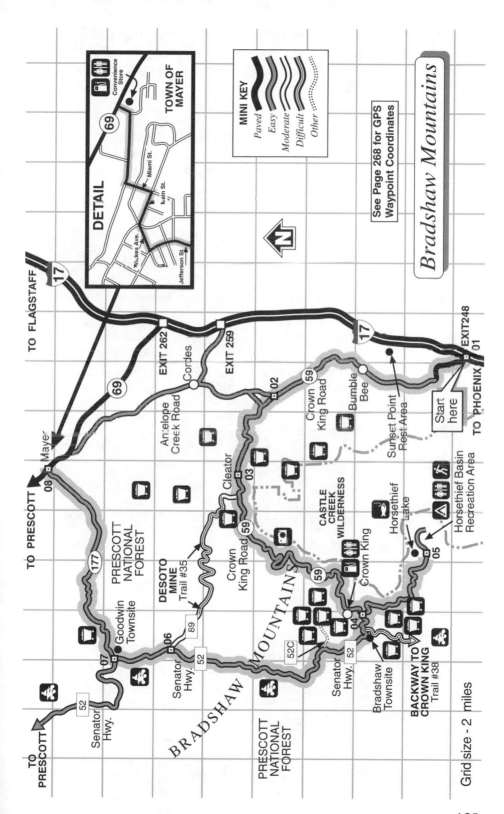

Bradshaw Mountains

MINI KEY

Paved
Easy
Moderate
Difficult
Other

See Page 268 for GPS
Waypoint Coordinates

DETAIL

TOWN OF MAYER

Convenience Store

69

Miami St.

Main St.

Wickes Ave.

Jefferson St.

N

TO FLAGSTAFF

17

EXIT 262

Cordes

EXIT 259

69

Mayer

TO PRESCOTT

08

Antelope Creek Road

Cleator

02

Crown King Road

59

Bumble Bee

Sunset Point Rest Area

Start here

17

EXIT 248

01

TO PHOENIX

03

59

Crown King Road

CASTLE CREEK WILDERNESS

Horsethief Lake

Crown King

Horsethief Basin Recreation Area

05

PRESCOTT NATIONAL FOREST

DESOTO MINE Trail #35

177

Goodwin Townsite

06

89

07

52

Senator Hwy.

52

52C

59

04

Senator Hwy.

52

Bradshaw Townsite

BACKWAY TO CROWN KING Trail #38

BRADSHAW MOUNTAINS

PRESCOTT NATIONAL FOREST

TO PRESCOTT

52

Senator Hwy.

Grid size - 2 miles

139

Stock Wrangler gets hung up while attempting to drive through narrow, rocky canyon.

Great views from top of highest ridge.

Narrow trail is very tippy in places.

The Cleator Bar is open on weekends only. Two trucks on right did not drive this trail.

Desoto Mine ◆35◆

Location: Southeast of Prescott between the Senator Highway and Cleator.

Difficulty: Difficult. A wild roller-coaster ride across some of Arizona's most remote backcountry. Pass through narrow creek beds with ever-changing boulder fields, then cross a series of ridges on a narrow, winding trail. Washed-out sections create hold-your-breath, tippy situations, especially for high-centered vehicles. Descents and climbs are very steep at times. Scratchy brush is guaranteed to produce Arizona pinstripes on any new paint job. Route-finding is sometimes confusing. Flash-flooding possible. Go prepared and travel with experienced four-wheelers. Help is a long way off.

Features: An out-of-the-way adventure sure to please any serious four-wheeler. Pass through mining country near the Desoto Mine.

Time & Distance: The trail itself is just under 12 miles and takes 4 to 5 hours. It is a considerable drive from any major city, so allow a full day for this trip.

To Get There:
   From Prescott: Take the Senator Highway south. *Reset your odometer when the pavement ends.* Make right turns at 3.6, 3.8, 5.2, and 13.3 miles. Turn left off Senator Highway on F.S. 89 at 16.4 miles [01].
   From Phoenix: Follow directions for *Bradshaw Mountains (Trail #34)*. Turn right off Senator Highway where the Desoto Mine Trail is shown. This point is about 43 miles from Exit 248 on Interstate 17. You can also drive the Desoto Mine Trail in the reverse direction. See **Reverse Directions** on next page.

Trail Description: Reset your odometer at the start [01]. Head uphill southeast on a rough single-lane road marked F.S. 89. Bear right at 1.4 miles where 89B goes left. Turn left into a rocky creek bed at 2.1 miles [02]. You'll climb out of the creek bed briefly to get around some large boulders, then rejoin F.S. 89 on the right at 2.3. A tippy spot at 2.5 goes around a concrete structure. At 2.8 miles start through a narrow, rocky canyon, the toughest part of the trail. The canyon dwindles after 3.0 miles and you begin climbing a high ridge. A steep descent down the other side brings several washed-out sections that test your articulation. When you reach bottom, the trail heads north in a brushy, dry creek bottom. Maps show this as Bear Creek. Watch carefully for an overgrown trail that comes out of the creek bottom

141

on the right at 4.0 miles [03]. This turn is almost impossible to see. If you miss it, you'll continue down the creek bottom to a windmill. Turn around and go back until you find the road that goes up the hill in a northeast direction. Once on the correct trail, you'll pass through a gate as you climb. You'll soon see the windmill below on the left.

At 4.7 miles [04] make a sharp left turn downhill onto F.S. 9268R. F.S. 89 continues straight. Trail 9268R is very tippy and has some hair-raising steep climbs. Brush is very tight. Pass through a gate at 5.1. You reach the top of a hill at 6.5 and start down again. The trail splits at 6.9 but comes back together. Pick your best line.

The road forks at 7.2 miles [05] at a cattle pond. Bear left on 9268R unless you want to take a side trip up the hill on the right. This road, 259B goes up to the Desoto Mine but is blocked on the other side. There's really not much to see at the top except a good view. This Forest Service road passes through dangerous private mining property. You must return to the cattle pond if you climb the hill.

Continuing left at the cattle pond on 9268R takes you around the hill on a very tippy road. Turn left when you reach 259B at a large rusty water tank at 8.5 miles [06]. Follow 259B east to Crown King Road at 11.7 miles.

Return Trip: Head east on Crown King Road past Cleator to Interstate 17 Exits 248 or 259. See map for *Bradford Mountains (Trail #34)*. The quickest way back to Prescott is to head north on Antelope Creek Road to Mayer then take Hwy. 69 west.

Reverse Directions: Turn north on 259B 1.3 miles [07] west of Cleator. Turn right at brown tank at 3.2 miles [06] on 9268R. Right at cattle pond at 4.5 [05]. Sharp right on F.S. 89 at 7.0 [04]. Turn left when you reach a dry creek bed at bottom of hill at 7.7 [03]. Zig-zag up steep, narrow trail to top of high ridge. Drop into rocky canyon on other side at 8.7. Follow rocky wash bottom until it intersects with F.S. 89 for the last time at 9.6 miles [02]. Follow F.S. 89 to Senator Highway at 11.7 [01]. Right goes to Prescott or Mayer. Left goes to Crown King and Interstate 17.

Services: None. Closest services are in Mayer. On weekends you can get a drink at the Cleator Bar.

Maps: Parts of this trail are shown on Prescott National Forest map. For GPS purposes, use USGS 7.5 minute map Battle Flat, Ariz. N3415-W11215/7.5

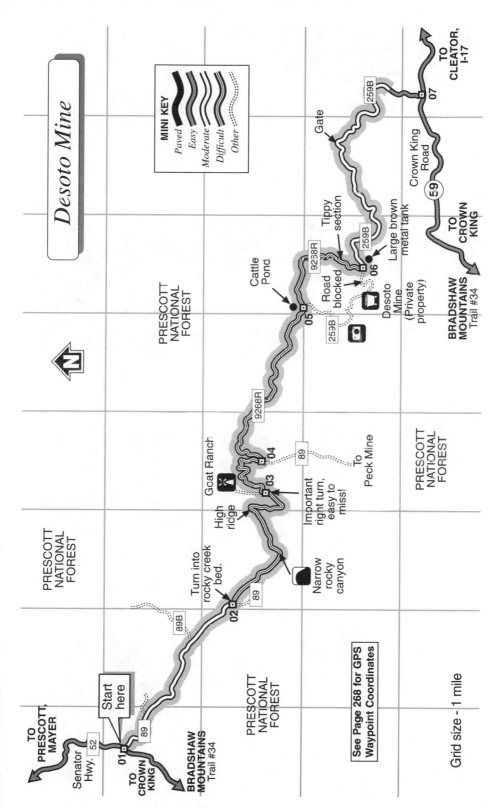

Desoto Mine

MINI KEY
Paved
Easy
Moderate
Difficult
Other

N

PRESCOTT NATIONAL FOREST

TO CLEATOR, I-17

259B

07

Gate

259B

Tippy section

Crown King Road

259B

06

Large brown metal tank

59

9258R

Cattle Pond

05

Road blocked

259B

Desoto Mine (Private property)

TO CROWN KING

BRADSHAW MOUNTAINS Trail #34

9266R

Goat Ranch

04

03

89

To Peck Mine

High ridge

Important right turn, easy to miss!

PRESCOTT NATIONAL FOREST

Turn into rocky creek bed.

Narrow rocky canyon

02

89

89B

PRESCOTT NATIONAL FOREST

TO PRESCOTT, MAYER

Senator Hwy. 52

Start here

01

89

TO CROWN KING

BRADSHAW MOUNTAINS Trail #34

See Page 268 for GPS Waypoint Coordinates

Grid size - 1 mile

Bradshaw's Grave.

Wickenburg Mountains.

The trail is fun to drive.

Sandy creek beds are susceptible to erosion.

Crucible left at UFO Mine.

Wickenburg Mountains 36

Location: Northeast of Wickenburg.

Difficulty: Moderate. This remote and rugged trail should not be taken lightly. It includes narrow, rocky shelf roads and steep inclines. Parts of the trail follow sandy creek bottoms which are highly susceptible to erosion. Be aware of the possibility of flash floods. Many side roads in the area can take you miles off course, so pay close attention to directions. The use of GPS is very helpful. Do not drive this trail alone. Use caution while exploring mines.

Features: Visit the well-marked grave of Isaac Bradshaw, namesake of the Bradshaw Mountains. Search for clues of historic Constellation City and Copperopolis Townsite. Enjoy beautiful mountain views and the solitude of a truly remote getaway. To learn more about this once-great mining area, I recommend a stop at the Wickenburg Museum in downtown Wickenburg. It is an outstanding museum with an extensive collection of mining memorabilia.

Time & Distance: Nearly 25 miles one way. The first half of the trip goes by quickly but the last part takes some time. Allow 5 to 6 hours for the round trip plus additional stopping time.

To Get There: From Phoenix, head north on Highway 60 to Wickenburg. Turn right on El Recreo Drive one block before McDonald's. From the west side of Wickenburg, go through town and over the Hassayampa Bridge. Turn left a block after McDonald's.

Trail Description: Reset your odometer as you get off Hwy. 60 [01]. Go north on El Recreo Drive, which quickly runs into Constellation Road. Continue straight. After a couple of miles the pavement ends. Bear right at 3.1 miles where Blue Tank Road goes left. Bear left at 4.2. Turn right off Constellation Road at 8.6 miles [02]. Make a left at 9.6. An important turn at 13.0 miles [03] is easy to miss. The main road swings right; you turn left, dropping down into a gully. Pass through a gate at 13.7. Leave gates the way you find them unless signs indicate otherwise. Bear left at 14.4 where a lesser road goes right, then left again at 14.8. At 15.0 pass through what was once Constellation City—not much left except a few concrete foundations and mine tailings on the right.

     Continue straight past Constellation City. At 15.6 pass through a gate and descend a steep, rocky shelf road. At 16.5 the road follows a low sandy wash that is highly susceptible to erosion. Watch carefully at 16.8

miles [04] where you make a hard right. Go by a cattle pond on the left at 18.2 then turn right at 18.8. Continue straight at 19.4 where a road joins on the left. Bear left at 20.3 and pass through a barbed wire gate. The trail drops into a wash then zigzags uphill to Bradshaw's Grave at 20.6 [05]. Continue past the grave and bear right at 21.0. At 22.3 pass through another gate on a descending shelf road. At 23.2 bear left where a road joins on the right. Go around a large green tank, then turn right. At the time of this writing, a crumpled truck trailer and old bulldozer marked this site at the UFO Mine [06]. Bear right following a shelf road along the hillside. At 23.6 turn left uphill. The road fades out about 24.6 miles [07] at the Copperopolis Townsite up the hill on the left. You'll have to look closely to find evidence that the town existed. The Copperopolis Mine is straight ahead in a northeast direction.

Return Trip: Return the way you came. There is an alternate way out downhill in a southeast direction along Castle Creek, but this road has become badly washed out. It's unlikely any repairs will be made to the road unless a local four-wheel drive club decides to do it. The road is barely passable for hard-core vehicles and the route is complex. Someone experienced would have to know the way.

Services: None along the trail. Return to Wickenburg.

Historical Highlights: The placard on Bradshaw's grave gives sole credit to Isaac Bradshaw as namesake to the Bradshaw Mountains. However, Isaac had four other brothers, three of whom initially came to Arizona. His brother William led the group. History is not clear as to whether William actually penetrated the mountains. We know he did placer mining on the east side of the mountains in Black Canyon and Turkey Creek. William later went on to establish the Ehrenberg Ferry across the Colorado River. He committed suicide in 1864 after an unsuccessful attempt in politics. After his brother's death, Isaac came into prominence when he reopened the "Bradshaw Diggings" which, at its peak, involved over 100 miners.

The Post Office in Constellation was established in 1901. By 1925 some 250 people sustained the town, which had a stage depot, store, saloon and dance hall. The town never produced much gold. Money was made from investors through promotions.

We know little about Copperopolis except that it had a post office in 1884 and lasted only about a year. Copper ore was its primary focus.

Maps: USGS 250,000 scale map Parker, Arizona. To see any detail requires a handful of 7.5-minute USGS maps. Constellation Road is shown on the Arizona Atlas and Gazetteer.

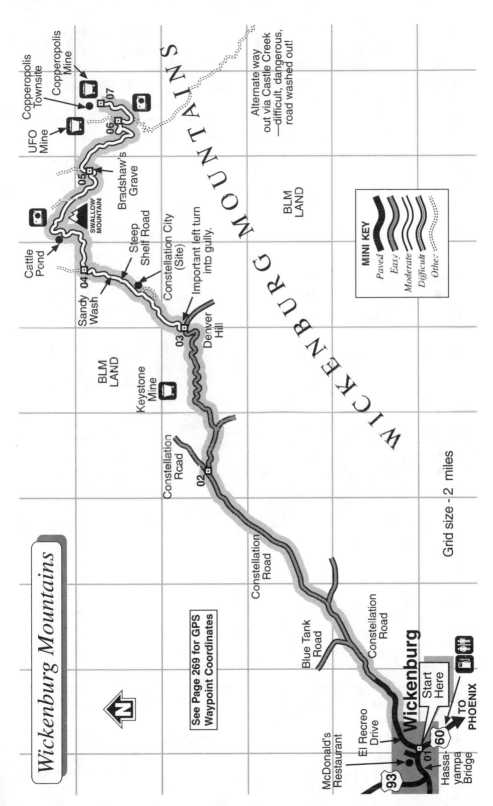

Wickenburg Mountains

WICKENBURG MOUNTAINS

Copperopolis Mine

Copperopolis Townsite

UFO Mine

Copperopolis Mine

07

06

05

Bradshaw's Grave

SWALLOW MOUNTAIN

Cattle Pond

Steep Shelf Road

Sandy Wash

04

Constellation City (Site)

Important left turn into gully.

03

Denver Hill

Alternate way out via Castle Creek —difficult, dangerous, road washed out!

BLM LAND

BLM LAND

Keystone Mine

Constellation Road

02

See Page 269 for GPS Waypoint Coordinates

Grid size - 2 miles

N

Constellation Road

Blue Tank Road

Constellation Road

McDonald's Restaurant

El Recreo Drive

Wickenburg

Start Here

60

TO PHOENIX

93

Hassayampa Bridge

01

MINI KEY	
Paved	
Easy	
Moderate	
Difficult	
Other	

Plentiful Saguaro in high Sonoran Desert.

Graded river bottom can be rough.

Castle Hot Springs Resort, well-maintained behind the palms.

Heed warnings.

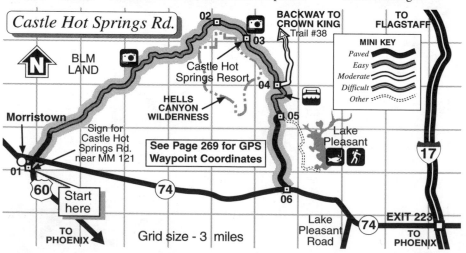

Castle Hot Springs Road 37

Location: Northwest of Phoenix, between Morristown and Lake Pleasant.

Difficulty: Easy. Graded gravel road that intermittently crosses and follows sandy creek bottoms. One stretch of road follows Castle Creek for 3 miles. The road is generally in good condition except after heavy rains and flash floods. High-clearance four-wheel drive is recommended because of sandy and potentially rocky conditions. Don't drive when rain is forecast. Route-finding is easy.

Features: Scenic drive through high Sonoran Desert near low mountain foothills. Drive by venerable Castle Hot Springs Resort (now closed to the public). Lake Pleasant offers boating, fishing and other water sports.

Time & Distance: Just under 48 miles from Morristown to Interstate 17. Allow 2 to 3 hours for the entire trip. Off-pavement portion is 28 miles.

To Get There: Head northwest from Phoenix on Hwy. 60 to Morristown. Turn right on well-marked Castle Hot Springs Road near mile marker 121.

Trail Description: Reset your odometer as you turn off Hwy. 60 [01]. Continue northeast on paved Castle Hot Springs Road as it crosses over State Highway 74 at 0.7 miles. Pavement changes to smooth gravel at 2.8 miles. At 8.8 the road dips into the first of many washes. The road gradually narrows. Rough conditions are possible if the road has not been graded since the last heavy rain. Bear right at 20.8 miles [02] and again at 21.7 miles. Continue on the road as it winds through private property at 22.4. The resort is reached at 23.5 miles [03]. Stay on the road at all times through this area. Follow posted signs. The road continues in Castle Creek for the next 3 miles before it improves. The *Backway to Crown King (Trail # 38)* goes left at 28.0 miles [04]. Turn right at 31.0 miles [05]. Straight takes you into the Lake Pleasant Recreation Area (fee required). Hwy. 74 is reached at 36.5 miles [06].

Return Trip: Left on Hwy. 74 to Exit 223 of Interstate 17 (about 11 miles). Right goes back to Morristown. You can also return to Phoenix/Glendale via Lake Pleasant Road, which departs south from Hwy. 74 six miles west of I-17.

Services: None. Closest gas and food is south on Lake Pleasant Road.

Maps: USGS 250,000 scale map Phoenix, Arizona, Arizona Atlas and Gazetteer.

Lake Pleasant.

Remains of Kentuck's Place.

Washouts common on steep sections.

Road winds through Bradshaw Mountains.

Nearing the end of the trail.

150

Backway to Crown King 38

Location: North of Phoenix, west of Interstate 17.

Difficulty: Difficult. Most of this route is easy to moderate; however, there are a few difficult places that will challenge stock vehicles. The road has gotten worse over the years, especially the steepest part in the last four miles. Erosion has exposed more rocks and deep ruts have formed. Aggressive stock vehicles with good articulation can get up this trail but they may need to stack rocks or be helped with a tow strap. This is a very popular trail on the weekends. Drive carefully and watch for ATVs and dirt bikes.

Features: This is a challenging four-wheel-drive route but is also a great historical tour. Your trip will be greatly enhanced if you learn a little about the area before you go. A book I've found most helpful is *Crown King and the Southern Bradshaws: A Complete History* by Bruce M. Wilson. It explains the history and development of the mines and mining towns with pictures from the past. Knowing how things looked back then will help you understand what remains today.

Time & Distance: The route as described here is 34.4 miles and takes 4 to 5 hours. Add to that a long drive to and from the trail. It's a full-day adventure from Phoenix.

To Get There: Take Interstate 17 to Cave Creek/ Carefree Exit 223. Head west on State Highway 74 about 11 miles. Turn right just past mile marker 19 on a major paved road.

Trail Description: Reset your odometer as you turn off Hwy. 74 [01]. Follow paved road north until it reaches Castle Creek Road at 5.5 miles. Turn left, after which the pavement ends. Turn right at 8.5 miles [02] following signs to Crown King. Bear left at 11.5. Pass through private property before crossing usually dry Cow Creek at 15.2 miles. Continue straight at 16.2 [03] where Champie Road joins on the left. Stay on the main road through a private residential area at 17.5. At 20.2 miles [04] turn right on a lesser road. It's marked with small painted boulders with arrows that point to CK (Crown King). The trail soon becomes rutted and steep. It splits at 22.4 then comes back together. Right is easier. Same thing at 23.9 but left is easier. Bear left at 24.7. Go either way at 25.9 miles. Bear right at 26.3.

Pass the "Burro John" Homestead on the left at 26.3 miles. A cattle guard marks the boundary of the Prescott National Forest at 26.4 miles [05].

151

At 26.8 watch for remains of "Kentuck's Place" on the left. A good place to stop for lunch is at Fort Misery, located in a clearing on the left at 27.4 miles.

Make an important right turn uphill at 30.4 miles [06] onto F.S. 192. This narrow shelf road starts easy but deteriorates quickly. Probably the worst spot on the trail is reached at 31.2. Stock vehicles may have to stack rocks here. A big water tank on the left at 31.3 [07] marks the location of the Oro Belle Townsite and Mine. A high rock wall cut into the bank on the right side of the road is a wall of a hotel. Remnants of the mine can be found on the hillside above. Turn up the tight switchback on the left and follow a narrow shelf road above the water tank. The road climbs rapidly with beautiful views of the road below. The solid rock walls that support the road were built by stone masons over 120 years ago. Bear right at 34.0. The road gets rough again before reaching the Senator Highway at 34.4 miles [08].

Return Trip: Turn right and follow Senator Highway downhill to Crown King. From there, follow Crown King Road to Cleator and Interstate 17 (see map). A long drive left on Senator Highway goes to Prescott and Mayer. See map for *Bradshaw Mountains (Trail #34)*.

Services: There's a single gas pump at the General Store in Crown King which is open everyday except major winter holidays. Crown King also has a restaurant, saloon, and cafe.

Historical Highlights: **"Burro" John Revello** was a colorful but unsavory character who operated a brothel and saloon near Oro Belle. His homestead once included a cabin where he lived with his prostitute wife. The Forest Service removed the cabin in the late 1970s. **"Kentuck's Place"** was a two-story cabin inhabited by an old Civil War veteran by the name of William "Kentuck" Bell. He lived there until he died at the age of 90 and is burried nearby. Others continued to live in the cabin until the late 1960s. **Fort Misery** was the name given to a small cabin built by Al Francis in the early 1900s. He hauled freight from Oro Belle to Crown King and apparently didn't think much of his job or his home. Only low walls of the cabin remain. **Oro Belle** mining operations started in the early 1880s but the town didn't get a post office until 1904. The saloon at Oro Belle was moved to Crown King and is still in operation today. **Crown King** remains as a living memorial to a golden era. Although scaled down from what it once was, much of the town still remains as it was over 100 years ago. Perhaps the biggest change is that the railroad no long runs through town. Today, it's a thriving tourist attraction and a great place to go in the summer to escape the desert heat.

Maps: Prescott National Forest, USGS 250,000 scale maps Prescott, Arizona, and Phoenix, Arizona, Arizona Atlas & Gazetteer.

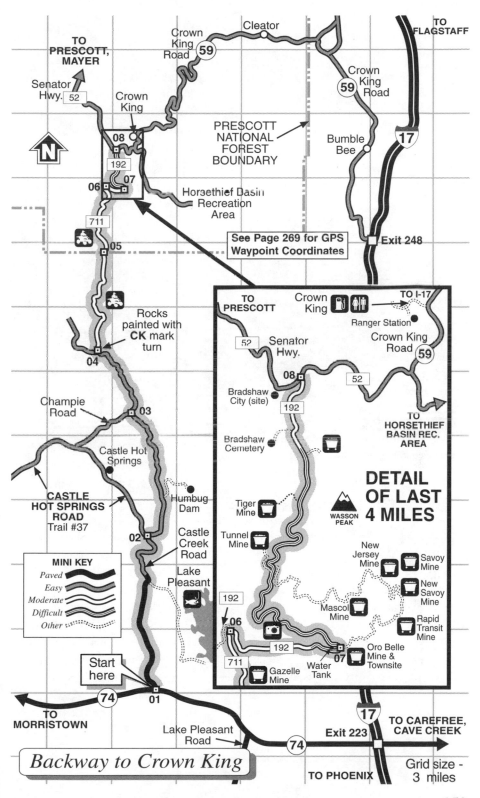

TO PRESCOTT, MAYER

Crown King Road **59**

Cleator

TO FLAGSTAFF

Senator Hwy. **52**

Crown King

Crown King Road **59**

08

192

N

07

06

711

05

PRESCOTT NATIONAL FOREST BOUNDARY

Bumble Bee

17

Horsethief Basin Recreation Area

See Page 269 for GPS Waypoint Coordinates

Exit 248

Rocks painted with **CK** mark turn

04

Champie Road

03

Castle Hot Springs

CASTLE HOT SPRINGS ROAD Trail #37

Humbug Dam

02

Castle Creek Road

Lake Pleasant

MINI KEY
Paved
Easy
Moderate
Difficult
Other

TO PRESCOTT

Crown King

TO I-17

Ranger Station

Crown King Road **59**

52

Senator Hwy.

08

52

Bradshaw City (site)

192

Bradshaw Cemetery

TO HORSETHIEF BASIN REC. AREA

Tiger Mine

DETAIL OF LAST 4 MILES

WASSON PEAK

Tunnel Mine

New Jersey Mine

Savoy Mine

New Savoy Mine

Mascot Mine

Rapid Transit Mine

192

06

192

711

Water Tank

07

Oro Belle Mine & Townsite

Gazelle Mine

Start here

74

01

TO MORRISTOWN

Lake Pleasant Road

74

Exit 223

17

TO CAREFREE, CAVE CREEK

TO PHOENIX

Backway to Crown King

Grid size - 3 miles

153

Turn left through this gate at 1.1 miles.

Remote country—don't go alone.

High water possible after heavy rains.

TO FLAGSTAFF

Gate on left

Start here

P

(Intermittent)

EXIT 236 TABLE MESA RD.

01

State Trust Land (permit required)

02

Private Ranch

41

(Intermittent)

New River

37

03

41

17

24

04

Cave Creek C.G.

Tonto N.F. Recreation Area (fee required for day use)

24

24

Sears-Kay Ruins

TONTO NATIONAL FOREST

17

MINI KEY
Paved
Easy
Moderate
Difficult
Other

See Page 269 for GPS Waypoint Coordinates

Cave Creek Road

05

Bartlett Dam Road

Cave Creek

Carefree

EXIT 223   Carefree Highway   06

74

TO PHOENIX   Grid size - 3 miles

New River Canyon

154

New River Canyon 39

Location: North of Phoenix and Carefree, southeast of Black Canyon City.

Difficulty: Moderate. Steep rocky climbs and washed-out conditions. Suitable for aggressive stock SUVs with high ground clearance and good articulation. Skid plates recommended. New River is often dry but can be deep after heavy rains. Remote backcountry; don't go alone.

Features: Passes through beautiful high Sonoran Desert into the Tonto National Forest. State Trust Land permit required (see introduction).

Time & Distance: About 20 miles through New River Canyon, 13 miles of gravel road and 23 miles of pavement. Allow 5 to 6 hours.

To Get There: Get off Interstate 17 at Table Mesa Road Exit 236.

Trail Description: Reset your odometer at the exit ramp on the east side of the freeway. [01]. Head east on Table Mesa Road. At 1.1 miles turn left through unmarked gate that allows you to bypass a private ranch. Cross river at 1.8 (may be dry). Stay left of gravel pit at 2.8. Cross cattle guard at 4.3 where F.S. Road 41 begins. Bear right at 4.4 miles [02]. Follow deteriorating road uphill past clearing at 5.2. Pass over high ridge. Cross river at 7.6 and 7.9. Tough spot after second crossing. Gates at 11.3 and 11.8 followed by tank and cabin. After a couple of rocky dips the road gets easier. Bear right at 13.7 miles [03] where F.S. 37 goes left. Road climbs through mountains before reaching F.S. Road 24 at 19.5 miles [04].

Reset your odometer at F.S. 24 [04]. Turn right and follow gravel/paved road south. Pass Cave Creek Campground (fee area) at 3.1 followed by hiking trailhead and toilet. Exit Tonto Recreation Area Seven Springs at 3.9 miles (fee required for day use). Sears-Kay Ruins on left at 13.0 (hike required to see ruins). Gravel road becomes paved Cave Creek Road at 13.3 miles [05]. Follow Cave Creek Road through town to Carefree Highway at 26.3 miles [06]. Interstate 17 is another 10 miles to the right.

Return Trip: Left at I-17 for Phoenix, right for Black Canyon City, Flagstaff.

Services: None on trail. Full services in Carefree and Cave Creek.

Maps: Tonto National Forest, three USGS 250,000 scale maps Phoenix, Holbrook and Mesa, Arizona, Arizona Atlas and Gazetteer.

Rocky and steep at the top.

Watch for this sign on Eagle Eye Road.

Registration box next to the observatory. Please let the BLM know you appreciate this road.

Ten miles of pure driving pleasure.

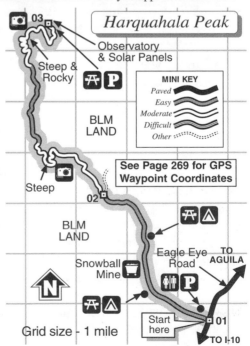

Harquahala Peak

03

Observatory & Solar Panels

Steep & Rocky

MINI KEY
Paved
Easy
Moderate
Difficult
Other

BLM LAND

See Page 269 for GPS Waypoint Coordinates

Steep

02

BLM LAND

Snowball Mine

Eagle Eye Road

TO AGUILA

N

Start here

01

TO I-10

Grid size - 1 mile

Location: Northwest of Phoenix, south of Aguila.

Difficulty: Moderate. Easy at the bottom, but the upper parts of the road are narrow, steep and rocky. Suitable for all SUVs with four-wheel drive and low-range gears.

Features: A BLM National Byway which climbs to the top of 5,681 ft. Harquahala Peak, the highest mountain in southwestern Arizona. At the top, find an observatory built by the Smithsonian Institution in use from 1920 to 1925. Also find modern solar collectors used by the Central Arizona Project. Camping and picnic places are provided along the road.

Time & Distance: Allow about an hour to reach the top, which is 10.6 miles.

To Get There: Follow Hwy. 60 northwest from Phoenix and west from Wickenburg to the small town of Aguila. Turn left on Eagle Eye Road and drive about 18 miles south. Watch for signs 1/2 mile past mile marker 9.

Trail Description: Reset your odometer when you turn right off Eagle Eye Road onto well-marked Harquahala Mountain Byway. [01]. There's a parking area and modern vault toilet on the right at 0.2 miles. An elaborate information kiosk tells you all about the mountain.

The drive to the top is interrupted by only one fork at 3.8 miles [02]. Bear left. From this point, the road gets steeper before leveling out again. The last few miles at the top are very steep and rocky. Those unfamiliar with this kind of terrain may find this part of the trip a little scary. A large parking area with a few picnic tables is on the right just below the summit. There's a smaller parking area at the summit at 10.6 miles [03]. Please sign in at the guest register so that the BLM knows you enjoyed this great road.

Return Trip: Return the way you came or head south on Eagle Eye Road. It intersects with Buckeye-Salome Road. Turn left to reach Interstate 10 at Exit 81. You can also come in this way, but it is less scenic.

Services: Just a vault toilet at the start. Closest full services in Wickenburg. Gas and food in Tonopah on Interstate 10 going back to Phoenix.

Maps: USGS 100,000 scale map Salome, Arizona 33113-E1-TM-100, Arizona Atlas and Gazetteer.

View from Belmont Mountain looking south.

Danger! Stay out of mines.

Start crosses flood plain.

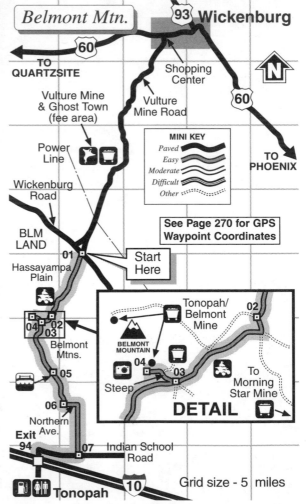

Belmont Mtn.

93 Wickenburg

60

TO
QUARTZSITE

Shopping
Center

N

Vulture Mine
& Ghost Town
(fee area)

Vulture
Mine Road

60

Power
Line

MINI KEY
Paved
Easy
Moderate
Difficult
Other

TO
PHOENIX

Wickenburg
Road

**See Page 270 for GPS
Waypoint Coordinates**

BLM
LAND

01

Start
Here

Hassayampa
Plain

Tonopah/
Belmont
Mine

02

**BELMONT
MOUNTAIN**

04
03
02

Belmont
Mtns.

04

03

To
Morning
Star Mine

05

Steep

DETAIL

06

Northern
Ave.

**Exit
94**

07 Indian School
Road

Grid size - 5 miles

Tonopah

10

158

Belmont Mountain 41

Location: Northwest of Phoenix, north of Tonopah.

Difficulty: Easy. Sandy washes and mild desert climbs. Steep and rocky just before Belmont Mine. Suitable for high-clearance stock SUVs.

Features: See the Tonopah/Belmont Mine high in the Sonoran Desert. Visit Vulture Mine—a rare opportunity to see a well-preserved gold mine and ghost town. Henry Wickenburg discovered the mine in 1863 and sold it for $100,000. This turned out to be a big mistake. It became one of the richest gold mines in Arizona and didn't shut down until 1942. The mine is now a commercial tourist attraction.

Time & Distance: About 22 miles off-pavement. Allow 2 to 3 hours for the trail and several more hours to get there and return.

To Get There: Head south on Vulture Mine Road from Hwy. 60 on the west side of Wickenburg between mile markers 108 and 107. Pass Vulture Mine on right at 11.6 miles. Go straight on sandy road when Vulture Mine Road reaches T at Wickenburg Road at 19.3 miles.

Trail Description: Reset your odometer when you leave pavement at the start [01]. Continue straight across a wide flood plain. Go straight where road goes right at 1.7. Turn left at a T at 5.8 miles [02]. Turn right uphill on lesser road at 5.9. Continue straight uphill through a 5-way intersection at 6.3 [03], then make an immediate left climbing a short, narrow, rocky shelf road. Park when it flattens out at the Tonopah/Belmont Mine at 6.6 miles [04]. After looking around and enjoying the views, head back down to the 5-way intersection [03], *reset your odometer* and turn right downhill. Cross a cattle guard by a metal water tank at 1.6. Continue straight when road joins on right at 1.9. Bear right at 3.0. Continue straight at 3.6 when road joins on right. Cross Central Arizona Project bridge at 4.6 [05]. Turn left at Northern Avenue at 7.3 miles [06]. Turn right at Silver Ranch and follow major road south. Pass large commercial cattle operation. Turn right on paved Indian School Road at 12.3 [07]. Interstate 10, Tonopah Exit 94 is reached at 15.4 miles

Return Trip: East on Interstate 10 to Phoenix, west to Quartzsite.

Services: Full services in Wickenburg, gas and food at Tonopah.

Maps: USGS 250,000 scale map Phoenix, AZ, Arizona Atlas and Gazetteer.

AREA 6

Northeast Phoenix, Apache Junction

42. Reno Pass
43. Sunflower Mine
44. Four Peaks
45. Telegraph Line Road
46. Bulldog Canyon
47. Apache Trail

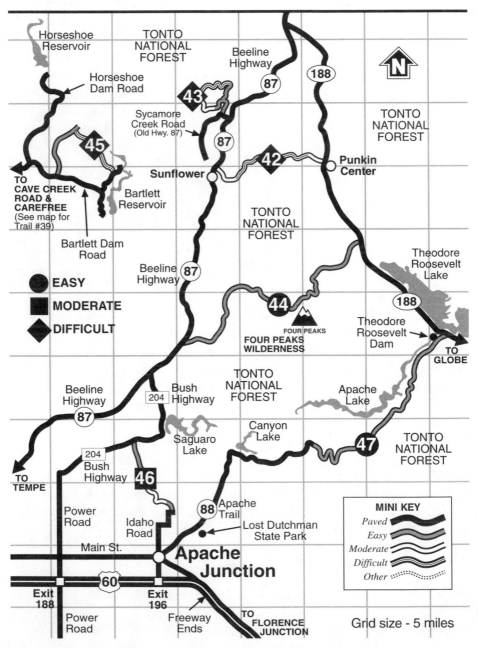

Horseshoe Reservoir

TONTO NATIONAL FOREST

Beeline Highway

188

N

Horseshoe Dam Road

43

Sycamore Creek Road (Old Hwy. 87)

87

TONTO NATIONAL FOREST

45

TO CAVE CREEK ROAD & CAREFREE (See map for Trail #39)

87

42

Punkin Center

Sunflower

Bartlett Reservoir

TONTO NATIONAL FOREST

Theodore Roosevelt Lake

Bartlett Dam Road

Beeline Highway 87

● **EASY**

■ **MODERATE**

◆ **DIFFICULT**

44

FOUR PEAKS

FOUR PEAKS WILDERNESS

188

Theodore Roosevelt Dam

TO GLOBE

Beeline Highway 87

204 Bush Highway

TONTO NATIONAL FOREST

Apache Lake

Saguaro Lake

Canyon Lake

47

TONTO NATIONAL FOREST

204 Bush Highway

46

TO TEMPE

Power Road

Idaho Road

88 Apache Trail

Lost Dutchman State Park

MINI KEY

Paved
Easy
Moderate
Difficult
Other

Main St.

Apache Junction

60

Exit 188

Exit 196

Freeway Ends

TO FLORENCE JUNCTION

Power Road

Grid size - 5 miles

160

AREA 6

Northeast Phoenix, Apache Junction

All of the trails in this area are located in the Tonto National Forest. The best known is *Apache Trail*, which, oddly, is not a trail at all. This wide gravel road is suitable for cars. It's included here because it's fun to drive and one of the most scenic backroads in America. This trail ends at historic Roosevelt Dam, gateway to massive Roosevelt Recreation Area. Those looking for more challenge will not be disappointed. Three trails in this section are rated difficult. My favorite is *Telegraph Line Road*, a supreme test of any vehicle's articulation as it meanders across gorgeous Sonoran Desert. *Reno Pass* is strictly for the hard-core crowd. This steep trail is a mix of tight brush, deep ruts, and a narrow, tippy shelf road. *Sunflower Mine* has some difficult terrain, but, fortunately, it starts after the mine. Much of this unusual mercury mine is still standing. Stock SUV owners looking for some challenge should head to spectacular *Four Peaks*. Still rated easy, this challenging, high-mountain road climbs above 5,000 feet with great views along the way.

Processing mill at Sunflower Mine, a.k.a. National Mine (Trail #43).

Good articulation or lockers needed.

Dangerous, narrow, tippy spot. Be careful.

Much of the trail is washed out.

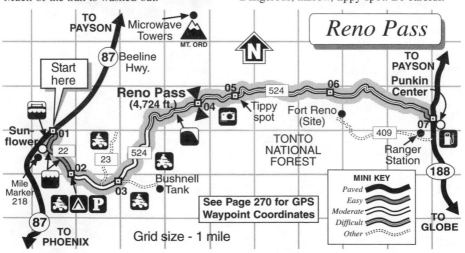

Reno Pass

TO PAYSON

Microwave Towers
MT. ORD

87 Beeline Hwy.

Start here

TO PAYSON
Punkin Center

Reno Pass
(4,724 ft.)

05
524
06

04
Tippy spot

Fort Reno (Site)

07

Sunflower

01
22
23
524

TONTO NATIONAL FOREST

409

Ranger Station

188

02

03
Bushnell Tank

Mile Marker 218

MINI KEY
Paved
Easy
Moderate
Difficult
Other

87
TO PHOENIX

See Page 270 for GPS Waypoint Coordinates

Grid size - 1 mile

TO GLOBE

162

Reno Pass 42

Location: Northeast of Phoenix between Sunflower and Punkin Center.

Difficulty: Difficult. Steep, narrow and extremely rutted. Very tight brush. Lockers recommended. East side descends narrow shelf road with one dangerous tippy spot, especially for full-size vehicles. Remote location.

Features: Route follows old military road built in 1863. Visit Fort Reno after completing trail. Take F.S. 409 west past ranger station from Hwy. 188.

Time & Distance: Just under 12 miles. Allow about 3 hours.

To Get There: Follow Hwy. 87 northeast past Sunflower near mile marker 218. Cross large bridge and turn right on wide gravel road. Follow sign to Bushnell Tank.

Trail Description: Reset your odometer as you turn right off Hwy. 87 [01]. Follow F.S. Road 22 as it swings south and weaves back and forth across Sycamore Creek. After a mile, the trail reaches a wide open area used for parking and camping. Continue south along the left side of this area, following signs for F.S. 22 at 1.1 miles [02]. Follow 22 and bear right at 1.8 where F.S. 23 goes left. Bear slightly right at 2.0 and pass a corral. You should be able to see microwave towers at the top of Mt. Ord to your left. Bear left at 2.4 miles [03] on F.S. 524 in the direction of Mt. Ord. Bear left again at 3.0. The trail deteriorates quickly. Continue straight through a gate at 5.6 before reaching Reno Pass at 5.7 [04]. Bear left and start downhill into Tonto Basin.

Go either way at 5.8. The trail descends quickly. A narrow spot at 6.6 is dangerous [05]. Be careful. Full-size vehicles will lean significantly. At 9.3 miles [06] go straight. Road 524 gets better but not for long. A lot of rough road remains. Stay in low range until you reach a major gravel road at 11.6. Turn right to reach Hwy. 188 at 11.9 miles [07].

Return Trip: Turn right and go a short distance to Punkin Center on the east side of Hwy. 188. Continuing south will take you around the southwest side of Roosevelt Lake to Globe. Left goes to Payson.

Services: Gas and food at Punkin Center and Spring Creek Store, about 8 miles south of Roosevelt Dam on 188. Full services in Globe.

Maps: Tonto National Forest, USGS 100,000 scale map Theodore Roosevelt Lake, AZ 33111-E1-TM-100, Arizona Atlas and Gazetteer.

The difficult part of the trail starts in this creek bed after the Sunflower Mine.

Ore chute below mine.

Gorgeous views from F.S. Road 201.

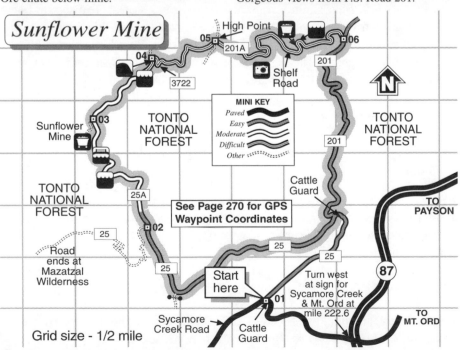

Sunflower Mine

High Point

05 ← 201A

04 ☐

3722

📷 Shelf Road

201

06

201

TONTO NATIONAL FOREST

03 Sunflower Mine

MINI KEY
Paved
Easy
Moderate
Difficult
Other

TONTO NATIONAL FOREST

201

TONTO NATIONAL FOREST

25A

Cattle Guard

See Page 270 for GPS Waypoint Coordinates

TO PAYSON

25

02

25

25

Road ends at Mazatzal Wilderness

25

Start here

Turn west at sign for Sycamore Creek & Mt. Ord at mile 222.6

87

Sycamore Creek Road

01

Cattle Guard

TO MT. ORD

Grid size - 1/2 mile

Sunflower Mine 43

Location: Northeast of Phoenix, north of Sunflower.

Difficulty: Difficult. Stock SUVs can reach Sunflower Mine. Difficult portion of the trail begins later. It becomes rocky and narrow with tight brush in places. One narrow shelf road with loose rock. Slippery when wet.

Features: See well-preserved mercury mine along scenic forest road.

Time & Distance: Allow about 4 hours for this 13-mile adventure.

To Get There: Take Highway 87 north and turn left on road marked to Sycamore Creek/Mt. Ord 0.6 miles past mile marker 222. Follow paved road 1.2 miles to bottom of hill and turn right at cattle guard on F.S. 25.

Trail Description: Reset your odometer at start [01]. Head north on F.S. 25. Swing left and cross second cattle guard at 1.1 miles. Bear left at next fork. Continue straight at 3.8 miles [02] on F.S. 25A. Road worsens. Cross creek at 4.8 and bridge at 5.1. Narrow road to Sunflower Mine goes uphill to left at 5.6 miles [03]. Walk 1/4 mile to mine (or drive if gate is open). Difficult part of trail begins at 5.1 as trail follows rocky creek bed. Make hard right up steep rock wall at 6.5 [04] on F.S. 3722. Turn right at T at 7.1. Several roads crisscross at top of hill at 7.4 miles [05]. Head southeast downhill on F.S. 201A. Driver's choice at 7.5; right is easier. Steep descent on narrow shelf road at 8.6. Watch for falling rock. At bottom of hill, trail swings left past two open mine tunnels, crosses creek, then heads in opposite direction. Climb steeply up washed-out road to F.S. 201 at 9.5 miles [06]. Turn right and head downhill. Return to start at 13.1 miles [01].

Return Trip: Return the way you came. North on Hwy. 87 goes to Payson.

Services: None on trail. Return to Phoenix or head north to Payson.

Historical Highlights: The Sunflower Mine (a.k.a. National Mine) produced mercury. Inside the processing building which still stands, you'll find a large pipe used to tumble a reddish-brown ore called cinnabar. The fine particles were burned in vertical furnaces with coke to produce mercury gas. The gas liquefied after being cooled in U-shaped tubes.

Maps: Tonto National Forest, USGS 7.5 minute map Reno Pass, AZ N3352.5-W11122.5/7.5, Arizona Atlas and Gazetteer.

Distinctive Four Peaks in distance.

Rocky and steep in places.

View from top looking west.

East side view of Roosevelt Lake.

Dry stream bed can be deep during rainy periods.

Four Peaks (44)

Location: Northeast of Phoenix on north side of Four Peaks Wilderness.

Difficulty: Easy. Graded dirt road but washed out and rutted in places. High clearance recommended. Four-wheel drive beneficial. Small stream crossings possible. Snow likely at top late fall and winter.

Features: Very popular mountain drive with several great hiking trails. Dispersed camping allowed. Make sure to pack out all trash. Heavily used ATV and dirt bike area. Stay on roads and trails at all times.

Time & Distance: Almost 28 miles of twisting, rough road. Allow 3-4 hours plus several hours travel time. Great full-day adventure if you return via Apache Trail (Trail #47). Turn right after crossing bridge at Roosevelt Dam.

To Get There: Take Highway 87 northeast from Phoenix. Turn right on well-marked dirt road to Four Peaks between mile marker 203 and 204.

Trail Description: Reset your odometer as you turn right off Hwy. 87 [01]. Head east on wide dirt road marked F.S. 143. Vault toilet and parking area on right at 0.7 miles. Go straight at 1.4. Swing left at 2.1 miles [02] staying on 143. Ignore many small side roads. Bear left at 4.3. Small water crossing possible at 10.1. Right at 10.6. Continue past Cline Hiking Trailhead at 11.1 miles [03]. Climb over ridge as Four Peaks comes back into view. Bear right after small stream at 13.7 (stream may be dry). Continue straight past Mud Spring Trailhead at 15.3. Reach highest point of trail at 18.2 miles [04]. F.S. 648 goes right to hiking trailhead to Four Peaks Wilderness.

Swing left at top [04] and start down. Make a right turn at 19.3. Pass microwave tower. Road is well-maintained the rest of the way. Beautiful views of Roosevelt Lake can be seen below. Turn left in front of knoll at 23.4 miles [05] or take fun loop around knoll (adds 0.1 miles). Reach Hwy. 188 at 27.8 miles [06] near mile marker 255.

Return Trip: Right for Roosevelt Dam, Globe and Phoenix. Left for Payson.

Services: Vault toilets near start. Gas at The Spring Creek Store 8 miles south of Roosevelt Dam on Hwy. 188. Full services in Globe.

Maps: Tonto National Forest, USGS 250,000 scale map Mesa, AZ, Arizona Atlas and Gazetteer.

Washouts common along the route.

A good test of articulation.

Fun to drive and great scenery.

"Edge of the Earth."

Telegraph Line Rd.

Verde River

TONTO NATIONAL FOREST

Devil's Hole

TONTO NATIONAL FOREST

Indian Spgs. Wash

05

42

04

03

Bartlett Flat

532

"Edge of the Earth"

1065

06

02

Bartlett Res.

1104

1064

42

MINI KEY
Paved
Easy
Moderate
Difficult
Other

Start here

01

532

See Page 270 for GPS Waypoint Coordinates

North Lake Road

459

07

TO CAVE CREEK ROAD & TOWN OF CAREFREE

Bartlett Dam Road

Bartlett Res.

Grid size - 1 mile

168

Telegraph Line Road 45

Location: North of Phoenix, east of Carefree and Cave Creek.

Difficulty: Difficult. Undulating sandy terrain with extreme washouts. Use caution to avoid rollovers. Lockers recommended.

Features: Beautiful Sonoran Desert overlooking Bartlett Reservoir and the Verde River. Camp and fish at the reservoir. This road was once a service road for a telegraph line. Look carefully along the trail for wooden stumps, remnants of old telegraph poles. A popular ATV and dirt bike area. Please stay on existing trails at all times to avoid further erosion.

Time & Distance: About 12 miles. Allow 4 hours. Add time for side trips.

To Get There: Get off Interstate 17 at Exit 223. Head east on Carefree Highway 12 miles and turn left on Tom Darlington Road. After 2 miles turn right on Cave Creek Road. Turn right on Bartlett Dam Road in another 6 miles. Drive 13 miles and turn left on North Lake Road after rest area. Turn left at information kiosk after 2.7 miles onto F.S. Road 42.

Trail Description: Reset your odometer at the start [01]. Bear left at 1.8 and 2.1. Driver's choice at 2.3. Right downhill at T at 2.4 miles [02]. Bear slightly left at 3.1 and cross Bartlett Flat. Trail worsens; watch for deep holes that can cause rollovers. Turn right down "Edge of the Earth" at 4.2 and follow wash to right. Bear left uphill at 4.4 miles [03]. (Nice spot for lunch by river if you go straight.) Turn right up steep hill out of wash at 4.8. Turn sharp left uphill at 5.2 miles [04]. (Straight is nasty so don't miss turn.) Turn left to exit at 6.2 [05] at Indian Springs Wash (or take side trip right to Devil's Hole).

    Reset odometer at Indian Springs Wash [05]. Driver's choice at 2.8. Left at 3.2 miles [06] where F.S. 1104 joins on right. Left at 3.5 where road joins on right. Choose best line at 3.6 through wide washed-out area (unless recently maintained). Bear right when roads join at 4.1 and 4.6. Stay on main road until you reach paved Bartlett Dam Road at 5.7 miles [07].

Return Trip: Go right on Bartlett Dam Road and return the way you came.

Services: None on trail. Return to Cave Creek or Carefree.

Maps: Indian Springs Wash is shown on Tonto National Forest map but F.S. 42 is not. For GPS purposes use USGS 100,000 scale map Theodore Roosevelt Lake, AZ 33111-E1-TM-100, Arizona Atlas and Gazetteer.

Loose rock presents some challenge.

Several steep sections.

Gate has combination lock. Get permit.

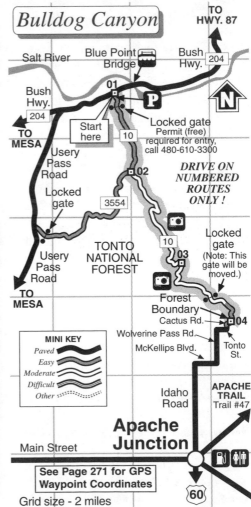

Sonoran Desert with mountain backdrop.

Bulldog Canyon

TO HWY. 87

Salt River

Blue Point Bridge

Bush Hwy. 204

Bush Hwy. 204

TO MESA

01

P

Start here

10

Locked gate
Permit (free) required for entry, call 480-610-3300

DRIVE ON NUMBERED ROUTES ONLY!

02

3554

10

03

Locked gate
(Note: This gate will be moved.)

Usery Pass Road

Locked gate

Usery Pass Road

TO MESA

TONTO NATIONAL FOREST

Forest Boundary
Cactus Rd.
Wolverine Pass Rd.
McKellips Blvd.

04

Tonto St.

MINI KEY

Paved
Easy
Moderate
Difficult
Other

Idaho Road

APACHE TRAIL
Trail #47

Main Street

Apache Junction

See Page 271 for GPS Waypoint Coordinates

60

Grid size - 2 miles

Bulldog Canyon 46

Location: Northeast of Mesa and north of Apache Junction.

Difficulty: Moderate. Several short, steep rocky climbs that require careful tire placement and some driving skill. Suitable for aggressive stock SUVs with high ground clearance. Go with a friend and carry a tow strap.

Features: A permit is required for this trail. It's easy to obtain and free. Carry it with you at all times. Call Mesa District Rangers at (480) 610-3300. This is a highly sensitive area and subject to closure. It has been adopted by Copper State 4-Wheelers Club, who fight to keep it open. Stay on trails and follow all rules or risk up to a $5,000 fine. The trail passes through scenic Sonoran Desert with views of Goldfield and Superstition Mountains.

Time & Distance: About 8 miles. Allow 2 to 3 hours.

To Get There: From Hwy. 60 east of Phoenix, head north from Exit 188 on Power Road which turns into Bush Highway north of town. Follow Bush Highway east and turn right 1.7 miles after Usery Pass Road. Refer to permit for combination of gate. Relock gate after passing through.

Trail Description: Reset your odometer at the start [01]. Follow easy road south. Continue straight across wash at 2.2 miles [02] on F.S. 10. (Right takes you on scenic drive to Usery Pass Road.) Road becomes more difficult so pay attention. Bear right at 2.7, 2.8 and 3.5 miles. Turn left at 5.2 and 5.4. Tough spot at 5.5 miles [03] as road curves downhill into a ravine. Steep, loose rock requires careful tire placement to climb out. Other challenges follow. Bear left at 6.3 then straight at 6.4. Reach locked gate at 7.3 miles. (Note: Plans are to move this gate closer to Forest Service boundary to stop people from using this area as a junkyard. Gate may be moved by the time you read this.) Pass through gate and turn left at T on good gravel road at 7.5. Bear right at Forest Service boundary at 8.4 miles [04]. The road weaves through a residential area, then zigzags right at Tonto, left at Wolverine Pass Road, right at McKellips Blvd., then finally left at Idaho Road. Idaho Road returns to Apache Junction and Highway 60.

Return Trip: Right on Highway 60 takes you towards Phoenix.

Services: None on trail. Full services in Apache Junction.

Maps: USGS 250,000 scale map Mesa, AZ, Arizona Atlas and Gazetteer.

Looking down from Fish Creek Hill as the trail heads east towards the Salt River.

Fish Creek Bridge.

East end of Apache Lake.

Allow time to visit these extensive ruins at Tonto National Monument.

172

Apache Trail (47)

Location: Between Apache Junction and Theodore Roosevelt Lake.

Difficulty: Easy. The road starts out paved then changes to well-maintained dirt suitable for passengers cars. Blind curves and tight switchbacks near cliff edges require utmost driver attention. The road is well-marked and easy to follow. Carry plenty of drinking water.

Features: The road weaves along mountainsides above the Salt River Valley then drops precipitously into the valley at Fish Creek Hill. Along the way you're treated to gorgeous views of Canyon Lake and Apache Lake. Both man-made reservoirs offer a full array of water sports including boating, water skiing and fishing. The trail can get quite congested on weekends and holidays. South of Apache Trail is the vast Superstition Wilderness with an extensive network of hiking trails and backpacking opportunities. The road skirts the edge the Salt River before climbing out of the valley at Theodore Roosevelt Dam which forms Roosevelt Lake. When full, the lake's shoreline measures 112 miles. This vast recreation area has just about everything for the outdoor enthusiast. There are many great four-wheel-drive roads in the surrounding Tonto National Forest. Not all are covered in this book.

Time and Distance: From Lost Dutchman State Park to Roosevelt Dam is about 39 miles. Driving time is approximately 3 hours. To fully enjoy everything along the way, including the ruins at the Tonto National Monument, plan a full day. It's a long drive back to Phoenix from Roosevelt Lake.

To Get There: From Phoenix take Highway 60 east to Apache Junction. Get off at Idaho Road, Exit 196, and head north. Turn right on Highway 88 and head northeast.

Trail Description: Reset your odometer at Lost Dutchman State Park [01]. On the way, you'll pass Goldfield, a reconstructed ghost town with mining tours and a museum. You'll pass overlooks and campgrounds before going by Canyon Lake Marina at 9.6 miles. Grab a bite to eat at Tortilla Flat, an interesting little stop at 11.7. Forest Road 80 goes left to the Horse Mesa Dam before the pavement ends at 17.2 miles [02]. F.S. 213 goes right to Tortilla Trailhead at 18.1. There's a large overlook at 19.0.
   Descend steeply down Fish Creek Hill to the Fish Creek Bridge at

20.7. Stop along the way for some great pictures. This is the narrowest and steepest part of the trip. There's another overlook on the left at the turn for Apache Lake Marina. This is a developed area with motels, restaurants and a gas station. The road skirts the edge of Salt River before reaching pavement below Roosevelt Dam at 37.5. Two large parking areas follow before reaching Highway 188 at 39.2 miles [03].

Return Trip: Turn right and head south on 88 to Highway 60 near Globe. From there, go east for Safford or west for Apache Junction and Phoenix. North on 188 goes to Payson.

On the way home, allow time to stop at *Tonto National Monument* about 3 miles south of Roosevelt Dam on Hwy. 88. See incredible Native American ruins built into a large cave on the hillside. It's a steep hike to the ruins, especially on a hot day.

Services: Gas is available at Apache Junction, Apache Lake Marina and at the Spring Creek Store on Highway 88 about 8 miles south of the dam. Find toilets at most of the overlooks, Canyon Lake Marina, Tortilla Flat, Apache Lake Marina and the Roosevelt Lake Visitor Center.

Historical Highlights: Just a foot trail for centuries, Apache Trail was developed to haul supplies for construction of the Roosevelt Dam in the early 1900s. Tales of the road's notoriety are described in detail at overlook kiosks along the route. Fish Creek Hill was the most challenging part of the road to build. Even today, this part of Apache Trail remains at a steep 10% grade. Former president Theodore Roosevelt attended the dedication of the dam in 1911. At that time, this was the primary route into Phoenix from the northeast. Decades later, concerns that the dam would not survive an earthquake resulted in construction of a new dam over the old one. At that time the dam was raised an additional 77 feet, which increased the capacity of the lake 20%. Today Apache Trail is a State Historic Road and National Scenic Byway.

Maps: Tonto National Forest, USGS 250,000 scale map Mesa, AZ, Arizona Atlas and Gazetteer.

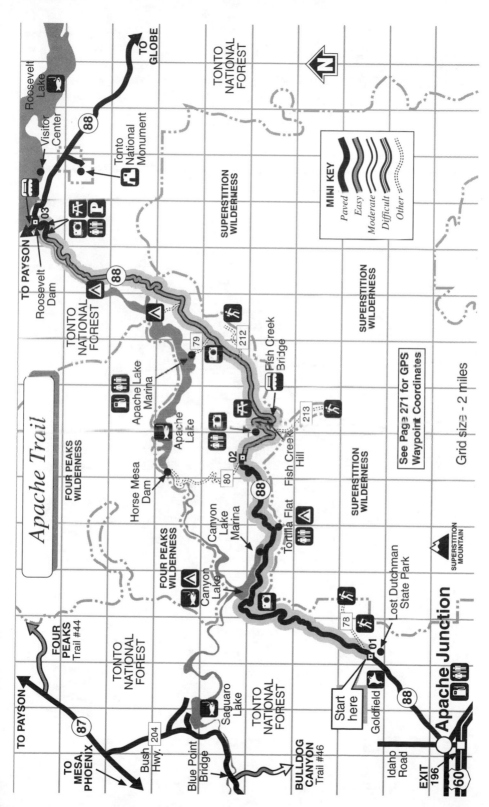

Apache Trail

MINI KEY
Paved
Easy
Moderate
Difficult
Other

TO GLOBE

Roosevelt Lake
Visitor Center
TONTO NATIONAL FOREST
Tonto National Monument
SUPERSTITION WILDERNESS

TO PAYSON
Roosevelt Dam
88
TONTO NATIONAL FOREST
03
79
212
Fish Creek Bridge
SUPERSTITION WILDERNESS

FOUR PEAKS WILDERNESS
Apache Lake Marina
Horse Mesa Dam
Apache Lake
213
Fish Creek Hill
02
80
88
See Page 271 for GPS Waypoint Coordinates

FOUR PEAKS WILDERNESS
Canyon Lake Marina
Canyon Lake
Tortilla Flat
SUPERSTITION WILDERNESS
SUPERSTITION MOUNTAIN

Grid size - 2 miles

TO PAYSON
87
FOUR PEAKS Trail #44
TONTO NATIONAL FOREST
Saguaro Lake
Bush Hwy. 204
TO MESA PHOENIX
Blue Point Bridge
TONTO NATIONAL FOREST
BULLDOG CANYON Trail #46

78
Start here
01
Goldfield
Lost Dutchman State Park

88
Apache Junction
Idaho Road
EXIT 196
60

175

AREA 7

Florence Junction,
Superior

48. Montana Mountain
49. Hackberry Creek
50. Woodpecker Mine
51. Ajax Mine
52. Martinez Cabin
53. Martinez Canyon
54. Jack Handle
55. Box Canyon
56. Coke Ovens
57. Walnut Canyon

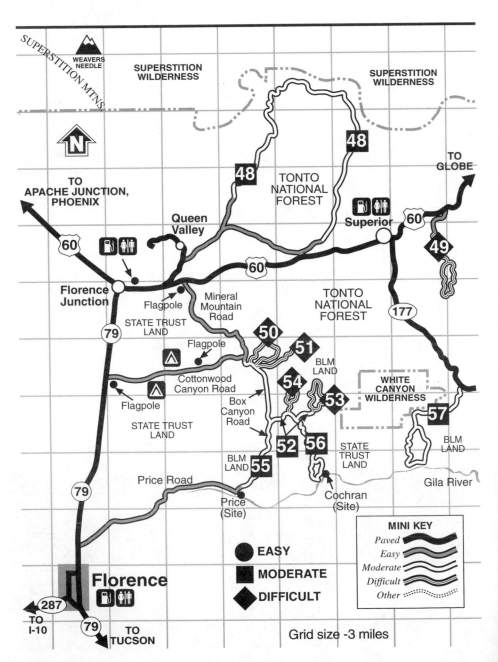

Florence Junction, Superior

Once you reach this rugged area east of Florence Junction, you won't have to travel far between trails. That's why the Arizona State Association of 4-Wheel-Drive Clubs comes here often for their annual jamboree. With miles of open land for dispersed camping, you can set up camp and enjoy an extended stay. The area is popular for four-wheeling and for ATVs. Much is state land so make sure you have a permit as described in the introduction. You'll note well-known trails like *Woodpecker Mine* and *Ajax Mine*. These boulder-strewn creek bottoms have been perennial favorites of the hard-core crowd. The centerpiece of the area, however, is *Martinez Canyon*, an incredible blend of extreme four-wheeling, beautiful scenery and intact mining structures. One obstacle on the trail, called *The Luge*, is very dangerous and for experts only. Moderate trails like *Box Canyon, Coke Ovens, Walnut Canyon* and *Montana Mountain* offer unique scenery and challenging terrain. Stock vehicles must have high-ground clearance, good articulation and skid plates. Area 7 has no easy trails.

High-centered Jeep on Woodpecker Mine, Trail #50.

Looking down on F.S. 172A near F.S. 650.

F.S. 650 follows creek in places. May be dry.

Straddle big ruts.

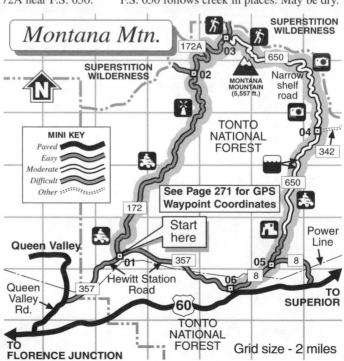

Montana Mtn.

SUPERSTITION WILDERNESS

172A

03

650

02

SUPERSTITION WILDERNESS

MONTANA MOUNTAIN (5,557 ft.)

Narrow shelf road

TONTO NATIONAL FOREST

04

342

MINI KEY
Paved
Easy
Moderate
Difficult
Other

650

See Page 271 for GPS Waypoint Coordinates

172

Start here

Queen Valley

01

357

Hewitt Station Road

357

Queen Valley Rd.

06

8

05

8

Power Line

TO SUPERIOR

60

TONTO NATIONAL FOREST

TO FLORENCE JUNCTION

Grid size - 2 miles

178

Montana Mountain 48

Location: Northeast of Florence Junction, northwest of Superior.

Difficulty: Moderate. Easy until F.S. 650 where it becomes narrow, steep and rutted. Stock vehicles with high ground clearance and good articulation can make it although some driving skill is necessary. Slippery at the top when wet. Dangerous ice can be present late fall and winter.

Features: Climbs to over 5,000 feet with panoramic desert and mountain views. Crosses many hiking trails into the bordering Superstition Wilderness. Popular area for ATVs and dirt bikes. Stay on existing trails at all times.

Time & Distance: Allow about 4 hours for this 30-mile trip.

To Get There: Take Hwy. 60 east from Florence Junction. Turn left on Queen Valley Rd. 1/4 mile past mile post 214. After 1.7 miles turn right on Hewitt Station Rd. F.S. 357. Go another 3.1 miles and turn left on F.S. 172.

Trail Description: Reset your odometer at F.S. 172 [01]. Bear right at 0.6 where F.S. 1900 goes left. Drivers choice at 3.9 across wash. The road climbs as you pass a windmill and corral at 7.5. Turn right on F.S. 172A at 9.4 miles [02]. Make another right on a steep, narrow road at 13.1 miles [03]. It's marked F.S. 650 farther up the hill. Do not cut switchback at 14.6; stay right. Stay left at 15.1. Narrow shelf road leans downhill at 15.3. Use caution if wet. Turn around if icy. Right downhill at 15.6. Go straight at 16.2 and 18.2 where hiking trails branch off. Continue right downhill at 19.3. Stay right at 22.0 miles [04] where F.S. 342 goes left. Left at Y at 22.8. Stay on widest part of road as many spurs branch off. Cross creek at 23.8. (Note: creek may be dry in summer.) Bear right and follow creek for a short distance at 24.0. Left out of creek at 24.2. Turn right on F.S. 8 at 28.2 miles [05]. Bear left over R.R. tracks at 29.3. Turn left on Hewitt Station Road at 30.0 miles [06] to connect to Highway 60 between mile markers 222 and 223.

Return Trip: Turn right on Highway 60 for Florence Junction, Apache Junction and Phoenix. Left for Superior, Miami and Globe.

Services: None on trail. There's a gas station and convenience store in Florence Junction. More services in Superior.

Maps: Tonto National Forest, USGS 250,000 scale map Mesa, AZ, Arizona Atlas and Gazetteer.

This spot near start is usually dry.

Steep rocky climbs with loose rock.

Hackberry Creek.

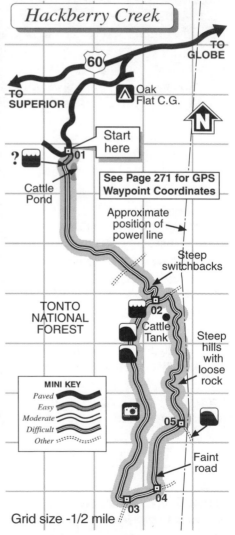

Hackberry Creek

60

TO GLOBE

TO SUPERIOR

Oak Flat C.G.

Start here

01

?

Cattle Pond

See Page 271 for GPS Waypoint Coordinates

Approximate position of power line

Steep switchbacks

02

TONTO NATIONAL FOREST

Cattle Tank

Steep hills with loose rock

MINI KEY
Paved
Easy
Moderate
Difficult
Other

05

Faint road

04

03

Grid size -1/2 mile

Hackberry Creek ◆49◆

Location: Southeast of Superior.

Difficulty: Difficult. Steep rocky climbs and descents. Follows narrow Hackberry Creek through several challenging boulder fields. Lockers and very high ground clearance recommended. Extreme terrain available on side roads. Don't go alone.

Features: Narrow valley surrounded by interesting rock formations. Very enjoyable hard-core run. Forest Service campground near the start.

Time & Distance: Just over 10 miles. Allow about 4 hours.

To Get There: Follow Highway 60 northeast past Superior. Turn right at sign for Oak Flat Campground near mile marker 231. Follow paved road south then east past the Oak Flat Campground. Turn left off paved road through gate after 1.5 miles. Close gate after passing through.

Trail Description: Reset your odometer at the gate [01]. Drop down a short hill to a flat spot and swing right. (This is a good place to air down.) Go around the right side of the cattle watering pond and head south. During rainy season, you may have to cross standing water. Continue straight uphill at 1.7 miles. Pick best way as you drop down steep, rocky switchbacks at 2.0. When you reach bottom at 2.4 miles [02], turn right and zigzag along Hackberry Creek. After several difficult rocky sections, cross open area after large rock at 4.6. Pass through fence at 5.0. Turn left at T at 5.1 miles [03].
     Important: At 5.4 miles [04] watch carefully for a faint road to the left Do *not* continue straight on a better road that goes under power lines. Turn left on the faint road. It becomes better defined as you continue north. Bear left at T at 6.1 miles [05]. (An extreme road goes uphill to the right.) Several challenging hills follow. Turn left at 7.6 and return to the start of Hackberry Creek at 7.8 [02]. Head north uphill the way you came in to the start of the trail at 10.2 miles [01].

Return Trip: Return to the gate at the start. Follow the paved road right to Hwy. 60. At Hwy. 60 turn left for Superior or right for Miami and Globe.

Services: None on trail. Return to Superior.

Maps: Tonto National Forest map shows only the paved road leading to the start of the trail. For GPS purposes use USGS 100,000 scale map Mesa, AZ.

Our group didn't attempt the "Firehole."

Okay, boys, who's going first?

One challenge after another.

Be careful around open mine shafts.

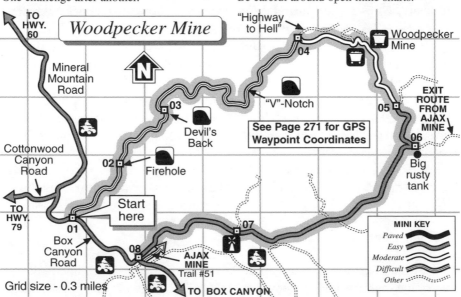

Woodpecker Mine

TO HWY. 60

"Highway to Hell"

Woodpecker Mine

04

N

Mineral Mountain Road

"V"-Notch

05

EXIT ROUTE FROM AJAX MINE

03

Devil's Back

See Page 271 for GPS Waypoint Coordinates

06

Cottonwood Canyon Road

02

Firehole

Big rusty tank

TO HWY. 79

Start here

01

Box Canyon Road

08

07

AJAX MINE
Trail #51

MINI KEY
Paved
Easy
Moderate
Difficult
Other

Grid size - 0.3 miles

TO BOX CANYON

Woodpecker Mine 50

Location: Southeast of Florence Junction, northeast of Florence.

Difficulty: Difficult. Trail follows normally dry creek bottom with large boulders and solid rock obstacles. Squeeze through narrow rock openings. Lockers and very high ground clearance required. Route-finding complex along exit route. Extreme obstacles can be bypassed. Flash floods possible.

Features: See Woodpecker Mine but watch for dangerous open mine shafts. State Trust Land permit required (call 602-364-2753).

Time & Distance: Difficult part of trail is just 2.3 miles. Entire loop back to start is 5.8 miles. Allow 3 to 4 hours if all goes well.

To Get There: From intersection of Hwys. 60 and 79 at Florence Junction, head east on Hwy. 60. Turn right at flagpole at 3.7 miles on Mineral Mountain Road. (Note: A red flag on flagpole indicates National Guard may be practicing. Trails are not affected but you may hear sounds of live ammunition being fired.) *Reset your odometer* and follow Mineral Mountain Road south. Bear left at 4.5 miles and go straight at 6.4. Ignore many small side roads. Turn left at start of trail at 6.7 miles.

Trail Description: Reset your odometer at the start [01]. Head north up rocky creek bed. Narrow at 0.1 with bypass right. The *Firehole* is on left at 0.5 miles [02], bypass right. More obstacles follow. *Devil's Back* at 1.0 miles [03], bypass left. Pick best line through more rocky terrain. *V-Notch* at 1.9. Woodpecker ends at 2.3 miles [04]. Turn right up steep bank out of wash. (Straight continues on extreme *Highway to Hell,* not covered in this book.)

Turn right at Y at 2.6 miles and left at mine shaft at 2.7. You are passing through area of Woodpecker Mine. Ignore side roads going uphill. Drop downhill to low spot then climb out and turn right on better road at 3.1 miles [05]. (Get a preview of Ajax Mine, Trail #51. The easy road that exits Woodpecker weaves through the creek bed of Ajax.) Bear right at 3.4 [06] and continue past windmill at 4.6 [07]. Run into Box Canyon Road at 5.3 [08]. It swings right back to start of Woodpecker at 5.8 [01].

Return Trip: Return the way you came or via Cottonwood Canyon Road.

Services: None on trail. Gas at Florence Junction. Full services in Florence.

Maps: USGS 7.5 minute map Mineral Mountain, AZ, N3307.5-W11107.5/7.5.

The trail changes with each rain storm.

Have fun but stay on the trail.

More challenge for full-size vehicles.

Looking for trouble? Try the upper part.

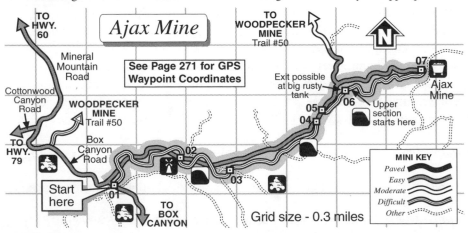

Ajax Mine

TO HWY. 60

TO WOODPECKER MINE
Trail #50

N

Mineral Mountain Road

See Page 271 for GPS Waypoint Coordinates

Cottonwood Canyon Road

07

Ajax Mine

Exit possible at big rusty tank

06

WOODPECKER MINE
Trail #50

05

04

Upper section starts here

TO HWY. 79

Box Canyon Road

02

03

Start here

01

TO BOX CANYON

Grid size - 0.3 miles

MINI KEY

Paved
Easy
Moderate
Difficult
Other

184

Ajax Mine 51

Location: Southeast of Florence Junction, northeast of Florence.

Difficulty: Difficult. Trail follows rocky creek bottom. Large boulders and narrow passages. Lower portion is very difficult; upper portion is extreme. Lockers and very high ground clearance required. Flash floods possible. Route-finding is very confusing. Stay in wash bottom as it weaves back and forth across exit road and other roads.

Features: Not much scenery except Ajax Mine. Strictly for the hard-core enthusiast. State Trust Land permit required (Call 602-364-2753).

Time & Distance: Lower portion is 2.2 miles. Add another 0.8 miles for upper portion. Return distance approximately the same. Allow 2 to 4 hours if all goes well.

To Get There: Follow directions to Woodpecker Mine (see previous trail). Continue past entrance to Woodpecker, cross wash and bear right. When road turns left and forks at 0.5 miles, bear right and drop into wash. Immediately turn left in bottom of wash. This is the start.

Trail Description: Reset your odometer at the start [01]. Head northeast in rocky wash. At 0.2 bear left staying in wash. The trail continues back-and-forth across exit route. Driver's choice at 0.4, left is easier. Stay right in the wash at windmill at 0.8 miles [02]. Bear right at 1.1 then go straight as several roads converge. At 1.2 miles [03], the exit road is on the left, and another road goes right. You stay in the wash between the two roads. Very tough obstacles follow. At 1.9 miles [04] the wash becomes impassable. Follow the exit road a short distance. Bear right back into wash at 2.0 [05]. The lower portion of Ajax concludes at a large rusty tank at 2.2 miles [06]. You can exit to left or continue in the wash.

      The remaining 0.8 miles of trail is extreme. I did not attempt the upper portion with my Cherokee. Two other very capable vehicles continued but one broke an axle within 1/4 mile, then it started to rain heavily. I walked the remainder of the trail. If you drive it, take plenty of spare parts.

Return Trip: Follow exit route back to start, then return the way you came.

Services: None on trail. Gas at Florence Junction. Full services in Florence.

Maps: USGS 7.5 minute map Mineral Mountain, AZ, N3307.5-W11107.5/7.5.

Superstition Mountains and Weaver's Needle as seen from one high ridge along trail.

Toughest spot on trail. Looks worse than it is.

Stage depot and well. Look but don't touch.

Trail can flood after heavy rain. Use caution.

Beautiful Sonoran Desert near canyon.

Martinez Cabin, a great place to stop for lunch. Make sure you pack out all your trash.

186

Martinez Cabin

Location: Southeast of Florence Junction, northeast of Florence.

Difficulty: Moderate. Most of the trail is easy except one moderate spot. A stock Suzuki Sidekick in our group had no problems. Some light brush rubs against vehicles near the end of the trail. Route-finding is complex so follow directions carefully. This is a remote and rugged area so carry plenty of water and be self-sufficient. Much of the trail follows wash bottoms where flash flooding is possible.

Features: A memorable drive through stark rocky canyons and gorgeous Sonoran Desert. Ends at spectacular Martinez Canyon, an historic mining area. Views of the Superstition Mountains and Weaver's Needle can be seen from high points along the route. Enjoy Martinez Cabin in the cool shade of giant cottonwoods at the end of the drive. Hike a half-mile to well-preserved Martinez Mine. Leave everything the way you find it and pack out all trash. Before you start this trip, make sure you have a State Trust Land permit as described in the introduction (call 602-364-2753).

Time & Distance: Martinez Cabin is almost 17 miles from Highway 79 as described here. Allow 5 to 6 hours for the round trip. If you stop along the way or hike to Martinez Mine, plan a full day. (Note: You can also come in via Mineral Mountain Road. See directions to Woodpecker Mine, Trail #50)

To Get There: From the intersection of Highways 60 and 79 at Florence Junction, drive south on Hwy. 79 about 5 miles. Turn left at a flagpole between mile posts 144 and 145 at Cottonwood Canyon Road. No-trespassing signs apply if you don't have a State Trust Land permit. (Note: A red flag on flagpole indicates National Guard may be practicing. Trails are not affected but you may hear sounds of live ammunition being fired.)

Trail Description: Reset your odometer when you turn off Highway 79 [01]. Follow Cottonwood Canyon Road east 5.1 miles [02] and cross cattle guard. Stop and register at box provided next to another flagpole. Bear left at 5.6 and 6.3. Continue straight through ranch gate at 6.6 and pass small log cabin. Bear right uphill out of wash at 6.9. Pass windmill at 7.5. Reach major T intersection with Mineral Mountain Road at 8.1 miles [03].

   Reset odometer and head south on Box Canyon Road [03]. Stay on road, avoiding wash at 0.1. Pass entrance to Woodpecker Mine (Trail #50) on left at 0.3 [04]. Cross wash and turn right following defined road. At 0.7 the road swings left then forks. Turn right and drop down into the wash. The start of Ajax Mine (Trail #51) is on the left [05]. Continue straight out of the wash. As the road swings left, bear right when it forks again at 0.8. Continue straight at 1.2 when a lesser road goes right. Bear right at 1.4. The road climbs to the top of a ridge at 1.9. Views of the Superstition Mountains and Weaver's Needle can be seen on the northern horizon. Follow the main road as it curves across the ridge and heads downhill. At 2.4 miles follow the main road right past a big metal tank. The road descends and gets rougher. The toughest spot of the trip is reached at 3.0 miles [06]. Stay right and place tires carefully as you drop down a high rocky ledge (see photo).

At 3.3 a corral on the right identifies the entrance to Axle Alley, a popular extreme trail not covered in this book. Follow wash downhill, keeping right as small off-shoots go left. Continue straight at 3.6 when a road joins on the left. Bear left at 3.9. At 4.2 miles, note historic stage depot on right. Don't disturb the structure. It's easily damaged.

At 5.2 miles [07] make an important sharp left turn uphill out of the wash. A yellow sign identified this spot when I drove the trail. Stay in wash at 5.5 as you go by another windmill. Continue straight at 6.0 over another high, scenic ridge. Bear right at 6.4 miles [08] at another windmill. Left is the entrance to Jack Handle (Trail #54). Bear left at 7.3 miles [09]. Right goes to the Coke Ovens (Trail #56). Bear left at a hard-to-see fork at 7.9 miles [10]. The road gets rougher. Note cave on right at 8.7. This one-time cantina and bordello is now home to many spiders. Martinez Cabin is reached at 8.8 miles [11]. To see Martinez Mine, hike another half mile east. Stay right in the rocky wash bottom when the road forks just east of the cabins. Again, look but don't touch. Pack out all trash. These structures are amazingly well-preserved; let's leave them that way.

Return Trip: Return the way you came. You can also exit the area by turning left at waypoint 7 and going out Box Canyon (Trail # 55). It runs into Price Road and reaches Highway 79 near Florence.

Services: None on trail. There's a gas station and convenience store in Florence Junction and full services in Florence.

Historical Highlights: Imagine this area as a booming mining center during the late 1800s. In addition to the Martinez Mine, you'll find the Columbia and Silver Belle Mines farther up the mountain. The two cabins at the end of the trail were lived in by the Villa Verde family until 1951, at which time a flash flood nearly swept the family away. For more information, see Arizona Highways January 1997 issue. It includes a great interview with Peter Villa Verde, who lived in the cabins as a boy.

Maps: For GPS purposes, use USGS 250,000 scale map Mesa, AZ. The Arizona Atlas and Gazetteer shows the main parts of the route.

188

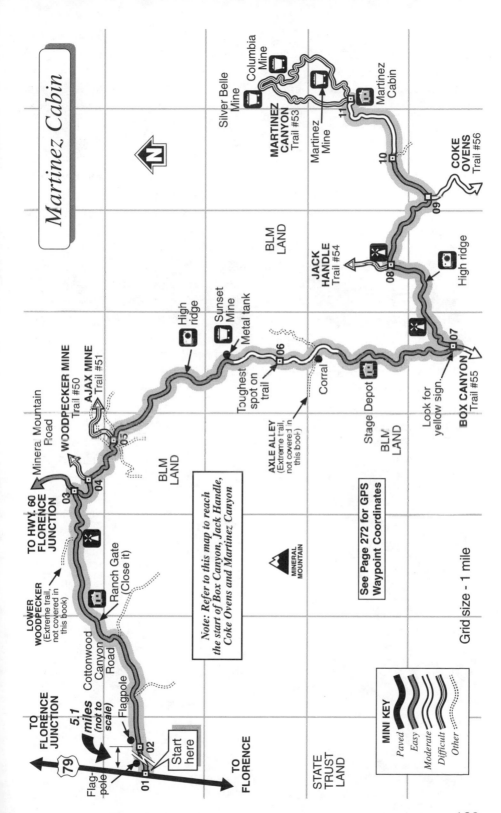

Martinez Cabin

189

Martinez Mill. Look but please stay out.

"The Luge" is dangerous.

Shelf road going up.

Bypass to "Luge" is steep.

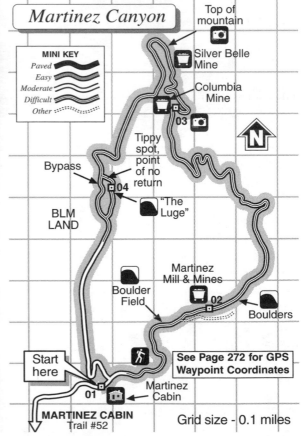

Martinez Canyon

MINI KEY
Paved
Easy
Moderate
Difficult
Other

Top of mountain

Silver Belle Mine

Columbia Mine

03

N

Tippy spot, point of no return

Bypass

04

"The Luge"

BLM LAND

Martinez Mill & Mines

Boulder Field

02

Boulders

Start here

See Page 272 for GPS Waypoint Coordinates

01

Martinez Cabin

MARTINEZ CABIN
Trail #52

Grid size - 0.1 miles

190

Martinez Canyon 53

Location: Southeast of Florence Junction, northeast of Florence.

Difficulty: Difficult and dangerous. Extremely steep with technically challenging rock obstacles. The most dangerous part is *The Luge*—a 10-foot-deep, 200-foot-long trench on a steep mountainside. *The Luge* has a bypass, but it is so steep you must slide down. This trail is for experts only.

Features: Absolutely stunning scenery, including remarkably intact Martinez Mill. Stay on the trail at all times. This is an environmentally sensitive area. Not sure how much longer this trail will remain open. State Trust Land permit required (call 602-364-2753).

Time & Distance: To reach this trail, you must first drive Martinez Cabin (Trail #52). Martinez Canyon is less than 3 miles but allow at least 2 hours. The entire trip, including Martinez Cabin, will take most of a day.

To Get There: Follow directions to Martinez Cabin (previous trail).

Trail Description: Reset your odometer at Martinez Cabin [01]. Continue northeast past the cabin. Bear right immediately, staying in a rocky wash. The trail soon gets difficult. A tough boulder field must be climbed before you see Martinez Mine. Stay left in the boulders just before the mine; the uphill road to the right is washed out. The mine is reached at 0.5 miles [02]. Challenging obstacles follow. Stay left at 0.6 and 0.9. The road climbs up a series of steep switchbacks. Go by Columbia Mine at 1.3 miles [03] and the Silver Belle Mine at 1.5. You reach the crest of the mountain and start down. Approach *The Luge* at 2.0. The bypass is straight down a steep, loose hill. Allow your wheels to turn enough to maintain steering as you slide down the hill. *The Luge* is on the left. When you see it, it's hard to believe anyone would drive down it. Most people use a safety strap attached to a vehicle behind. The last man down has to do it without a strap. *The Luge* reconnects to the trail below. When you reach the bottom of the hill at 2.6 miles, turn right for Martinez Cabin.

Return Trip: Return the way you came or via Box Canyon.

Services: None on trail. Gas at Florence Junction. Full services in Florence.

Maps: USGS 7.5 minute map Mineral Mountain, AZ, N3307.5-W11107.5/7.5.

Narrow spot made more difficult under unusual wet conditions.

High ridge portion of the trail.

Flooded road on way to trailhead.

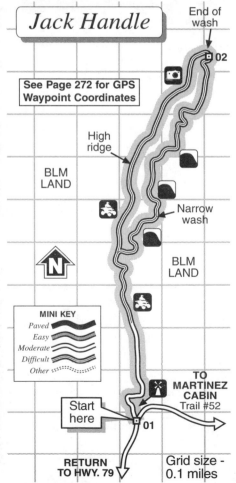

Jack Handle

End of wash

□ 02

See Page 272 for GPS
Waypoint Coordinates

High ridge

BLM
LAND

Narrow
wash

BLM
LAND

N

MINI KEY
Paved
Easy
Moderate
Difficult
Other

TO
MARTINEZ
CABIN
Trail #52

Start
here

□ 01

RETURN
TO HWY. 79

Grid size -
0.1 miles

Jack Handle ◆54◆

Location: Southeast of Florence Junction, northeast of Florence.

Difficulty: Difficult. A short, narrow canyon with little room to maneuver. Rock obstacles are challenging with sharp edges to cut tires if you get careless. One obstacle appears to be an opening cut through solid rock and is barely wide enough to squeeze through. Large vehicles will have problems on this trail. Brush and tree branches are very tight. I took out a rear window on my Cherokee on a thick tree limb hidden in the brush. Frankly, I found this trail more suited for ATVs than Jeeps. The day I ran the trail it was raining heavily with water pouring over the rocks.

Features: A long drive to a short trail. Add this trail to another when you haven't had enough wheeling for a day. State Trust Land permit required as described in the introduction to this book (call 602-364-2753).

Time & Distance: Only 2.2 miles. Our group of 6 vehicles took 2 hours.

To Get There: Refer to directions for Martinez Cabin (Trail # 52). Jack Handle turns off Martinez Cabin trail after 14.5 miles and is shown on Martinez Cabin map as Waypoint 8 (page 189). A windmill marks the start of Jack Handle. If you enter the area via Mineral Mountain Road rather than Cottonwood Canyon Road, the trip is a bit shorter. See Woodpecker Mine (Trail #50) to come in this way.

Trail Description: Reset your odometer at the start of Jack Handle [01]. Turn left at the windmill and head north up a wash. Stay in the wash; do not climb out on any side roads. The first obstacle is reached at 0.4 miles and more obstacles follow in quick succession, including the one that turns left through the rock cut. The trail is blocked at 0.9 miles. You must turn right up a steep bank out of the wash then drop back into it. Exit the wash again up tight switchbacks at 1.2 miles [02]. Bear left heading south along the top of a scenic ridge. You'll drop down switchbacks into the original wash at 1.7 miles. Continue straight back to the start of the trail at 2.2 miles [01].

Return Trip: Return the way you came or via Box Canyon.

Services: None on trail. Gas at Florence Junction. Full services in Florence.

Maps: USGS 7.5 minute map Mineral Mountain, AZ, N3307.5-W11107.5/7.5.

Some small rocky challenges in the canyon.

No place to be in a flash flood.

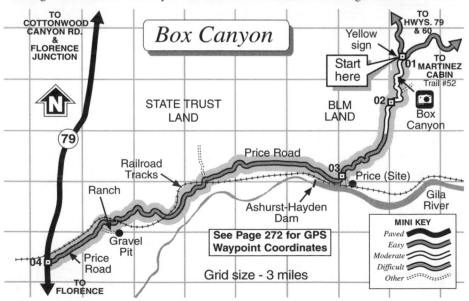

Looking back towards Box Canyon from beautiful Sonoran Desert along Price Road.

Box Canyon

TO
COTTONWOOD
CANYON RD.
&
FLORENCE
JUNCTION

TO
HWYS. 79
& 60

Yellow
sign

Start
here

01

TO
MARTINEZ
CABIN
Trail #52

N

STATE TRUST
LAND

BLM
LAND

02

Box
Canyon

79

Price Road

Railroad
Tracks

03

Price (Site)

Ranch

Ashurst-Hayden
Dam

Gila
River

MINI KEY
Paved
Easy
Moderate
Difficult
Other

Gravel
Pit

See Page 272 for GPS
Waypoint Coordinates

04

Price
Road

Grid size - 3 miles

TO
FLORENCE

Box Canyon 55

Location: Southeast of Florence Junction, northeast of Florence.

Difficulty: Moderate. It's tempting to rate this trail easy but there are several moderate-size rocks to get over. Stock SUVs with good ground clearance should be okay. You may bottom out occasionally but damage is unlikely. The trail is a bit tougher driven uphill in the opposite direction. Stay off this trail if rain is expected. This canyon is extremely dangerous when flooded. The walls of the canyon are too steep to climb out. Route-finding is easy.

Features: A unique and scenic drive through a narrow, steep-walled canyon. Use as alternate exit route from the area. State Trust Land permit required as described in the introduction to this book (call 602-364-2753).

Time & Distance: Almost 16 miles as described here. Add another 13.3 miles to reach the trailhead from Hwy. 79 via Cottonwood Canyon Road. Allow about 1-1/2 hours for the trail plus time to get there.

To Get There: Refer to directions for Martinez Cabin (Trail # 52). Box Canyon departs from Martinez Cabin trail after 13.3 miles and is shown on Martinez Cabin map as Waypoint 7 (page 189). Instead of turning left at the yellow sign, continue straight down the wash.

Trail Description: *Reset your odometer at the start by yellow sign* [01]. Continue south in a wide wash. Cross a cattle guard as the wash narrows. Swing left into the canyon at 0.4. The canyon narrows to a single lane with several challenging rocks to get over. Bear right at 1.5 and exit the canyon at 2.0 miles [02]. Follow tire tracks as the road zigzags in and out of a shallow wash. Bear left at 3.8. The road gradually becomes more defined. Bear right at a fork at 5.2 miles [03] and head west. The left fork dead ends at a R.R. trestle at Price Townsite. Swing left and cross R.R. tracks at 9.7. Bear right and cross tracks at 11.4. Cross wide wash at 13.0. Bear left and cross tracks last time at 13.3. Turn right immediately and go through ranch. Road joins on left at 13.8. Continue west to Hwy. 79 at 15.7 miles [04].

Return Trip: Florence is a short distance left, Florence Junction is right.

Services: None on trail. Full services in Florence.

Maps: USGS 7.5 minute map Mineral Mountain, AZ, N3307.5-W11107.5/7.5.

This big step is toughest spot on trail.

Difficult ledge road on optional exit route.

Descending series of rocky steps.

Coke ovens are in excellent condition.

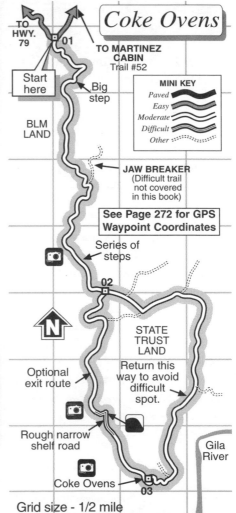

Coke Ovens

TO HWY. 79

01

Start here

TO MARTINEZ CABIN
Trail #52

Big step

BLM LAND

MINI KEY
Paved
Easy
Moderate
Difficult
Other

JAW BREAKER
(Difficult trail not covered in this book)

See Page 272 for GPS Waypoint Coordinates

Series of steps

02

N

STATE TRUST LAND

Optional exit route

Return this way to avoid difficult spot.

Rough narrow shelf road

Coke Ovens

Gila River

03

Grid size - 1/2 mile

Coke Ovens

Location: Southeast of Florence Junction, northeast of Florence.

Difficulty: Moderate. Steep climbs, tippy shelf roads and challenging rock obstacles. Stock vehicles should have high ground clearance and good articulation. Skid plates recommended. Very remote location. Don't drive alone.

Features: See unique, beehive-shaped ovens near the Cochran Townsite. This area was closed for a time but is now open. Please help keep the area clean. State Trust Land permit required (call 602-364-2753). The ovens were used in the early 1900s to make coke, a clean-burning fuel used in blast furnaces to produce iron ore. Coke was made by baking a mixture of different kinds of coal at high temperature without contact with air.

Time & Distance: Almost 21 miles one way. Allow 6 to 7 hours for the complete round-trip.

To Get There: Refer to directions for Martinez Cabin (Trail # 52). Coke Ovens trail departs from Martinez Cabin trail after 15.4 miles and is shown on Martinez Cabin map as Waypoint 9 (page 189).

Trail Description: Reset your odometer as you turn right at the start [01]. Head south on a narrow, rocky road. Climb over a tall rock ledge at 0.5. Great scenery unfolds as you cross a series of ridges. Continue straight at 2.3 down a long hill with big steps. Bear left at a fork at 2.7 miles [02]. Turn left at a T at 3.1 then right downhill at 3.4. Bear right at a major Y at 4.2, then left downhill at 4.8. Pass through an open gate at 5.0. Bear left downhill into the trees at 5.1. Drop into a sandy area and weave through tall brush. Pass remains of caretaker's house before reaching Coke Ovens at 5.3 miles [03]. Cochran Townsite is located across the river east of the ovens.

Return Trip: Return the way you came or via a slightly more difficult route that departs from behind the Coke Ovens. Turn right at the south end of the Coke Ovens and head straight uphill. Cross a narrow ledge road followed by a large rock step at 6.0. Bear left at Y at 6.9. Bear left at T at 7.4 miles [02]. You are now heading out the way you came in.

Services: None on trail. Gas at Florence Junction, full services in Florence.

Maps: USGS 7.5 minute maps Mineral Mountain, AZ, N3307.5-W11107.5/7.5 and North Butte, AZ, N3300-W11107.5/7.5

Scenic buttes tower over the trail at every turn.

Our group stops for lunch in one of the sandy wash bottoms.

Group repairs rain damage to the trail.

Recent heavy rains had damaged the trail.   Some water still flowing after recent rains.

Walnut Canyon

Location: South of Superior, southeast of Florence Junction.

Difficulty: Moderate. Winding, rutted road with moderate climbs and descents. Narrow in a few places. Our group drove the trail following a period of torrential rains. Several places were badly washed out, which required some rock-stacking for several stock vehicles in our group. While the road is well defined most of the way, one section crosses a low sandy area along the Gila River. Rains had washed away previous tire tracks making route-finding difficult. Skid plates and high ground clearance recommended for stock vehicles. Brush may lightly touch your vehicle. Go with other vehicles in case you need help.

Features: A photographer's dream. Beautiful Sonoran Desert with towering red buttes on all sides of the trail. A fun drive offering real adventure. Hike into the nearby White Canyon Wilderness area north of the trail. A small part of this trail crosses State Trust Land so it's best to have a State Trust Land permit as described in the introduction of this book (call 602-364-2753). This is also a popular ATV area. Stay on existing trails at all times.

Time & Distance: Just under 20 miles, but driving is slow the entire way. Allow at least 5 to 6 hours.

To Get There: From Phoenix and Apache Junction, take Highway 60 east to the town of Superior. On the east side of town, head south on paved Highway 177. Turn right at the top of a hill on well-graded Battle Axe Road 0.9 miles past mile marker 159.

Trail Description: Reset your odometer as you turn right off Highway 177 [01]. Follow Battle Axe Road south. After coming over a rise, turn right onto a lesser road at 1.3 miles [02]. Shift into four-wheel drive as the road becomes rutted. Bear left into a sandy wash at 1.7. Bear left at a Y at 4.3. Right goes to a parking area and hiking trail into the White Canyon Wilderness. Climb rocky switchbacks to a T at the top of a hill at 5.1 and turn right. At 5.3 miles [03] turn left at a Y. This starts the loop portion of the trail. You will return to this point later.

You'll climb to a high point with beautiful views before descending a series of badly washed-out switchbacks. Careful tire placement is necessary but our group of mostly stock vehicles managed fine. A particularly bad washed-out spot at 8.2 required considerable rock-stacking. Turn right into a flat, sandy wash at 8.3 miles [04]. We stopped here for lunch. Continue down this wash and turn right into a smaller wash at 9.3 miles [05]. Continue straight across a small wash at 9.8 and climb a small hill. At 10.7 miles [06] turn right heading north in a wide, confusing wash. Work your way from the right side of the wash to the left side, maneuvering around tall weeds. Just make sure you keep heading north. At 11.9 miles [07] watch carefully for a small road that comes out of the wash to the left, almost reversing direction. A small rock with a white painted arrow marked this location when I drove the trail.

The trail becomes more defined again. A badly washed-out spot at 12.5 required more rock-stacking. Over time, these bad wash-outs get easier as more people fill in the holes. You may have no trouble at all. Bear right at a Y at 12.7 miles. Right is an alternate route to the Coke Ovens (Trail #56). Bear left at another Y at 12.8. This section of the trail is very scenic. At 14.5 miles [03] you return to the start of the loop portion of the trail. Turn left and go out the way you came in.

Return Trip: Turn left at Highway 177 to return to Superior. When you reach Highway 60, turn left for Phoenix or right for Globe.

Services: None on trail. Some services in Superior. We stopped at an ice cream stand west of Highway 177 near Highway 60.

Maps: USGS 7.5 minute maps Teapot Mountain, AZ, N3307.5-W11100/7.5 and Grayback, AZ, N3300-W11100/7.5

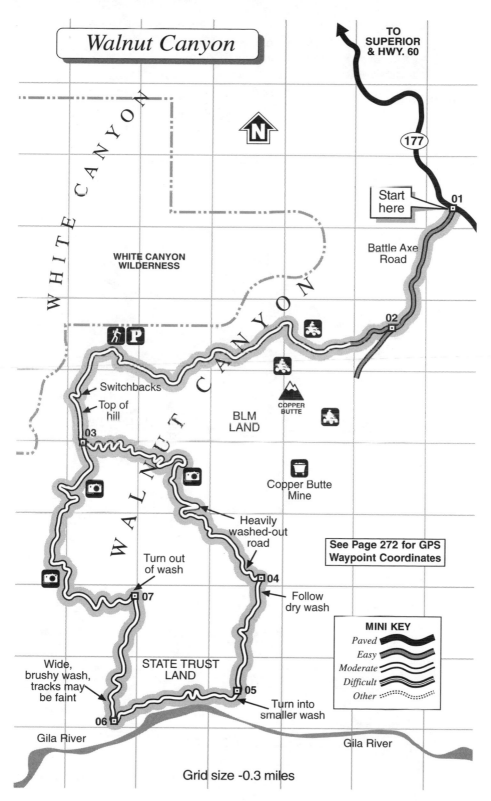

Walnut Canyon

TO SUPERIOR & HWY. 60

177

Start here

01

Battle Axe Road

02

WHITE CANYON

WHITE CANYON WILDERNESS

WALNUT CANYON

N

Switchbacks

Top of hill

03

BLM LAND

COPPER BUTTE

Copper Butte Mine

Heavily washed-out road

Turn out of wash

07

04

Follow dry wash

See Page 272 for GPS Waypoint Coordinates

STATE TRUST LAND

Wide, brushy wash, tracks may be faint

05

Turn into smaller wash

06

Gila River

Gila River

MINI KEY
Paved
Easy
Moderate
Difficult
Other

Grid size -0.3 miles

AREA 8

Quartzsite, Yuma

58. Plomosa Mountains
59. Sand Bowl OHV Area
60. Dripping Springs
61. Palm Canyon
62. Castle Dome Mountains
63. Laguna Mountain Ridge

202

Quartzsite, Yuma

Travel to Quartzsite in the middle of Arizona's hot summer and you'll find a pleasant little town of about 3,000 people. Come back six months later and you won't believe your eyes. Motorhomes are stretched across the desert as far as the eye can see. People flock to the area to enjoy mild winter temperatures and extremely cheap camping fees. Winter population is estimated to peak around 250,000. The BLM estimates that over one million people attend numerous gem shows and swap meets between October and March. Despite the fact that some of the land in the area is off-limits to the public (i.e., Yuma Proving Ground), there's plenty of open land left for four-wheeling and backcountry exploration. This includes the use of ATVs and dirt bikes. Most of the trails are easy to moderate and appeal to those looking for a relaxing way to spend a day searching for stone cabins or rock souvenirs. Even the *Sand Bowl OHV Area* has much easy terrain to enjoy, provided you don't attempt to drive up the soft side of a steep sand dune. Not all trails are a walk in the park. *Laguna Mountain Ridge, Dripping Springs* and *Castle Dome Mountains* have a few surprises to delight those looking for more challenge. *Dripping Springs* even offers some optional difficult terrain.

Well-preserved cabin at Big Eye Mine in the Castle Dome Mountains (Trail #62).

203

Crossing one of the small sand dunes. Plomosa Mountains to right of picture.

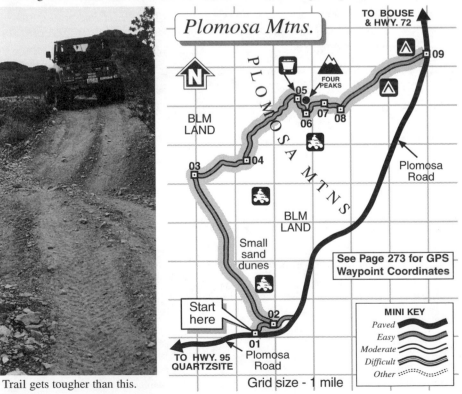

Trail gets tougher than this.

Plomosa Mtns.

TO BOUSE & HWY. 72

PLOMOSA MTNS

FOUR PEAKS

BLM LAND

05
06 07 08
09

03 04

Plomosa Road

BLM LAND

Small sand dunes

See Page 273 for GPS Waypoint Coordinates

Start here

02

01
Plomosa Road

TO HWY. 95 QUARTZSITE

Grid size - 1 mile

MINI KEY

Paved
Easy
Moderate
Difficult
Other

204

Plomosa Mountains (58)

Location: Between Quartzsite and Bouse. Southeast of Parker.

Difficulty: Easy. Mostly flat desert with minor steep climbs across occasional washes. Some rocky terrain as you pass through a low spot in the Plomosa Mountains. Blowing sand can quickly hide the trail. GPS is very helpful under these conditions. Suitable for stock SUVs with high ground clearance. Very hot in summer. Carry plenty of water.

Features: Little-used trail is great for a quiet and relaxing getaway. Small sand dunes along the way are fun to cross. Enough challenge to be interesting. Good area for ATVs and dirt bikes.

Time & Distance: About 14 miles. Allow 1-1/2 to 2 hours.

To Get There: Head north on Highway 95 from Quartzsite or south from Parker. Turn east on Plomosa Road between mile markers 114 and 115. Go east 6.5 miles and turn left on an unmarked gravel road.

Trail Description: Reset your odometer as you turn off Plomosa Road [01]. Head northeast on a wide gravel road 0.5 miles [02] and turn left on a faint single lane road. Sometimes a ribbon marks the turn. Head north crossing perpendicular to a series of washes. Side roads branch off, but you continue north. Begin crossing small sand dunes after a couple of miles. Bear right at a Y at 5.3 miles [03] and head east towards small mountain peaks. Bear right at 6.4 and left at 7.0 [04]. Continue straight as a road joins on the left at 7.6. Continue straight at 9.5 miles [05]. Continue straight over a hump at 9.9. The road to the left dead ends at a mine. Bear left at 10.0 miles [06] where roads intersect in a triangle. You should be circling around the tallest of four peaks on your left. At 10.6 you come over a rise and the road becomes faint. Continue straight about 150 feet until the road reappears. Bear right at a T at 10.8 miles [07] as the terrain flattens out. Cross a wash at 11.2 [08] and immediately bear left at a T. In the wintertime, motorhomes will be camped across this broad area. Plomosa Road is reached at 14.0 miles [09].

Return Trip: Left goes to Bouse and Highway 72. Right goes back to Highway 95 and Quartzsite.

Services: Good restaurant in Bouse. Full services in Parker and Quartzsite.

Maps: USGS 100,000 scale map Blythe CA-AZ, 33114-E1-TM-100.

Parking area has vault toilet and sheltered picnic table.

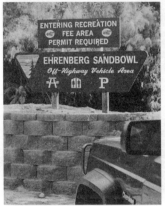

A fee of $5 per vehicle.

Go anywhere inside the Sand Bowl boundary.

Be careful on steep climbs.

CA.

Colorado River

Sand Bowl

10 Ehrenberg EXIT 1

10 TO QUARTZSITE

01 Major Truck Stop

Frontage Road

See Page 273 for GPS Waypoint Coordinates

STATE LAND

Colorado River Frontage Road

BLM EHRENBERG SAND BOWL

STATE LAND

P

02 Start here

BLM EHRENBERG SAND BOWL

MINI KEY

Paved
Easy
Moderate
Difficult
Other

Grid size - 0.5 miles

206

Sand Bowl OHV Area ◆59◆

Location: South of Ehrenberg on the western border of Arizona.

Difficulty: Difficult. Don't be fooled by what, at first glance, looks easy. Some of these slopes are very steep. If you slide into soft sand you can quickly get sideways on the hill, lose control and roll over. Air down as much as possible to improve traction. SUVs okay on easier slopes.

Features: A fun little playground for ATVs, dirt bikes, SUVs and Jeeps. Go anywhere inside the boundary. Pay $5.00 per vehicle at the site.

Time & Distance: No set distance. Play as long as you like.

To Get There: Take Interstate 10 to Ehrenberg, located on the western border of Arizona. Get off at Exit 1. Take the Frontage Road on the south side of the freeway west 0.4 miles. Go past the large truck stop and turn left on a wide dirt road [01]. Head south 1.0 miles and turn left at the sign for the Ehrenberg Sand Bowl OHV Area [02].

Trail Description: Go anywhere inside the borders of the park. You'll quickly discover that even the most capable vehicles will want to stick to existing trails which are firm enough to support a vehicle. Ascending steep virgin slopes is nearly impossible. Use caution when approaching the top of a hill. Make sure no one is coming up the other side. Pack out your trash and leave the area the way you found it.

Other Areas: There is a larger non-fee area south of the Sand Bowl that is open to OHVs, SUVs and Jeeps. This long strip of land is located between the Colorado River Frontage Road and the Yuma Proving Ground. Look for signs at various points where roads enter the area. The signs are misleading. Vehicles are allowed but they must stay on marked trails only. Stay out of the Trigo Mountains Wilderness farther south. You can cross the Yuma Proving Ground on Cibola Road only.

Return Trip: Return the way you came.

Services: There is a modern vault toilet at the parking area and a sheltered picnic table. Full services available at the truck stop you passed coming in.

Maps: BLM Arizona Access Guide, Ehrenberg-Cibola Area. USGS 7.5 minute map Blythe CA-AZ, N3330-W11430/7.5, Arizona Atlas & Gazetteer.

The first part of the trail is quite easy.

Narrow canyon before Dripping Springs.

More hills on the last part of the trip.

Remains of stone cabin at Dripping Springs.

The more difficult alternate exit route. Okay for aggressive stock vehicles.

Dripping Springs 60

Location: East of Quartzsite.

Difficulty: Moderate. This trail starts easy and gradually worsens. The last mile before Dripping Springs is challenging and requires some backroad driving experience. High ground clearance and good articulation are needed to drive up a couple of steep, rutted banks and squeeze through a narrow rocky canyon. The last part can be hiked but it is strenuous. Many roads crisscross the area and it's easy to get lost. GPS is highly recommended. You need not get all the way to Dripping Springs to have fun. Serious four-wheelers will want to take the more difficult exit route after Dripping Springs. Dangerously hot in summer. Flash floods possible.

Features: This area is dotted with historic mines and stone cabins. Stay clear of the Gold Nugget Mine, which is still active. Dripping Springs has a stone cabin and terrific Native American petroglyphs. In at least one place, the petroglyphs have been vandalized. Because of this, the BLM may eventually have to stop vehicles from driving all the way to Dripping Springs. Report any vandalism to the BLM immediately. Don't disturb or remove anything and pack out all trash.

Time & Distance: There are several different ways to reach Dripping Springs. The way described here is 6.3 miles one way. Allow 3 to 4 hours for the round trip. The alternate exit route doesn't take much longer.

To Get There: Get off Interstate 10 at Exit 26, about 8 miles east of Quartzsite. Head southeast on a rough macadam road and turn right after 0.4 miles. Watch for yellow "Primitive Road" sign.

Trail Description: Reset your odometer where the primitive road starts [01]. After 1.0 miles [02] turn right onto a single-lane road at sign for "Gold Nugget Road." (The Gold Nugget Mine is left.) Follow a wide wash south, staying to the left side of the wash. Turn right out of the wash at 1.4 miles [03]. Bear right at a fork at 2.2 miles. Turn left at the next fork at 2.4 miles [04]. (A right turn here would take you to the Belle of Arizona Mine and some stone cabins.) Bear left at 3.1 and 3.5 miles. The road gets rougher as you drop into and climb out of a wash. At 3.9 bear right and drop down a steep bank into a wash. Make a hard left turn at 4.1 miles [05]. Stay on the best traveled road as many smaller roads branch off. The road winds around several open mine shafts so be careful. Make a right uphill at 4.4 miles, drop into a wash, and then climb back out. Bear left at 4.7. (Right goes to the Dos Picachos Mine.) Make a right at 5.0 then another right at 5.1 miles [06], dropping into a narrow wash. Bear right in the wash. Go less than 0.1 miles and turn right out of the wash up a steep, rutted bank. This is the toughest spot on the trail. It may require a little speed to get up this short hill. Some may prefer to walk from here.

After this short challenge, continue straight up a hill. When you reach the top at 5.7, turn left and continue down the other side. You have a choice of two places to turn left. Both are steep and tippy with loose gravel. Don't get sideways. At the bottom of the hill the trail enters a narrow rocky canyon. Go slowly and you should have no problem. Large vehicles will find this section more difficult. The canyon forks at 6.1 miles [07]. Turn left and climb a steep, short hill to Dripping Springs at 6.3 miles [08]. You'll see low walls of a stone cabin. Hike around the area to see petroglyphs. A hiking trail to the left leads uphill to Dripping Springs. Water drips from the roof of a small cave all year, unusual in Arizona.

When you're done exploring several good hiking trails in the area, drive back down the hill to the fork in the narrow canyon. Right takes you out the way you came in. Left is a difficult alternate exit. Aggressive stock vehicles can make it.

Alternate exit route (difficult): Reset your odometer at the fork in the narrow canyon [07] *and turn left.* Drop down a ledge at 0.2. A tough spot at 0.5 miles [09] is called the Waterfall. You leave the high walls of the canyon following a wide sandy wash. Continue straight at 2.8 miles [10] when a road joins on the left. Head northwest on an improving road. At 6.6 miles [11] you enter the La Posa North Camping Area, although it may not be obvious if no campers are around. Swing left off the main road at 9.9 miles [12] and head east. Exit the campground to reach Hwy. 95 at 10.7 miles [13].

Return Trip: At Interstate 10, turn left for Quartzsite and right for Phoenix. If you took the alternate exit, turn right on Hwy. 95 for Quartzsite and left for Yuma.

Services: None on trail. Full services in Quartzsite.

Maps: USGS 7.5 minute maps Plomosa Pass, AZ, 33114-F1-TF-024 and Crystal Hill, AZ, 33114-E1-TF-024. The Arizona Atlas and Gazetteer shows the start of the trail and some of the alternate exit route.

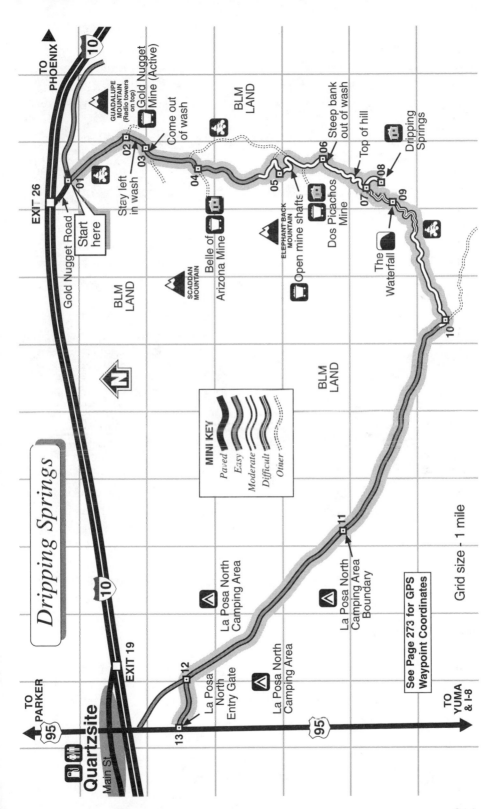

Dripping Springs

TO PHOENIX

TO PARKER

10

Quartzsite
Main St

95

EXIT 19

EXIT 26

Gold Nugget Road

Start here

01

Stay left in wash

02

GUADALUPE MOUNTAIN (Radio towers on top)

Gold Nugget Mine (Active)

03

Come out of wash

04

05

BLM LAND

06

Steep bank out of wash

Top of hill

08

07

Dripping Springs

09

Dos Picachos Mine

Open mine shafts

ELEPHANT BACK MOUNTAIN

Belle of Arizona Mine

SCADDAN MOUNTAIN

BLM LAND

The Waterfall

10

N

MINI KEY
Paved
Easy
Moderate
Difficult
Other

BLM LAND

11

La Posa North Camping Area

La Posa North Camping Area Boundary

La Posa North Camping Area

La Posa North Camping Area

12

La Posa North Entry Gate

13

95

TO YUMA & I-8

See Page 273 for GPS Waypoint Coordinates

Grid size - 1 mile

95

10

211

Entering the Kofa National Wildlife Refuge. Follow all posted regulations.

Looking back at entry road from hiking trail.

Binoculars will help to see the palm trees.

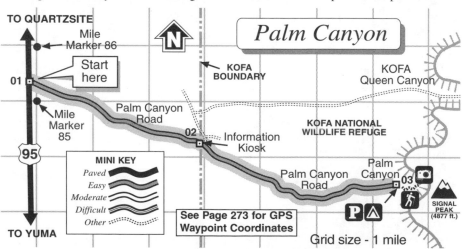

TO QUARTZSITE

Mile Marker 86

Start here

01

Mile Marker 85

95

TO YUMA

N

KOFA BOUNDARY

Palm Canyon Road

02

Information Kiosk

MINI KEY

Paved
Easy
Moderate
Difficult
Other

See Page 273 for GPS Waypoint Coordinates

KOFA Queen Canyon

KOFA NATIONAL WILDLIFE REFUGE

Palm Canyon Road

Palm Canyon

03

SIGNAL PEAK (4877 ft.)

P

Grid size - 1 mile

Palm Canyon

Palm Canyon 61

Location: Between Quartzsite and Yuma, east of Highway 95 in the Kofa National Wildlife Refuge.

Difficulty: Easy. A graded gravel road suitable for all but the lowest-slung passenger cars. Rough washboard surface with a few small ruts. A four-wheel-drive side trip to Queen Canyon branches off from this road. A kiosk at the entry to the refuge has brochures with regulations and a map showing all the designated four-wheel-drive roads in the area. You must stay on numbered routes only. Some of the other roads in the refuge are rough with a few challenges, including Castle Dome Mountains (Trail #62).

Features: This short, scenic trip introduces you to the Kofa National Wildlife Refuge—665,400 acres of pristine desert and low, rugged mountains. The refuge is home to bighorn sheep, desert tortoise and other interesting wildlife. This trip ends at a small parking area with a few designated campsites. A short (1/2-mile), rocky hiking trail climbs steeply to a spot where you can see small native palm trees growing out of steep canyon walls. This is one of only two or three places in Arizona where palm trees grow naturally. All other palm trees in Arizona are transplanted.

Time & Distance: It's 7.2 miles from Highway 95 to the parking area at Palm Canyon. Takes less than 1/2 hour one way. Add time for the hike.

To Get There: Turn east off Highway 95 between mile markers 85 and 86 onto Palm Canyon Road. (Located about 18 miles south of Quartzsite.)

Trail Description: *Reset your odometer as you turn off Highway 95* [01]. Head east on a wide gravel road. A large sign identifies the entrance to Kofa National Wildlife Refuge at 3.4 miles [02]. Read all posted regulations and pick up a brochure at the kiosk. Continue east to the parking area at 7.2 miles [03]. Park and hike uphill to the palms. This is a strenuous hike on a hot day. Make sure you have plenty of water.

Return Trip: Return the way you came. Turn right at Highway 95 for Quartzsite and left for Yuma.

Services: None. Return to Quartzsite or Yuma.

Maps: Kofa National Wildlife Refuge brochure, USGS 100,000 scale map Trigo Mountains AZ-CA, 33114-A1-TM-100, Arizona Atlas & Gazetteer.

Heading south from Junction 60. Castle Dome Mountains in distance.

Cave once inhabited by Native Americans.   A few rough spots along the way.

Approaching cabins at the Big Eye Mine. You must hike up a rough road about a mile.

Castle Dome Mountains 62

Location: Between Quartzsite and Yuma, east of Highway 95 in the Kofa National Wildlife Refuge.

Difficulty: Moderate. Starts as a easy washboard gravel road but changes to single lane with minor obstacles. Mostly easy except for one moderate spot at McPherson Pass. This spot requires good articulation and high ground clearance. Suitable for aggressive stock SUVs. This trail crosses many miles of hot desert. Carry plenty of water and travel with another vehicle.

Features: Travel through rugged parts of the Kofa National Wildlife Refuge. Perhaps you'll catch a glimpse of some of the abundant wildlife, which includes desert bighorn sheep, mule deer, coyote, cottontail, bobcat, fox and golden eagle. Visit a cave once inhabited by Native Americans. Cross rocky McPherson Pass through the Castle Dome Mountains. Hike to well-preserved cabins at Big Eye Mine. Stop at the Castle Dome Mines Museum and learn about the area's extensive mining history.

Time & Distance: About 54 miles. Allow about 5 hours on the trail plus traveling time. Add extra time for the uphill hike to the Big Eye Mine.

To Get There: Travel north from Yuma or south from Quartzsite on Highway 95. Turn east on King Road between mile markers 76 and 77 (about 29 miles south of Quartzsite). If you are approaching from the south, a large "King Valley" sign identifies the turn.

Trail Description: Reset your odometer as you turn off Highway 95 [01]. Head east on a wide gravel road. Enter the Kofa National Wildlife Refuge at 1.8 miles. Stop at the unmanned information kiosk and pick up a free brochure that explains rules and regulations. Most important is to stay on numbered routes only. Find a complete map of the refuge on the back of the brochure.

Continue east and turn right at 2.2 miles [02] at Junction #42. Follow this two-track road south. Watch for a cave on the left at 4.9 miles. Stop here and hike a very short distance up a rocky slope. Note the smooth, rounded holes in the cave floor where Native Americans used pestles to grind corn. Continue south on the road to a parking area at 5.1 miles [03]. Signs direct you on a short walk to the Horse Tanks. Turn around and head back to King Road.

Reset your odometer when you get back to King Road at 8.0 miles

[02] and turn right. At 4.1 miles [04], watch for a sign for McPherson Pass and turn right at Junction #60. Head south across the desert with views of Castle Dome Peak in the distance. At 10.3 miles [05] turn right at Junction #53. McPherson Pass is crossed at 13.5 miles. It's not a high pass so you may not be aware that you are going over a pass. The hardest spot on the trail is reached at 14.1 miles. Fortunately, it's downhill. Stock vehicles with high ground clearance can get through with careful tire placement. The Castle Dome Mountains provide dramatic views to the left. By 18.9 miles the road becomes easier as you weave through an area of many mines. Go straight at 19.2 and left at 19.3. The entrance to the Castle Dome Mines Museum is on the right at 20.3 miles. Continue straight or take time to visit the museum.

Bear left at 21.0 miles [06] at Junction #75 to visit the Big Eye Mine. This is the best part of the trip. A sign says it's 11 miles to the mine but it's actually closer to 16 miles. Bear left at 34.4 miles. Either way is okay at 36.5 as the trails merge later. The trail ends at a turnaround area at 37.3 miles [07]. You must walk the last mile uphill on a rough road to the mine. The hike is worth it. The cabin at the mine is extremely well-preserved. When I was there (Dec. 2000), old mining papers were still lying on tables inside the cabin. Make sure you leave everything exactly as you find it.

After visiting the mine, go back out the way you came in. Turn left when you reach Junction #75. Highway 95 is about 8.5 miles southwest. The last couple of miles before you reach Highway 95 are paved.

Return Trip: Quartzsite is about 50 miles to the right at Highway 95. Yuma is about 30 miles to the left. The end of this trip is about 24 miles south of where you started on Highway 95.

Services: None on trail. Return to Quartzsite or Yuma.

Maps: Kofa National Wildlife Refuge brochure, USGS 100,000 scale maps Trigo Mtns, AZ-CA, 33114-A1-TM-100 and Yuma, AZ-CA-Baja California Norte, 32114-E1-TM-100, Arizona Atlas & Gazetteer.

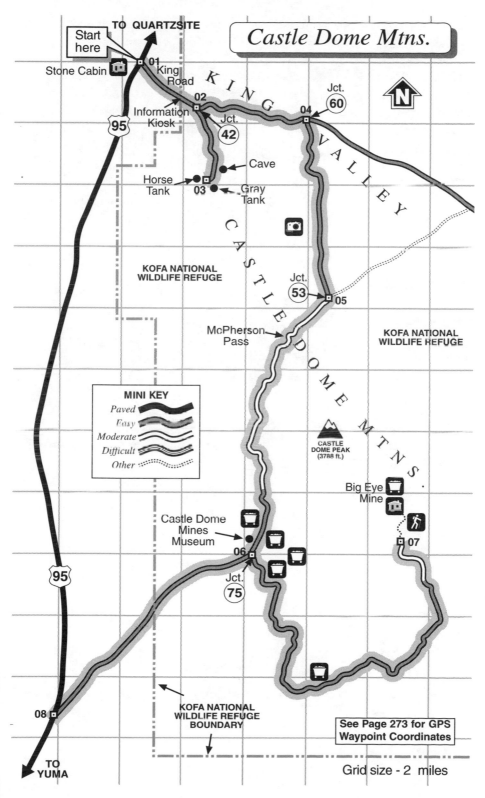

Castle Dome Mtns.

TO QUARTZSITE

Start here

01

Stone Cabin

King Road

02 — Jct. 42

Information Kiosk

95

Cave

Horse Tank

03 — Gray Tank

KING VALLEY

Jct. 60 — 04

N

KOFA NATIONAL WILDLIFE REFUGE

CASTLE DOME MTNS.

Jct. 53 — 05

McPherson Pass

KOFA NATIONAL WILDLIFE REFUGE

CASTLE DOME PEAK (3788 ft.)

Big Eye Mine

07

MINI KEY
Paved
Easy
Moderate
Difficult
Other

Castle Dome Mines Museum

06

Jct. 75

08

95

KOFA NATIONAL WILDLIFE REFUGE BOUNDARY

TO YUMA

See Page 273 for GPS Waypoint Coordinates

Grid size - 2 miles

Looking west towards California's fertile farming country.

The ridge is narrow and steep.

Yuma can be seen from the highest point.

Laguna Mtn. Ridge

Kool Corner

Mittry Lake Road

BLM LAND

04

Canals

03

L A G U N A   M T N S .

N

TO YUMA (via Laguna Dam Road)

02

Tiny Church Steeple

TO QUARTZ-SITE

MINI KEY
Paved
Easy
Moderate
Difficult
Other

See Page 274 for GPS Waypoint Coordinates

Mining Area Gravel Pit

Mile Marker 40

95

Start here

01

McPhaul Suspension Bridge (Closed)

Grid size - 1 mile

TO YUMA

218

Laguna Mountain Ridge 63

Location: Northeast of Yuma.

Difficulty: Moderate. A narrow, steep road along the top of a ridge. The road turns sharply, creating dangerous blind turns. You may need a spotter to avoid driving off the trail. Suitable for stock high-clearance SUVs. Route-finding is very confusing.

Features: Moon-like landscape with views of Yuma and California. A unique four-wheeling experience.

Time & Distance: The trail measures 7.3 miles. Allow about 2 hours.

To Get There: From Hwy. 95 turn west on a hard-to-see paved road near mile marker 40. Go southwest about 2 miles and bear right at the suspension bridge. After another 0.8 miles turn right into a gravel pit.

Trail Description: *Reset your odometer at the gravel pit* [01]. This private land is constantly changing but there should be a path through the area. Head northwest to a road that climbs up the hillside. Watch for white stakes marking the road. Be careful at the top at 1.0 as the road turns sharply and blindly to the right. Bear right at 1.8 and right again at a T at 2.7 miles [02]. Immediately bear left then right at two quick forks. At 3.9 bear right downhill. Bear left at a T at 4.0. Bear right and weave through a valley at 4.1 miles [03] as the road swings north towards power lines. Bear right at 4.3 then cross under the power lines at 4.7. Drop down a hill as the road narrows. After crossing a badly washed-out spot, the road gradually improves. Bear left at 5.8 miles. Turn right when you reach a canal at 5.9 miles. The road goes around the end of the canal and heads in the opposite direction at 6.4. Follow the edge of the canal southwest and turn right at 7.0. Weave right then left around a building before reaching Mittry Lake Road at 7.3 miles [04]. This spot is shown on maps as Kool Corner.

Return Trip: Left goes back to Highway 95 north of Yuma. Right weaves through the Mittry Lake Wildlife Area and connects to Imperial Dam Road. From there, turn right to exit the Yuma Proving Ground back to Hwy. 95.

Services: None. Return to Quartzsite or Yuma.

Maps: USGS 100,000 scale map Yuma AZ-CA-Baja California Norte, 32114-E1-TM-100.

64. Oatman Massacre Site
65. Butterfield Stage Route
66. Organ Pipe Cactus
   National Monument

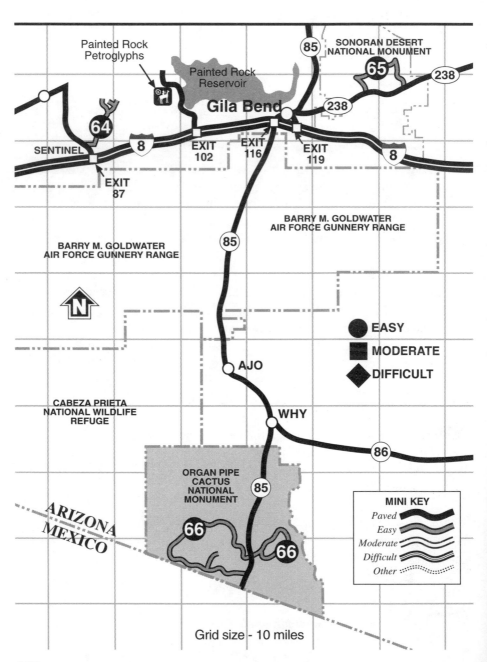

Grid size - 10 miles

220

Gila Bend, Sentinel, Why

The three trails in this area are all easy, scenic drives. They were selected for their historical and educational interest rather than for four-wheeling challenge. To fully appreciate the *Oatman Massacre Site* and *Butterfield Stage Route* requires some knowledge of the historical events that occurred there. Because most space in this book is given to directions, history buffs will likely want to do some additional reading before heading to these trails. Everyone should try to make the trip to *Organ Pipe Cactus National Monument*. It's a long drive from Phoenix and Tucson but most will find the trip rewarding. It's a chance to study the desert in a wide-open setting with few people around to spoil the experience. The monument has two separate drives. I found the longer, 51-mile Puerto Blanco Drive on the west side of the monument more of a true desert experience. The road is all dirt, less traveled and more remote. The Ajo Mountain Drive on the east side is more scenic, partly paved, shorter (21 miles) and has more traffic. Pick up booklets at Visitor Center that explain features along the routes. This is a wonderful opportunity for kids and adults to learn about the Sonoran Desert All trails in Area 9 are dangerously hot in summer.

Butterfield Stage Route (Trail #65) as it passes through the Maricopa Mountains.

221

Rare wet road on way to massacre site.

Stage route east of site; note wheel tracks.

Spot where Oatman family was attacked.

Oatman family grave.

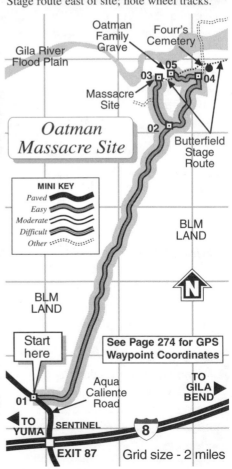

Oatman Family Grave

Fourr's Cemetery

Gila River Flood Plain

05

03

04

Massacre Site

02

Oatman Massacre Site

Butterfield Stage Route

MINI KEY
Paved
Easy
Moderate
Difficult
Other

BLM LAND

BLM LAND

Start here

See Page 274 for GPS Waypoint Coordinates

01

Aqua Caliente Road

TO YUMA

SENTINEL

TO GILA BEND

8

EXIT 87

Grid size - 2 miles

Oatman Massacre Site 64

Location: West of Gila Bend, north of Sentinel.

Difficulty: Easy. Wide graded dirt road narrows to two-track near massacre site. High-clearance 2-wheel drive adequate. Remote, desolate location.

Features: Visit historic site where Oatman family was attacked by Indians. See parts of Butterfield Stage Route and nearby grave sites.

Time & Distance: About 10.6 miles from start to massacre site plus 4.5 more miles to circle back to the Oatman family grave. Allow 1 to 2 hours plus considerable travel time to reach Sentinel.

To Get There: Take Interstate 8 to Sentinel, Exit 87, and head north 1.3 miles on paved Aqua Caliente Road.

Trail Description: Reset your odometer at the start [01]. Head east on a wide dirt road that swings north after 0.8 miles. Turn left on faint two-track road at 9.1 miles [02]. Watch for cairns. Bear right at a fork at 9.9 miles. Massacre site is reached at 10.6 miles [03]. Rocky road that climbs hill east of massacre site is part of the Butterfield Route (note wheel tracks in rock).

    To drive to the Oatman family grave, return to main dirt road [02] *and reset odometer.* Turn left weaving through rocky area. Bear left at 1.9 between fence posts. Turn left at 2.2 miles [04] across cotton fields. Jog left then right at 2.5. Road swings right before ending next to tall brush at 3.0 miles [05]. Walk short distance southwest to grave site in brush.

Return Trip: Return the way you came.

Services: Closest services in Gila Bend about 30 miles east on Interstate 8.

Historical Highlights: In 1851, traveling what later became the Butterfield Stage Route, Royce Oatman was determined to get to California with his wife and five children. While struggling with tired oxen to climb the rocky hill east of the marker, they were savagely attacked by Indians. Three children survived: Olive, age 16; Mary Ann, age 10; and Lorenzo, age 14. Mary Ann and Olive were taken by the Indians. Mary Ann died in captivity but Olive survived to live with the Indians for five years. Lorenzo was badly beaten but managed to struggle back to civilization to tell his story. The family was buried 0.3 miles east and slightly north of the massacre site.

Maps: USGS 250,000 scale map Ajo, AZ-Sonora, 32112-A1-TM-250.

Crossing the Maricopa Mountains.

Toughest spot on trail.

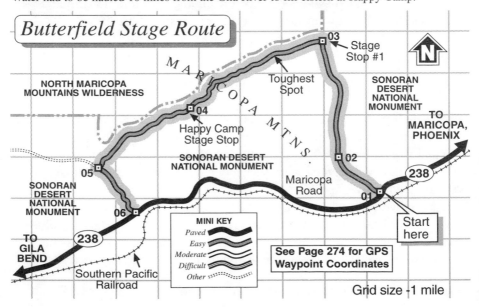
Water had to be hauled 10 miles from the Gila River to fill cistern at Happy Camp.

Butterfield Stage Route

N

03 Stage Stop #1

NORTH MARICOPA MOUNTAINS WILDERNESS

Toughest Spot

SONORAN DESERT NATIONAL MONUMENT

TO MARICOPA, PHOENIX

04

Happy Camp Stage Stop

MARICOPA MTNS.

SONORAN DESERT NATIONAL MONUMENT

Maricopa Road

02

05

238

SONORAN DESERT NATIONAL MONUMENT

01

Start here

06

MINI KEY
Paved
Easy
Moderate
Difficult
Other

TO GILA BEND

238

Southern Pacific Railroad

See Page 274 for GPS Waypoint Coordinates

Grid size -1 mile

Butterfield Stage Route 65

Location: Southwest of Phoenix between Maricopa and Gila Bend.

Difficulty: Easy. Two-wheel drive adequate most of the way when dry. A bit rougher through the Maricopa Mountains. Suitable for stock SUVs. Dangerously hot in summer. Carry plenty of water and travel with someone.

Features: This section of the Butterfield Stage Route is inside the Sonoran Desert National Monument and is directly adjacent to a wilderness area. It is imperative that you remain on the designated route at all times.

Time & Distance: More than 12 miles off pavement. Allow 1 to 2 hours.

To Get There: From the intersection of Highways 347 and 238 just north of Maricopa, head west 23.2 miles on Hwy. 238. Turn north on dirt road at signs for Butterfield Stage Route. (Just east of mile marker 19.)

Trail Description: Reset your odometer as you turn north off Highway 238 [01]. Follow dirt road northwest. Bear right at 1.4 miles [02]. This fork is marked with a large pile of rocks. Road can be hard to see if previous tire tracks have been blown over. Turn left at 4.5 miles [03] onto well-marked Butterfield Stage Route. Sign register and review information at kiosk. Continue straight across gully at 5.8 miles. This is the toughest spot on trail. Bear right out of wash at 6.7 miles. Continue west through Happy Camp stage stop at 8.3 miles [04]. Bear left at T at 11.1 miles [05] and reconnect with Highway 238 at 12.5 miles [06].

Return Trip: Turn left to return to Maricopa or right for Gila Bend.

Services: None. Full services in Maricopa or Gila Bend.

Historical Highlights: It took John Butterfield just one year to establish a mail, freight and passenger route from Missouri to San Francisco after he was awarded a government contract in 1857. Setting up and running the stage line required coordination of approximately 800 employees, 1,000 horses, 700 mules, 800 sets of harnesses and 250 stage coaches and wagons. About 200 stage depots and waystations had to be stocked with food, hay, grain, water and other supplies. Each driver completed a 60-mile leg of the route. The entire 2,800-mile trip took 22 to 25 days. The Arizona portion of the route was abandoned and moved north in 1861 because of the Civil War.

Maps: USGS 250,000 scale map Phoenix, AZ, N1 12-7, Series V502.

Organ Pipe Cactus at left along Puerto Blanco Drive.

Arch seen from Ajo Mountain Drive.

Corral at Bonita Well.

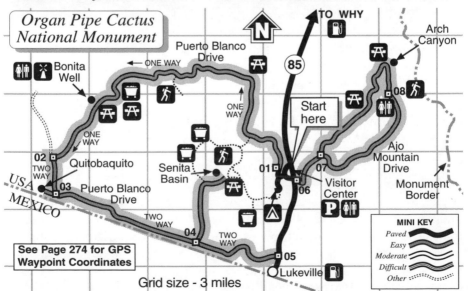

Organ Pipe Cactus National Monument

TO WHY

Arch Canyon

Puerto Blanco Drive

← ONE WAY

85

Bonita Well

ONE WAY

08

ONE WAY

Start here

ONE WAY

02
TWO WAY

Quitobaquito

Senita Basin

Ajo Mountain Drive

03 Puerto Blanco Drive

01

07

Monument Border

06

Visitor Center

TWO WAY

04

TWO WAY

05

USA
MEXICO

See Page 274 for GPS Waypoint Coordinates

Lukeville

Grid size - 3 miles

MINI KEY
Paved
Easy
Moderate
Difficult
Other

Organ Pipe Cactus Nat. Mon. 66

Location: Southwest of Phoenix along U.S./Mexico border. About halfway between Tucson and Yuma.

Difficulty: Easy. Well-maintained dirt roads suitable for most passenger cars. Ajo Mountain Drive has short stretches of pavement on steeper sections. Dangerouly hot in summer. Carry plenty of water. Route-finding easy.

Features: Drive through dramatic Sonoran Desert on two lightly traveled loop roads. See abundant desert flora and wildlife including the Organ Pipe Cactus, common in Mexico but rare in the United States. Booklets, which explain numbered features along routes, are available at Visitor Center for a small fee. Enjoy hiking trails and nature walks. Campground includes 208 spaces for RVs up to 35 feet in length. Water is available but no hook-ups or showers. Entry fee to enter monument is $5 per vehicle and is good for 7 days. Camping is additional. Call 520-387-6849 for more information.

Time & Distance: The 51-mile Puerto Blanco loop takes 3 to 4 hours. The 21-mile Ajo Mountain loop takes 1 to 2 hours. Add time for stops and hikes.

To Get There: Take Hwy. 85 south from Phoenix or Hwy. 86 west from Tucson. (Allow about 3 hours.) From the town of Why, continue south on Hwy. 85 about 23 miles to the Visitor Center on right.

Trail Description: Follow signs at Visitor Center to start of trails.
    Puerto Blanco Loop: Reset odometer where pavement ends [01]. Follow well-marked, one-way road past mines, picnic areas and hiking trails. Vault toilet at 18.4 miles. Turn left at T at 22.2 miles [02]. Two-way traffic begins here. Turn left again at 24.0 miles [03]. (Add 0.8 miles if you take side trip right to Quitobaquito.) Continue straight at 32.6 miles [04]. (Add 9.0 miles if you take side trip left to Senita Basin.) Hwy. 85 is reached at 37.6 miles [05]. Turn left to return to Visitor Center.
    Ajo Mountain Loop: Reset odometer at start [06]. Follow well-marked road east. Bear left at 2.1 miles [07]. Toilet and picnic area at 11 miles [08]. Left at 18.2 [07]. Back to Hwy. 85 at 20.3 miles [06].

Return Trip: Return the way you came.

Services: Gas and food in Why and Lukeville. Full services in Ajo.

Maps: Organ Pipe Cactus National Monument brochure, USGS 250,000 scale map Lukeville, AZ, Arizona Atlas & Gazetteer.

AREA 10

Tucson, Oracle, Nogales

67. Backway to Mt. Lemmon
68. Rice Peak
69. Charouleau Gap
70. Chimney Rock
71. Chivo Falls
72. Gunsight Pass
73. Gardner Canyon
74. Bull Springs Road
75. Patagonia Mountains

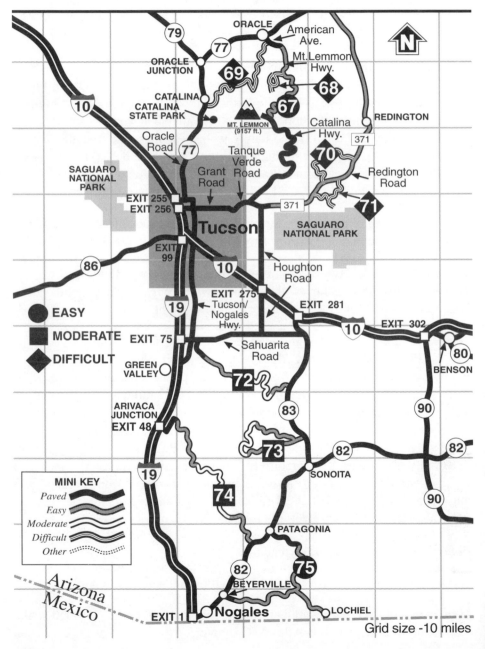

EASY

MODERATE

DIFFICULT

MINI KEY

Paved
Easy
Moderate
Difficult
Other

Grid size -10 miles

Tucson, Oracle, Nogales

This area includes four outstanding hard-core trails. At the top of the list is *Charouleau Gap*—long, scenic and an extreme test of articulation. One obstacle, called "The Step," is tough on U-joints. Drivers with a heavy foot should be handy with tools and carry plenty of spare parts. Menacing *Chivo Falls* is popular with local rock crawlers because it is close to Tucson and has a beautiful lunch spot below impressive (when flowing) Chivo Falls. *Rice Peak* and *Chimney Rock*, not quite as tough as the first two, are still serious trails. SUV owners looking for challenge, but without the rock bashing, will enjoy three outstanding moderate trails: *Gunsight Pass*, *Gardner Canyon* and *Bull Springs Road*. These trails offer driving thrills with dramatic views as they wind through high mountain country in the cool Coronado National Forest. Drivers who prefer easy stuff won't be disappointed either—no flat, boring roads here. The *Backway to Mt. Lemmon* twists and climbs dramatically to near 9,000 feet on a teeth-chattering Odyssey. The *Patagonia Mountains* trip is the smoothest ride and features historic ghost towns like Harshaw and Duquesne. The halfway point of this trip literally ends at the border fence to Mexico in the hamlet of Lochiel.

Photo by Craig Becwar

Crowd turns its attention to the next victim at "The Step" on Charouleau Gap (Trail #69).

229

This 25-mile-long road covers a straight-line distance of only about 10 miles.

Watering hole next to the road.

Fall color had started in late November.

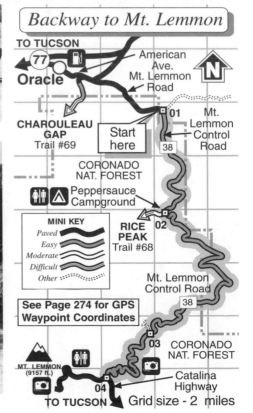

Backway to Mt. Lemmon

TO TUCSON

77

Oracle

American Ave.
Mt. Lemmon Road

N

01

Mt. Lemmon Control Road

CHAROULEAU GAP
Trail #69

Start here

38

CORONADO NAT. FOREST

Peppersauce Campground

MINI KEY
Paved
Easy
Moderate
Difficult
Other

RICE PEAK
Trail #68

02

Mt. Lemmon Control Road

38

See Page 274 for GPS Waypoint Coordinates

03

CORONADO NAT. FOREST

MT. LEMMON
(9157 ft.)

Catalina Highway

04

TO TUCSON

Grid size - 2 miles

230

Backway to Mt. Lemmon 67

Location: Northeast of Tucson, southeast of Oracle.

Difficulty: Easy. Well-maintained dirt road but very bumpy. Low range is helpful to climb the last few miles up the backside of Mt. Lemmon. Two-wheel drive, high-clearance adequate in dry weather. Snow and ice possible near top in late fall. Avoid during the winter.

Features: A fun, lightly-used backcountry road to popular Mt. Lemmon. Usually driven from south side on busy Catalina Highway. Camp in Coronado National Forest's Peppersauce Campground (fee area).

Time & Distance: About 25 miles as described here. Allow 2 to 3 hours plus time to reach Oracle north of Tucson. The descent from Mt. Lemmon on the Catalina Highway also takes a while.

To Get There: Head north on Oracle Road (Highway 77) from Tucson. Stay on Highway 77 all the way to Oracle. Turn right on American Avenue just past mile marker 100. Bear right on Mt. Lemmon Road after 2.4 miles. Turn right after another 3.2 miles where the road turns to dirt. This is called the Mt. Lemmon Control Road and marks the start of the trip.

Trail Description: Reset odometer at the start [01]. Follow this major dirt road south as it winds down into a valley. At 5.1 miles [02] you'll go by the Peppersauce Campground. This is the turn for Rice Peak (Trail #68) but you continue straight. The road is marked F.S. 38 inside the Coronado National Forest. Lesser roads branch off but the main road is obvious. Continue straight at 15.9 where another road goes left. Bear left at 18.5 miles [03]. The road climbs with great views of the valley below. Four-wheel drive was needed when our group ran into snow and ice on the road in late November. Continue uphill on pavement past the Mt. Lemmon Fire Department before reaching the Catalina Highway at 25.1 miles [04].

Return Trip: Left takes you downhill back to Tucson. Right takes you uphill to the top of Mt. Lemmon and the Mt. Lemmon Ski Area.

Services: Gas and food in Oracle, full services in Tucson. Drinking water and toilets at Peppersauce Campground.

Maps: Coronado National Forest (Safford and Santa Catalina Ranger Districts), USGS 250,000 scale map Tucson, AZ, Arizona Atlas & Gazetteer.

Typical conditions part way up.

High ground clearance needed.

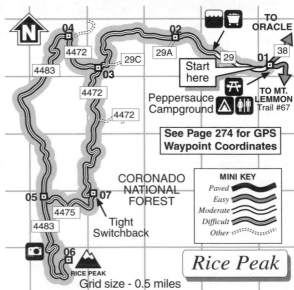

Stay out of old mines.

N

04

4472

02

TO ORACLE

4483

29C

29A

29

38

03

4472

Start here

01

4472

Peppersauce Campground

TO MT. LEMMON
Trail #67

See Page 274 for GPS Waypoint Coordinates

CORONADO NATIONAL FOREST

MINI KEY
Paved
Easy
Moderate
Difficult
Other

05

07

4475

4483

Tight Switchback

06

Rice Peak

RICE PEAK

Grid size - 0.5 miles

Rice Peak 68

Location: Northeast of Tucson, southeast of Oracle.

Difficulty: Difficult. Suitable for aggressive stock vehicles with good articulation, skid plates and an experienced driver. Steep at the top. Dangerous if snow-covered or icy. Route-finding complex. Some brush.

Features: A challenging run with broad views from the 7,577-ft. summit. Camp at the Forest Service Peppersauce Campground (fee area).

Time & Distance: From Peppersauce C.G. to summit is 5.8 miles. Return trip 5.6 miles. Allow about 4 hours plus travel time. Combine with Trail #67.

To Get There: Follow directions to *Backway to Mt. Lemmon (Trail #67)*. Turn right at Peppersauce Campground.

Trail Description: Reset odometer at Peppersauce Campground [01]. Road follows Peppersauce Wash west. The trail is tight and overgrown in places. Low gear is needed early. Cross creek and note mine on right at 0.6. Bear right at 1.1 miles [02] and left at 1.9. Bear right on FS 29C at 2.1. Quickly make another right on F.S. 4472 at 2.2 miles [03]. Make a left at 2.7 miles [04] on F.S. 4483. Stay right at 3.1 on 4483. Bear right uphill to reach peak at 4.5 miles [05]. You'll come back to this spot. Bear left at 5.1 at tight switchback. More switchbacks follow. It's steep and loose just before the top, which is reached at 5.8 miles [06]. Parking tight. Walk west for best views.

Reset odometer at top and return to fork at 1.2 miles [05]. Turn right to go out a different way than you entered. Steep descent with washouts at 1.8. Signs recommend you pull ahead then back down tight switchback at 1.9 miles [07]. Bear left down another tight switchback at 2.5. Continue straight at 2.9 where F.S. 4472 goes right. Bear right when you get back to original trail at 3.5 miles [03]. Go out the way you came in. Peppersause Campground is reached at 5.6 miles [01].

Return Trip: Turn left to return to Oracle or right to go the *Backway to Mt. Lemmon* (Trail #67).

Services: Gas and food in Oracle, full services in Tucson. Drinking water and toilets at Peppersauce Campground.

Maps: Coronado National Forest (Safford and Santa Catalina Ranger Districts), USGS 250,000 scale map Tucson, AZ, Arizona Atlas & Gazetteer.

Large ruts common on most of the trail.

"The Step"—tough on U-joints.

The "Elevator Shaft" is long and steep.

Water depth varies at the "Car Wash."

Coming down the west side.

Charouleau Gap ◆69◆

Location: Northeast of Tucson, south of Oracle and east of Catalina.

Difficulty: Difficult. For serious four-wheelers only. No stock vehicles. Lockers or winch recommended. Extreme articulation needed for deep washouts and gullies. Climb several steep hills with loose rock. One water crossing is deep during rainy periods. One rock obstacle called "The Step" often requires assistance. Aggressive drivers may break parts. Trail is very long and remote. Route-finding is difficult at the end. Go with a group and be prepared for surprises.

Features: Fun, challenging and scenic. One of the most popular hard-core runs in the state. A must drive for any serious four-wheeler. Crosses the Santa Catalina Mountain range in the Coronado National Forest.

Time & Distance: Less than 20 miles but almost all must be driven slowly. Allow 5 to 7 hours plus travel time. Allow additional time if you're traveling with a large group.

To Get There: Head north on Oracle Road (Highway 77) from Tucson. Stay on Highway 77 all the way to Oracle. Turn right on American Avenue just past mile marker 100. Go 2.1 miles to Maplewood Street on the right.

Trail Description: *Reset odometer as you turn right at Maplewood Street* [01]. Head west on Maplewood and turn left at 0.1 on Estill Road. Head south and bear right on Viento at 0.4. Road changes to dirt. Turn right at 0.7 on Callas. Wide spot at gate at 0.9 is good place to air down. Pass through gate and immediately bear right. (Leave gates the way you find them unless posted otherwise.) Turn right again at 1.0 miles [02] where F.S. 4487 goes straight. You immediately encounter bad washouts. Driver's choice at 1.1. Pick your line carefully. Left is harder at 1.8. Bear right down steep hill at 2.3 (bypass is left). Continue straight at 2.4. Stay on main road as smaller roads branch off.

Continue straight at 3.6 miles past windmill on left. Straight again at 4.0. Bear left at fork at 4.2. The road drops into a valley at 4.5 miles [03] and begins a long, steep climb up the "Elevator Shaft." Bear right at 6.3 on F.S. 736. Continue straight down rocky challenge at 6.6. Cross in and out of creek in Del Oro Canyon starting at 7.0. "Car Wash" is reached at 7.3 miles [04]. Heading straight across creek is easier. Turning left and following creek is deepest part. Make a sharp right uphill at 7.5 miles. Climb a short, rocky hill and immediately turn right at the top.

235

At 8.2 miles [05] you cross a creek just before "The Step"—a very difficult, high, rocky ledge. Short wheel-base vehicles tend to go over backwards. I broke a front U-joint on my Cherokee because I refused to use my winch or take a strap. I made the repair but lost over an hour. Stay on the trail; don't try to bypass this obstacle. After "The Step," you'll pass Coronado Camp, a small cabin on the left at 8.5 miles. Red Ridge Hiking Trail goes left at 9.7 miles [06]. You bear right heading north for a short distance.

After a long up-and-down climb on a narrow shelf road, you reach Charouleau Gap, marked by a cattle guard at 13.1 miles [07]. Great views of Catalina as you descend the other side. At 15.3 miles, F.S. 4496 goes right; you continue straight. From here, the trail includes huge ruts and rocky ledges. Many side roads branch off. Do your best to follow the trail downhill, staying to the right when in doubt. After crossing a broad area of rock, bear right at a T at 17.0 miles [08]. Continue straight when a road joins on the left at 17.8. A creek crossing follows. Stay under telephone lines for a distance. Stay between fences on each side of the road before reaching the end of the trail at 19.3 miles [09]. Sign in at the information kiosk and let the Forest Service know you enjoyed this trail.

Return Trip: Turn left on the paved road after the kiosk. This is Lago Del Oro Parkway. Go south 3.1 miles and turn right on Golder Ranch Road. Oracle Road is reached in another 1.2 miles. Turn left for Tucson.

Services: None on trail. Gas and food in Oracle, full services in Tucson.

Special Note: The west end of the trail was slated to be closed a few years ago. The local four-wheel drive club, the Tucson Rough Riders, fought successfully to keep the trail open. This is the reason the exit point is fenced on both sides of the road where it cuts across private land. Respect the fences and the rights of the property owners as you pass through. Charouleau Gap remains an Adopt-a-trail of the Tuscon Rough Riders. Do your part to keep the trail in good shape. Stay on the trail at all times and pack out your trash.

Maps: Coronado National Forest (Safford and Santa Catalina Ranger Districts), USGS 250,000 scale map Tucson, AZ, Arizona Atlas & Gazetteer.

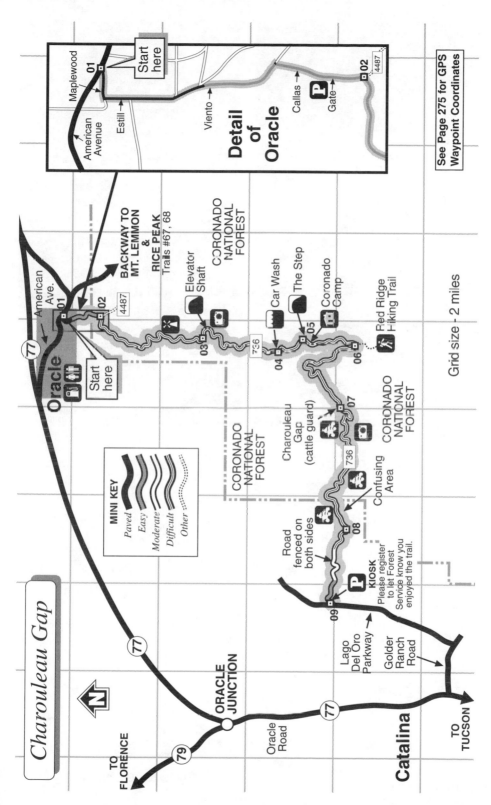

Charouleau Gap

See Page 275 for GPS Waypoint Coordinates

Detail of Oracle

Start here

Maplewood
American Avenue
Estill
Viento
Callas
Gate

BACKWAY TO MT. LEMMON & RICE PEAK
Trails #67, 68

Elevator Shaft

CORONADO NATIONAL FOREST

Car Wash
The Step
Coronado Camp
Red Ridge Hiking Trail

American Ave.

Start here

Oracle

CORONADO NATIONAL FOREST

MINI KEY
Paved
Easy
Moderate
Difficult
Other

Charouleau Gap (cattle guard)

CORONADO NATIONAL FOREST

Confusing Area

Road fenced on both sides

KIOSK
Please register to let Forest Service know you enjoyed the trail.

Lago Del Oro Parkway
Golder Ranch Road

Grid size - 2 miles

TO FLORENCE

ORACLE JUNCTION

Oracle Road

Catalina

TO TUCSON

N

237

Roughest spot on trail.

Wrong way around Chimney Rock.

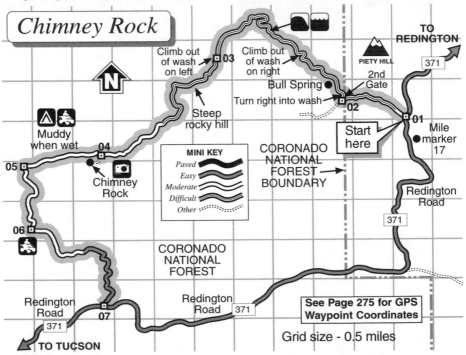

Chimney Rock

TO REDINGTON

PIETY HILL

371

Climb out of wash on left 03

Climb out of wash on right

2nd Gate

Bull Spring ●

Turn right into wash 02

Steep rocky hill

N

01

Start here

Mile marker 17

Muddy when wet

04

CORONADO NATIONAL FOREST BOUNDARY

05

Chimney Rock

MINI KEY
Paved
Easy
Moderate
Difficult
Other

Redington Road

371

06

CORONADO NATIONAL FOREST

Redington Road 371

See Page 275 for GPS Waypoint Coordinates

Redington Road

371

07

TO TUCSON

Grid size - 0.5 miles

Chimney Rock ◀70▶

Location: East of Tucson.

Difficulty: Difficult. Much of trail follows a narrow, rocky wash with very tight brush. Good articulation, high ground clearance and skid plates recommended. Aggressive stock vehicles can make it but brush will likely scratch new paint. Route-finding is confusing at times. GPS is helpful.

Features: Chimney Rock is a popular ATV and camping area. Most people enter from the easier south side. The trail described here comes in the lesser-used back way. Leave gates as you find them. The corridor along Redington Road is heavily used. Weekends are very busy.

Time & Distance: It's 17 miles to the start of the trail on bumpy Redington Road. The trail measures 8.4 miles and takes 3 to 4 hours.

To Get There: Head east from Tucson on Tanque Verde Road, which becomes Redington Road as it leaves town. Turn left 0.4 miles past mile marker 17. This rough, single-lane road is a public road despite posted signs; however, you must stay on the road as it crosses private land the first mile.

Trail Description: Reset odometer as you turn off Redington Road [01]. Pass through first gate at 0.4 miles. Many more gates follow and not all are mentioned here. Bear right and drop into wash after second gate at 0.9 miles [02]. Pass through another gate at Bull Spring at 1.2. Follow wash, climbing out briefly on the right at 1.9 and 3.6. The wash is very rocky in places. Climb out of the wash on the left side at 3.8 miles [03]. Road gets better after steep rocky hill at 4.7. As you approach Chimney Rock, turn right at T at 6.3 miles [04] and continue heading east around right side of Chimney Rock. Turn right at another T after gate at 6.4. Do your best to stay on the main road as many spurs branch off. Turn left heading south after passing through another gate at 7.2 miles [05]. Cross cattle guard and pass through last gate at 8.1. Bear left at 8.2 miles [06]. Do not follow wash to right. Redington Road is reached at 8.4 miles [07].

Return Trip: Turn right to return to Tucson.

Services: None on trail. Return to Tucson.

Maps: Coronado National Forest (Safford and Santa Catalina Ranger Districts), USGS 7.5 minute map Piety Hill, AZ, N3215-W11030/7.5.

Descending Three Feathers.

Typical challenges along the route.

Chivo Falls during rainy period.

High water at Italian Trap.

Location: East of Tucson.

Difficulty: Difficult. Narrow, rocky trail that drops into Tanque Verde Canyon then follows the canyon creek bottom. Usually, the creek is relatively dry, but during rainy periods deep crossings are possible. One obstacle called "Three Feathers" has various routes from which to choose, some more difficult than others. The last 0.1 miles before Chivo Falls is difficult and tippy, but this part can be walked. Generally, this trail is driven by modified vehicles, but aggressive stock vehicles can probably get through with some help. There are no monster obstacles, but you can find tough stuff if that's what you want. Lockers, high ground clearance and skid plates recommended. Route-finding is complex. Don't drive this trail alone.

Features: This great hard-core trail features Chivo Falls. During wet periods, water flows over a high rock ledge and drops dramatically to a pool below. This cool, shaded halfway point on the route is a popular place to stop for lunch.

Time & Distance: Just under 10 miles. Allow 4 to 5 hours.

To Get There: From Exit 256 at Interstate 10 head east on Grant Road. This flows into Tanque Verde Road which becomes Redington Road as it leaves town. Turn right through an opening in a fence about a half mile after mile marker 7. The road is marked on the fence as F.S. 4417.

Trail Description: Reset odometer as you turn right off Redington Road [01]. There's a broad rocky area inside the fence but no clear start to the road. Head straight through the fence in a southeast direction and the road will become more obvious. After a short distance the road starts downhill and turns left in a northeast direction. Bear right downhill at 0.2 miles. The road heads south then northeast again. Continue straight at 0.5. Bear right at 0.8 miles [02] to the top of "Three Feathers." A path down the right side is the easiest route. Hardest route is far left.

    The road goes right and crosses a cattle guard at 2.2 miles [03]. Cross another cattle guard at 2.4. At 2.5 cross a small earthen dam at Chiva Tank. Bear right at a T at 2.8 miles [04] staying on F.S. 4417. The road left is an alternate route back to Redington Road. Bear left over a cattle guard at 3.2 miles [05]. The road to the right is called Redington Loop, not covered in this book. Bear right for Chivo Falls at 3.3 miles [06] on F.S. 4405. You will come back to this point later. Cross creek at 3.4 then bear right. Cross another cattle guard and drop down a steep bank. Bear left at 4.1 miles. F.S. 4405 continues to the right. Descend a steep, rocky hill. The trail gets tougher as you near Chivo Falls. I stopped at 4.4 miles [07]. The last part was very tippy. You have to walk up a short, rocky hill to see the falls. It's a very pretty spot even if the falls are not flowing.

Reset your odometer and return to the intersection 1.0 miles back [06]. Turn right and follow F.S. 4426. After crossing a creek bed at 1.2 miles, continue straight where a road goes left. Continue straight at 1.5 miles [08] where a road goes right. Cross another creek and cattle guard before 2.4 miles [09]. At this point, the trail follows the creek bed, weaving in and out. It may be dry or quite deep depending on the time of year. The deepest part will be at 2.9 miles. You can follow the creek or drive along the right side at the deepest part. This area is called the "Italian Trap". It is very rocky with various routes from which to choose. Continue straight leaving the creek at 3.2 miles [10]. A metal tank marks this spot. Bear left after passing through a gate at 3.3. The road is easier for a while but gets rocky again. Bear right at a T at 5.1 miles. Continue straight at 5.2 before reaching Redington Road at 5.3 miles [11].

Return Trip: Turn left to return to Tucson. Right takes you on a long trip to Redington. You may wish to explore other marked trails in this popular four-wheel-drive and ATV area.

Services: None on trail. Return to Tucson.

Maps: Coronado National Forest (Safford and Santa Catalina Ranger Districts), USGS 7.5 minute maps Piety Hill, AZ N3215-W11030/7.5 and Aqua Caliente Hill, AZ 32110-C6-TF-024.

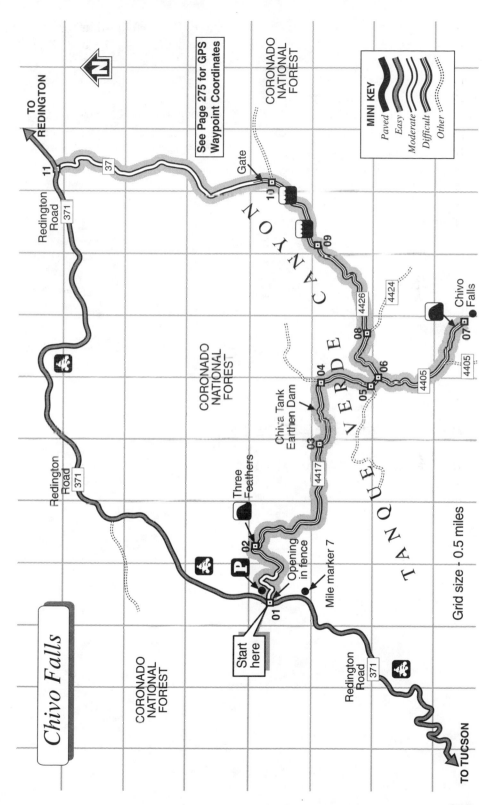

Chivo Falls

TO REDINGTON

Redington Road 371

11

37

See Page 275 for GPS Waypoint Coordinates

Gate

10

09

CORONADO NATIONAL FOREST

CANYON

4426

4424

08

07

Chivo Falls

4405

4405

06

05

04

CORONADO NATIONAL FOREST

Chiva Tank Earthen Dam

VERDE

03

4417

Three Feathers

02

P

Opening in fence

01

Mile marker 7

TANQUE

Start here

CORONADO NATIONAL FOREST

Redington Road 371

Redington Road 371

Grid size - 0.5 miles

TO TUCSON

MINI KEY

Paved
Easy
Moderate
Difficult
Other

243

Starting down the west side of Gunsight Pass.   One of many graves in Helvetia Cemetery.

Popular area for ATVs. Just make sure to stay on numbered routes only.

Remains of adobe structure east of Helvetia Townsite.

Gunsight Pass 72

Location: Southeast of Tucson, east of Green Valley.

Difficulty: Moderate. Narrow, rocky trail climbs steeply to an elevation over 5,000 feet. Rutted with loose rock in several places. Suitable for aggressive stock vehicles with high ground clearance. Some backcountry driving experience recommended. Don't go alone.

Features: Old mining road with beautiful views from Gunsight Pass and Lopez Pass at the top of the Santa Rita Mountains. This is a popular ATV area. Make sure you stay on numbered routes only and follow Tread Lightly guidelines. Stop at Helvetia Townsite—not much left but a few adobe walls. Examine historic gravesites in Helvetia Cemetery.

Time & Distance: A short drive from Tucson. The trail is more than 23 miles off pavement. Allow 3 to 4 hours.

To Get There: Follow Highway 83 south from Exit 281 of Interstate 10. Turn right 0.4 miles south of mile marker 47. Watch for a sign for Rosemont Junction after a rest area on the right side of the road.

Trail Description: Reset odometer as you turn right off Highway 83 [01]. Follow a well-graded road west. There's an information kiosk on the right at 0.4 miles with a map of the Santa Rita Area. Some of the route numbers do not agree with what is actually posted on the trail. Continue on the main road as it follows a wash starting at 1.1 miles. Bear right out of the wash at 2.4 miles. Bear right where F.S. 4064 goes left at 2.6 miles [02]. This is Rosemont Junction. Stay on the left side of this wash as lesser roads go right. Bear left at a concrete tank where F.S. 4051 goes right at 2.9 miles. Bear left at 3.0 miles. Turn right at 3.3 miles [03], following a sign to Gunsight Pass. Stay right of a tank at 4.1. Bear right on F.S. 4051 at 4.2 miles [04] where 4059 goes left. At 4.3 make two right turns very close together. Continue straight over a rise at 5.1. Make a sharp left uphill on F.S. 505 at 5.4 miles [05]. Gunsight Pass is reached at 6.0 miles [06]. Pass between two wooden posts and start down the other side. You might want to stop here for a few pictures.

A shortcut goes left at 6.3 miles. Turn right to continue. Lopez Pass is reached at 6.6 miles [07]. Go between fence posts and make a soft right downhill. Make a left at 6.9 and another left 100 feet beyond that. Follow sign to Sycamore Canyon. Bear left through a gate at 7.3 miles [08]. At 9.0 turn left at a T. Go left uphill at 9.5 [09]. Continue uphill through a badly washed out section at 11.3. The shortcut mentioned earlier joins on the left at 11.5 miles [10]. Bear right on the main road at 11.9. Continue straight at 12.2 as the road gets easier. Ignore side roads. Helvetia Townsite is on the right at 13.2 miles [11]. Part of an old adobe structure remains just east of the townsite. Roads converge at 13.7 miles. Stay slightly left uphill; do not go into the wash. Bear left at a major T at 14.0. You're now on Helvetia Road. Watch for Helvetia Cemetery on the right at 14.8 miles [12]. It's worth your time to stop a few minutes. Continue to follow the main road as it curves to the right and heads northwest. Helvetia Road becomes Santa Rita Road when you reach pavement at 23.3 miles.

Return Trip: Continue northwest on Santa Rita Road. It soon turns north and runs into Sahaurita Road. Left takes you to Interstate 19. Right takes you to Houghton Road, which goes north to the east side of Tucson.

Services: Rest area just before the start on Highway 83. None on trail. Full services in Tucson.

Maps: Coronado National Forest (Nogales Ranger District), Santa Rita Off-Highway Vehicle Access map issued by the Forest Service, USGS 7.5 minute maps Helvetia, AZ, 31110-G7-TF-024 and Empire Ranch, AZ, 31110-G6-TF-024, Arizona Atlas & Gazetteer.

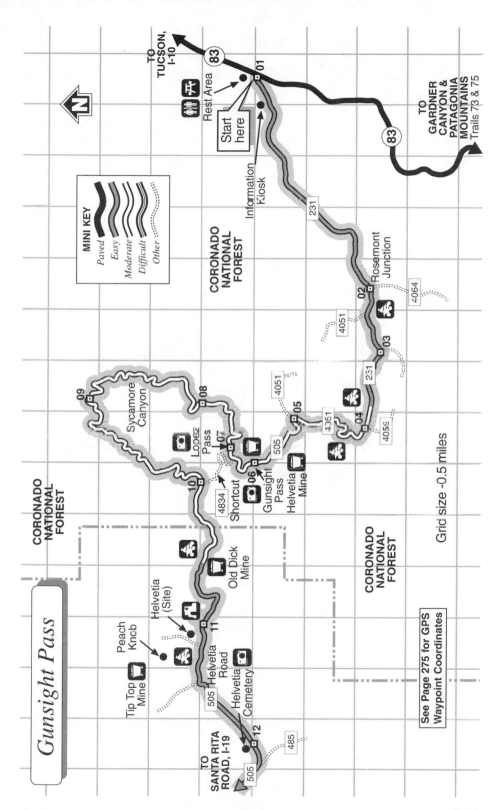

Gunsight Pass

MINI KEY

Paved
Easy
Moderate
Difficult
Other

TO TUCSON, I-10

83

Rest Area

Start here

Information Kiosk

83

TO GARDNER CANYON & PATAGONIA MOUNTAINS
Trails 73 & 75

01

231

CORONADO NATIONAL FOREST

Rosemont Junction

02

4051

4064

03

231

4051

04

4351

05

4058

Sycamore Canyon

09

08

Lopez Pass

07

505

06

Shortcut

4834

Gunsight Pass

Helvetia Mine

10

CORONADO NATIONAL FOREST

Old Dick Mine

Grid size - 0.5 miles

Helvetia (Site)

Peach Knob

Tip Top Mine

Helvetia Road

11

505

Helvetia Cemetery

TO SANTA RITA ROAD, I-19

505

12

485

See Page 275 for GPS Waypoint Coordinates

247

Gate is open to drive to Kentucky Camp on Saturdays. You must hike at other times.

Watch for livestock on the road.

This is the toughest spot on the trail.

The road before Kentucky Camp is easy.

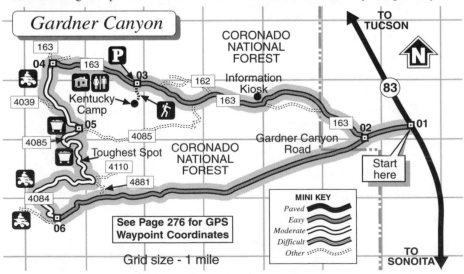

Gardner Canyon

CORONADO NATIONAL FOREST

163
04
4039
163
P
03
162
Information Kiosk
163
Kentucky Camp
4085
05
4085
Toughest Spot
4110
4084
4881
06

CORONADO NATIONAL FOREST

Gardner Canyon Road

163
02
01
83

Start here

TO TUCSON

N

TO SONOITA

See Page 276 for GPS Waypoint Coordinates

Grid size - 1 mile

MINI KEY
Paved
Easy
Moderate
Difficult
Other

Gardner Canyon 73

Location: Southeast of Tucson.

Difficulty: Moderate. Mostly easy except for one rocky hill. Suitable for high clearance stock SUVs. Can be muddy when wet.

Features: Many side roads in the area to explore—some are difficult. Visit historic Kentucky Camp. Popular ATV area. Stay on marked roads.

Time & Distance: Loop described here is 18.3 miles. Allow 2 to 3 hours.

To Get There: Take Hwy. 83 south from Exit 281 of Interstate 10. Turn right 0.7 miles south of mile marker 38 on well-marked Gardner Canyon Rd.

Trail Description: Reset your odometer at the start of Gardner Canyon Road [01]. Turn right on F.S 163 at 0.8 miles [02]. Bear right at 1.7 and soon enter Coronado National Forest. Turn left at 2.8. Continue straight at 3.1 past information kiosk. Continue straight, following signs to Kentucky Camp at 3.9. Right at 4.2. Park on left at 5.3 miles [03] for Kentucky Camp. Hike 1/4 mile to camp. (Gate is open on Saturdays to drive down.)
Continue northwest on F.S. 163 from Kentucky Camp hiking trail-head. Straight at 6.8. At 7.0 miles [04] turn left where 163 goes straight. Possible muddy area if wet. Bear left at 7.8 where F.S. 4039 goes right. Bear right at 8.4 miles [05] on F.S. 4085. Left at 8.7. Bear left twice after Snyder Mine at 8.9. Toughest spot on trail at 9.5. Bear left at 9.8. Bear right at 10.0 where F.S. 4110 goes left. Immediately bear right again where F.S. 4881 goes left. This is a difficult shortcut. Stay left on F.S 4085 at 10.7. Left again at 11.2 and join F.S. 4084. A difficult Jeep trail goes right at this point. To return to Hwy. 83, turn left when you get back to Gardner Canyon Road at 11.9 miles [06]. There are additional roads to explore if you turn right.

Return Trip: At Hwy. 83 turn left for Tucson or right 4 miles to Sonoita.

Services: Modern vault toilet at Kentucky Camp. Gas in Sonoita.

Historical Highlights: Kentucky Camp served as headquarters for the Santa Rita Water and Mining Company in 1904. Buildings are being restored by volunteers. Main building is small museum. One cabin is bed & breakfast.

Maps: Coronado National Forest, USGS 100,000 scale map Fort Huachuca, AZ, 31110-E1-TM-100, Santa Rita Off-Highway Vehicle Access Map.

Trail climbs over 5,000 feet across the Santa Rita Mountains.

Adobe ruins of post office at Alto Camp.

Boulder partially blocks road.

Frontage Rd.
Elephant Head Rd.

Bull Springs Rd.

EXIT 48

Mt. Hopkins Road

Start here

MT. WRIGHTSON WILDERNESS

N

01

ARIVACA JUNCTION

143

MT. HOPKINS (Observatory)

MT. WRIGHTSON

19

02

03

CORONADO NATIONAL FOREST

MINI KEY

Paved
Easy
Moderate
Difficult
Other

Alto Camp

04

Squaw Gulch Road

05

See Page 276 for GPS Waypoint Coordinates

TO PATA-GONIA

06

Grid size - 3 miles

TO NOGALES

82

Bull Springs Road

Location: South of Tucson between Arivaca Junction and Patagonia.

Difficulty: Moderate. Narrow, rocky shelf road at higher elevations. Suitable for high clearance stock SUVs. Remote location.

Features: Little-used mining road crosses Santa Rita Mountains from Interstate 19 to Hwy. 82 south of Patagonia. See mines along the route and adobe ruins at Alto Camp, once a community of several hundred people. The post office was active until 1933.

Time & Distance: About 24 miles. Allow 3 to 4 hours plus travel time.

To Get There: Get off Interstate 19 at Arivaca Junction Exit 48 south of rest area. Cross under freeway and take Frontage Road north less than 2 miles to Elephant Head Road. Head east 1.5 miles and turn right on Mt. Hopkins Road towards Whipple Observatory. Continue another 4.8 miles southeast and turn right at sign for Bull Springs Road.

Trail Description: *Reset your odometer at the start of Bull Springs Road* [01]. Bear right at 2.1 miles. Continue straight through wash at 3.1. At 3.7 cross cattle guard into National Forest. This starts F.S. 143. Pass mines at 4.4 and 4.5. Stay right on F.S. 143 at 4.8 miles [02]. Road gradually worsens as you pass corral at 5.5. Mileage sign at 6.1 conflicts with one at start. Neither is correct. Cross creek and climb hill at 6.4. Bear right uphill at 7.1 where F.S. 4079 goes left. Climb over 5,000 feet, the highest point on the trail at 8.1 miles [03]. Some say abandoned vehicles, seen as you come down the other side, were dumped by illegal drug runners from Mexico. Bear right through complex intersection at 10.8. Note mine on left at 11.0. Stay left at 11.4. See Alto Camp on right at 12.5 miles [04]. Leave National Forest at 13.1. Do not stray from main road as you cross private ranch. Bear right at 18.8 miles [05] where Squaw Gulch Road goes left. Bear right at 23.7. Cross Patagonia River (water depth varies) before reaching Hwy. 82 at 24.1 miles [06].

Return Trip: Left to Patagonia, Sonoita and Tucson; right to Nogales.

Services: Public toilets at town park in Patagonia. Gas in Sonoita. Full services in Tucson and Nogales.

Maps: Coronado National Forest (Nogales R.D.), USGS 100,000 scale map Fort Huachuca, AZ, 31110-E1-TM-100, Arizona Atlas & Gazetteer.

One of several well-preserved structures in privately owned Duquesne.

Descending from the Patagonia Mountains towards Mexico.

Ore bin next to Duquesne Road on way to Nogales.

Patagonia Mountains 75

Location: South of Tucson, southeast of Patagonia and northeast of Nogales. Part of the road reaches the Arizona/Mexico border.

Difficulty: Easy. Well-maintained dirt road suitable for high-slung passenger cars in dry weather. Side trip to Duquesne is a bit rougher but suitable for stock SUVs. Four-wheel drive may be needed when wet. Possible high water crossings during heavy rains.

Features: This scenic mountain drive reaches five forgotten backcountry towns: Harshaw, Mowry, Washington Camp, Duquesne and Lochiel. Harshaw and Duquesne are legitimate ghost towns with interesting buildings still standing. Lochiel was once a border crossing point into Mexico. This is a popular ATV recreation area although many side roads are now closed because of excessive surface damage. You must stay on numbered routes only. It is interesting to note that the Border Patrol uses ATVs to patrol this area for drugs and illegal aliens.

Time & Distance: Almost 42 miles from the point you leave Highway 82 at Patagonia until you return to Highway 82 at Beyerville. Allow 4 to 5 hours for this part of the trip. This is a full-day adventure if you add travel time from Tucson.

To Get There: Take Highway 83 south from Tucson. At Sonoita, connect with Highway 82 south to Patagonia. As you come into Patagonia, turn left on a small road just south of the post office. This road is just before a small town park.

Trail Description: *Reset odometer as you turn off Highway 82 at the post office* [01]. Head east less than 100 feet and turn left on Harshaw Avenue, which later changes to Harshaw Road. Harshaw Road continues all the way to Duquesne Road and has various route number designations. The paved portion of the road heads north for a short distance then turns east. About 3.2 miles bear right on F.S. 58, staying on a mostly paved road. Bear right again at 6.1 [02] miles on F.S. 49, after which the pavement finally ends.

The ghost town of Harshaw is on the left at 8.0 miles [03]. On the right is the Harshaw Cemetery. Continue south on Harshaw Road as lesser roads branch off. At 12.8 miles [04] F.S. 214 goes left to remains of the town of Mowry. Only a few adobe walls remain. (These directions do not include the half-mile round trip to Mowry.) Continue south on Harshaw Road until it intersects with Duquesne Road at 16.6 miles [05]. Duquesne Road joins on the right. You will continue south from this point on Duquesne Road and return to this point later. Pass through Washington Camp at 16.8. The town has quite a history, but some buildings are occupied so it appears more like an old residential area. At 17.3 miles [06] turn right on a lesser, rougher road in the direction of Duquesne. (This road was marked F.S. 126 but the Coronado Forest map shows the road as F.S. 128. It is marked 128 at the other end.) You pass through Duquesne at 17.9 miles. Although the town is a ghost town, it is privately owned and the land is for sale. Hopefully, new owners won't tear down the old buildings. Bear left at 18.0 and 18.8 miles. Continue south when you reintersect with Duquesne Road at 19.1 miles [07].

The road becomes sandy and dusty as you descend. Broad views of the valley below are a striking contrast to the mountain terrain you are leaving. Note the Fray Marcos de Niza Historical Monument and Cemetery on the right at 22.4 miles. A road goes left at 22.7. You continue straight across a cattle guard until you reach the border fence at Lochiel at 22.9 miles [08].

Turn around and reset your odometer at Lochiel. Head back the way you came. This time, when you reach the turn for Duquesne, stay right on the main road at 3.8 miles [07]. Bear left at 5.8 miles [05] when you reach the intersection of Duquesne and Harshaw Roads mentioned earlier. An interesting ore bin hangs over the road just around the corner. Beautiful views follow as you descend towards Nogales. You reach pavement at 17.2 before intersecting with Highway 82 at 18.8 miles [09].

Return Trip: Turn left for Nogales where signs direct you to Interstate 19. Right goes back to Patagonia and Tucson.

Services: Nothing along the route. Nogales is a fairly large town with fast food restaurants and department stores. The city park in Patagonia has public restrooms.

Historical Highlights: In 1880, **Harshaw** had its own newspaper, seven saloons, a mile-long main street, over 200 buildings and a population of about 2,000. Just two years later, the town was 80% vacant. A major fire and failure of its rich silver mine led to the town's demise. Both **Washington Camp** and **Duquesne** were major mining camps in the 1880s, each with populations of about 1,000 residents. The two towns worked closely together to support mining operations in the area. **Lochiel** had its own post office in 1884. It later became an important border crossing point but closed in 1980.

Maps: Coronado National Forest (Nogales Ranger District), USGS 250,000 scale map Nogales, AZ, Arizona Atlas & Gazetteer.

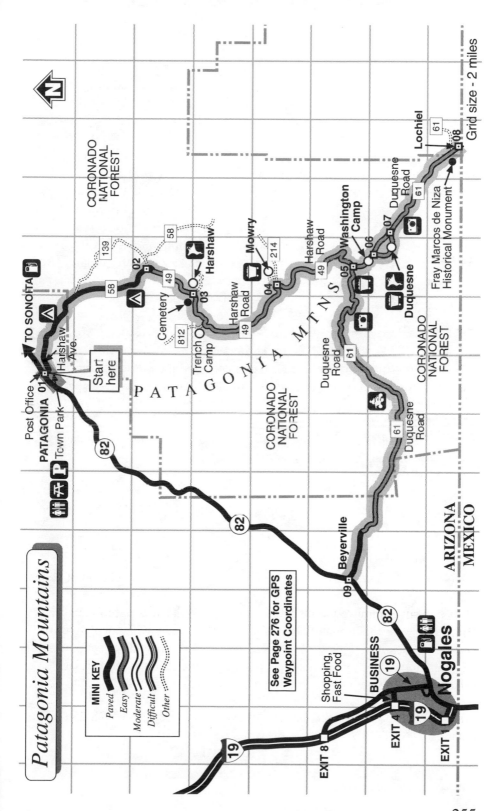

Patagonia Mountains

MINI KEY
Paved
Easy
Moderate
Difficult
Other

See Page 276 for GPS Waypoint Coordinates

Grid size - 2 miles

CORONADO NATIONAL FOREST

P A T A G O N I A   M T N S

CORONADO NATIONAL FOREST

CORONADO NATIONAL FOREST

TO SONOITA

Post Office
PATAGONIA 01
Town Park
Harshaw Ave.
Start here

58
139
58
02
49
Harshaw
Cemetery
Trench Camp
812
03
Harshaw Road
49
49
Harshaw Road
Mowry
214
04
05
Harshaw Road
06
Washington Camp
07
Duquesne Road
61
Duquesne
Fray Marcos de Niza Historical Monument
Lochiel
61
08
61
61
Duquesne Road
61
Duquesne Road

82
82
Beyerville
09
82

ARIZONA
MEXICO

Shopping, Fast Food
BUSINESS
19
19
Nogales
EXIT 4
EXIT 8
EXIT 1

19

255

Sedona's Broken Arrow (Trail #23), rated difficult.

APPENDIX

Telegraph Line Road (Trail # 45), rated difficult.

GPS Basics

What is GPS? GPS stands for Global Positioning System. Satellites circle the earth and broadcast signals to receiving units below. These signals allow you to determine your position on the earth. Five to 12 satellites can be picked up at any one time. A GPS unit with 12-satellite capability has the best chance of determining your position quickly.

Is GPS necessary? No. Some people prefer to rely on instinct, orienteering and map-reading skills. In many areas roads are well defined and easy to follow. You may travel with people who are familiar with the trail or you may prefer hiring a guide. Most of the trails in this book can be driven without the use of GPS.

Then why should I buy a GPS unit? It's the fastest and easiest way to determine your position. Like any new device, you'll wonder how you got along without it.

What kind of GPS unit do I need? There are many brands and models in all price ranges. It depends on your needs. Don't get one with less than 12 parallel satellite channels. It's handy to be able to download and upload data to a computer, but this is not required. Many GPS units have built-in maps. The amount of detail in the maps is usually a function of price.

How complicated is it to use a GPS unit? My GPS unit came with a small 100-page user's manual. It took a little time to read but it was simple and easy to understand. After a little practice, using the unit becomes second nature. Basic units are much simpler.

What are waypoints and trackpoints? Waypoints are important locations you choose to mark along your route, like where you start, key intersections along the way, and your final destination. Waypoints are recorded when you consciously hit a button. Trackpoints are automatically recorded as you move along. They're often referred to as a breadcrumb trail.

How accurate is GPS? It's gotten much better since the government reduced the *Selective Availability* error. Prior to that they scrambled the signal, allowing a worst-case error of about a 300-ft. radius. Clinton's announcement on May 1, 2000, says that error is now down to 20 meters or about 60 ft. Subsequent tests of the new system are showing even better accuracy. Future supplimental projects, like the FAA's Wide Area Augmentation System (WAAS), promises even more accuracy.

Do I need a computer to use a GPS unit? No, but if you have a computer, you'll be able to do a lot more. You can download waypoints and trackpoints to your home computer onto digital maps and see exactly where you went. You can print maps showing your exact route. You can save a large number of routes to upload to your GPS unit anytime you want. You can exchange routes and maps with friends. You can store many detailed maps in the computer at a very low cost per map. You can see a much bigger picture of a map than what you see on your tiny GPS screen. You can use maps with more detail.

If you use a laptop, you can take it with you and follow your progress on the screen. You can download hundreds of waypoints and trackpoints instantly into your GPS unit and avoid the tedious task of entering them by hand. Most GPS units don't have a keypad, so entering numerical data takes a long time without a computer.

Is a laptop easy to use in the field? No. It's hard to find a good place to set it up. The screen is hard to see in the sun. It's exposed to damage from dust and vibration. I keep mine in its case much of the time and pull it out when I need it. Despite these drawbacks, it has been indispensible at times and saved me many hours of wandering around aimlessly. I know I'll never get lost when I have it with me.

I already have paper maps. Will a GPS unit help me? Yes. You can plot your GPS location on any map that has tick marks along the edge for latitude/longitude or UTM coordinates. You can get a general idea where you are by sighting across the map. To determine your exact position, you'll need to draw lines. (A template is needed with UTM.) Large fold-out maps can be awkward in the car. I like the handy booklet-style format of an atlas like the DeLorme *Arizona Atlas & Gazetteer* or Benchmark's *Arizona Road & Recreation Atlas*.

What's UTM (Universal Transverse Mercator)? It's an alternative to using Latitude/Longitude coordinates. Many people prefer it because it's easier to plot on a map. Most topo maps have ruled UTM grid lines. Others argue that UTM is not as accurate as Lat./Long. Some maps may have only one set of coordinates. Most GPS units give coordinates both ways. Both are given in this book.

What maps do I need? Again it depends on your needs. The greatest amount of detail is shown on USGS 7.5 minute maps, but many maps are needed to cover a large area. Forest Service maps are practical when you're on forest land but don't help in other areas. The BLM also has maps but they vary in quality. Your best buy is an atlas-style map that covers an entire state. If you're using a computer, several companies now offer statewide map packages with the same detail as 7.5 minute maps. A state the size of Arizona requires about 6 CDs for these rasterized maps. The packages also include the software to manipulate the data. Vector quality maps have less detail but cover more area.

What's the difference between rasterized and vector maps? A rasterized image looks like a photograph of the original map. It takes a lot of computer space. When you zoom out you lose detail. Up close, however, it has the best detail. A vector map is a line conversion and looks more like a drawing in flat color. It lacks detail, but looks the same as you zoom in and out. It doesn't require as much computer space and can be downloaded directly into some new GPS units.

What's mapping software do? Among other things, it allows you to manipulate maps on the screen, download and upload your waypoints and trackpoints, save map images and print them out. It finds the next map as you run off the page and switches automatically to the next map when you're moving in your vehicle with your GPS on.

What specific equipment and maps do you use, Mr. Wells? I use a Garmin II Plus GPS receiver. I bought two additional accessories— a dash mount and a computer cord. The computer cord is split with one part that goes to my cigarette lighter which powers the GPS unit. I've never needed an outside antenna.

I have a Dell Inspiron 7000 laptop with a 14.5″ screen, 4 gig HD, 64 MB ram, and 300 MHz. It has two 4-hour batteries, but since I don't leave the computer on all the time, I've never needed the second battery.

I use a CD map package called All Topo Maps by iGage. The Arizona set includes 1,953 USGS 7.5 minute maps, 73 USGS 1:100,000-scale maps and 26 USGS 1:250,000-scale maps. Because of what I do, I have special needs that the average person doesn't. The maps are complete with collars and are as close as you can get to using a real USGS map. The software has an excellent search tool with a large data base. When I have questions, I have no problem getting through on their toll-free tech support number.

What other mapping software is available?
Several other companies have similar mapping packages. National Geographic (now merged with Wildflower) has a statewide rasterized package that's great for the average user. The maps are seamless so you don't have to jump from map to map. They also have small locator maps in the corner of the screen that allow you to figure out your general location more quickly. The maps are enhanced and show shaded relief. The software is very intuitive and easy to use.

DeLorme's strength lies in their vector map package called *Topo USA*. Because vector maps use less computer space, you can buy the entire United States for about the same price as one state of rasterized maps. They also sell smaller regions for even less.

Perhaps the most versatile package is Maptech's *Terrain Navigator 2001*. It has many handy features including the ability to switch back and forth between seamless and individual maps. I also like it's ability to display two maps side by side. The quality of the maps is excellent and it's very user friendly. Like DeLorme, Maptech has a 3-D mode that's a lot of fun, but for everyday use, I prefer using flat topographic maps. Maptech requires that you install each of its CDs, so installation takes a little longer.

Mapping software retails from about $50 to $150 depending upon brand, coverage, and type of graphics. You generally get more coverage with vector maps, but you sacrifice detail. Before you buy, check out everything on the market. There's new software coming out all the time. I can only report what's available today.

How much did you spend on your GPS equipment? My equipment is about two years old now, so take that into consideration. The Garmin II Plus was about $250 plus a little more for the accessories. My Dell laptop was about $3,000. I recently checked the cost of the iGage mapping package; it still sells for about $120. I also carry many folding maps that would be expensive to replace.

I don't want to spend that much but would still like to have a GPS unit. What can I do? The most important thing a GPS unit does is tell you where you are. A simple unit will do that. You can buy a quality GPS unit with basic features for about $100. If you don't have any maps, invest in a DeLorme *Arizona Atlas and Gazetteer*. This has maps of the entire state for about $20. With this you can plot your general position quickly and easily. Simply look along the edge of the map for longitude and latitude. I use this method about 95% of the time.

If you have a home PC, I'd definitely spend a little more for a GPS unit that can download and upload data to your computer. The first time you try to key waypoints into your GPS unit, you'll know why a computer is important.

How can I learn more about GPS? The first thing I did was buy and read a book called *GPS Made Easy* by Lawrence Letham. It explained GPS in easy-to-understand terms. Finding information about GPS units, different brands, etc., is more difficult.

You can find excellent information on the Internet. Check out 4x4books.com, which sells GPS equipment and mapping products. They show and compare most GPS products and have the latest information on new products. You can also contact the manufacturers directly. (See appendix for addresses and telephone numbers.)

Note: The author is not sponsored by any manufacturer.

GPS Waypoint Coordinates

The following table lists waypoints for each trail. Waypoints are shown in Latitude/Longitude and UTM coordinates. All coordinates were recorded after *selective availability error* was reduced by the U.S. government on May 1, 2000. No coordinate should be in error by more than a radius of 20 meters or approximately 60 feet. All coordinates were compiled using All Topo Maps (iGage) software (DATUM=NAD27). Only significant intersections or special features were assigned waypoints.

Wpt.	Mile	Latitude North	Longitude West	UTM Easting	UTM Northing	Zone	Turn*
1. TOROWEAP OVERLOOK							
01	0	36° 52' 44.8"	112° 38' 50.2"	353190E	4082526N	12	L
02	23.0	36° 37' 07.7"	112° 50' 33.5"	335223E	4053965N	12	S
03	40.3	36° 28' 11.4"	113° 01' 47.2"	318137E	4037775N	12	S
04	46.6	36° 23' 20.2"	113° 03' 31.8"	315342E	4028857N	12	L
05	54.1	36° 17' 11.7"	113° 03' 50.0"	314646E	4017511N	12	S
06	57.6	36° 14' 22.0"	113° 04' 22.2"	313731E	4012298N	12	L
07	60.3	36° 12' 53.8"	113° 03' 21.8"	315180E	4009549N	12	T
08	-	36° 12' 41.4"	113° 04' 58.2"	312765E	4009218N	12	-
2. FIRE POINT, TIMP POINT							
01	0	36° 24' 04.6"	112° 07' 44.0"	398769E	4028849N	12	R
02	2.1	36° 24' 39.6"	112° 08' 55.5"	397002E	4029948N	12	L
03	3.2	36° 23' 47.5"	112° 09' 02.6"	396806E	4028345N	12	S
04	4.4	36° 22' 54.4"	112° 08' 31.7"	397556E	4026698N	12	R
05	10.3	36° 22' 13.8"	112° 14' 17.6"	388922E	4025554N	12	S
06	11.1	36° 22' 22.1"	112° 15' 06.7"	387700E	4025825N	12	S
07	17.6	36° 21' 23.0"	112° 21' 23.2"	378292E	4024132N	12	T
08	3.8	36° 23' 00.5"	112° 17' 25.9"	384248E	4027055N	12	L
09	7.9	36° 22' 55.0"	112° 21' 20.2"	378407E	4026966N	12	T
10	8.1	36° 24' 07.6"	112° 14' 04.3"	389298E	4029057N	12	R
3. SADDLE MOUNTAIN ROAD							
01	0	36° 24' 03.9"	112° 07' 42.5"	398807E	4028827N	12	L
02	1.4	36° 23' 35.1"	112° 07' 03.9"	399758E	4027926N	12	R
03	8.1	36° 20' 16.0"	112° 03' 33.1"	404943E	4021734N	12	S
04	13.6	36° 18' 10.7"	112° 59' 38.7"	410746E	4017810N	12	T
05	-	36° 24' 06.9"	112° 03' 46.8"	404679E	4028853N	12	T

---

* R = Right   L = Left   S = Straight   D = Driver's Choice   T = Turnaround

Wpt.	Mile	Latitude North	Longitude West	UTM Easting	UTM Northing	Zone	Turn*
4. POINT SUBLIME							
01	0	36° 13' 28.5"	112° 03' 32.3"	404825E	4009177N	12	R
02	11.9	36° 15' 21.5"	112° 11' 56.7"	392274E	4012806N	12	L
03	17.9	36° 11' 54.4"	112° 14' 59.1"	387640E	4006482N	12	T
04	-	36° 22' 13.8"	112° 14' 17.6"	388922E	4025554N	12	L
5. SOUTH BASS TRAILHEAD							
01	0	35° 59' 24.6"	112° 07' 22.1"	398786E	3983241N	12	-
02	4.9	36° 00' 33.5"	112° 11' 23.1"	392778E	3985435N	12	S
03	14.9	36° 03' 31.9"	112° 19' 20.6"	380898E	3991085N	12	L
04	22.7	36° 06' 18.3"	112° 25' 50.7"	371205E	3996355N	12	R
05	29.7	36° 11' 02.0"	112° 22' 33.4"	376272E	4005020N	12	T
6. GRANDVIEW LOOKOUT							
01	0	35° 58' 07.4"	112° 07' 39.3"	398329E	3980865N	12	-
02	2.7	35° 57' 15.0"	112° 05' 17.3"	401867E	3979212N	12	L
03	6.9	35° 57' 35.6"	112° 01' 38.8"	407349E	3979786N	12	R
04	9.9	35° 55' 38.1"	112° 03' 21.6"	404733E	3976194N	12	L
05	18.8	35° 56' 29.6"	111° 56' 28.1"	415112E	3977674N	12	L
06	20.1	35° 57' 21.8"	111° 57' 14.0"	413977E	3979293N	12	D
07	21.5	35° 58' 05.1"	111° 58' 17.2"	412407E	3980645N	12	L
08	1.8	35° 58' 05.0"	111° 56' 43.7"	414750E	3980617N	12	T
7. SLEEPING PRINCESS							
01	0	35° 11' 43.6"	114° 25' 56.3"	733779E	3897539N	11	-
02	0.4	35° 11' 57.1"	114° 25' 45.7"	734037E	3897962N	11	L
03	2.3	35° 13' 28.5"	114° 26' 02.2"	733547E	3900768N	11	R
04	3.8	35° 13' 52.1"	114° 25' 04.5"	734987E	3901532N	11	L
05	4.6	35° 14' 02.7"	114° 25' 41.5"	734043E	3901835N	11	L
06	6.0	35° 13' 59.2"	114° 24' 39.8"	735606E	3901768N	11	S
07	7.2	35° 14' 26.7"	114° 24' 20.5"	736071E	3902629N	11	S
08	1.8	35° 15' 21.8"	114° 23' 19.8"	737561E	3904367N	11	L
09	6.5	35° 18' 53.2"	114° 24' 38.3"	735407E	3910829N	11	R
10	8.1	35° 19' 06.3"	114° 23' 13.8"	737531E	3911289N	11	S
11	14.7	35° 18' 05.1"	114° 18' 21.4"	744967E	3909600N	11	R
12	19.8	35° 13' 36.4"	114° 18' 21.7"	745186E	3901322N	11	D
8. CHLORIDE MINES							
01	0	35° 24' 51.3"	114° 11' 54.0"	754403E	3922389N	11	S
02	1.9	35° 24' 28.4"	114° 10' 15.4"	756910E	3921756N	11	S
03	3.4	35° 23' 57.6"	114° 09' 35.1"	757954E	3920836N	11	L
04	4.4	35° 24' 26.0"	114° 09' 05.9"	758666E	3921734N	11	S
05	6.0	35° 24' 58.6"	114° 08' 59.8"	758790E	3922743N	11	S
06	7.8	35° 26' 14.4"	114° 09' 27.4"	758026E	3925057N	11	L
07	9.8	35° 27' 08.6"	114° 10' 08.8"	756934E	3926696N	11	S
08	15.1	35° 27' 05.3"	114° 13' 50.3"	751351E	3926437N	11	S
09	18.6	35° 25' 03.3"	114° 16' 23.0"	747606E	3922572N	11	D

Wpt.	Mile	Latitude North	Longitude West	UTM Easting	UTM Northing	Zone	Turn*

9. PASS CANYON

Wpt.	Mile	Latitude North	Longitude West	UTM Easting	UTM Northing	Zone	Turn*
01	0	35° 04' 43.3"	114° 26' 56.8"	732581E	3884549N	11	-
02	0.3	35° 04' 56.7"	114° 26' 42.2"	732940E	3884973N	11	R
03	3.2	35° 05' 50.1"	114° 24' 28.9"	736275E	3886705N	11	R
04	5.8	35° 07' 20.0"	114° 25' 05.8"	735267E	3889451N	11	R
05	7.1	35° 08' 20.8"	114° 24' 39.4"	735887E	3891341N	11	L
06	2.3	35° 07' 07.4"	114° 25' 46.6"	734246E	3889037N	11	S
07	4.0	35° 07' 05.0"	114° 27' 18.2"	731927E	3888902N	11	L
08	5.2	35° 06' 23.1"	114° 26' 46.6"	732760E	3887632N	11	L
09	5.9	35° 05' 55.9"	114° 26' 41.5"	732911E	3886795N	11	L

10. SECRET PASS

Wpt.	Mile	Latitude North	Longitude West	UTM Easting	UTM Northing	Zone	Turn*
01	0	35° 11' 39.3"	114° 24' 24.7"	736101E	3897469N	11	-
02	0.7	35° 11' 08.3"	114° 24' 13.2"	736416E	3896520N	11	L
03	1.5	35° 10' 47.0"	114° 23' 43.9"	737174E	3895883N	11	L
04	2.8	35° 10' 39.9"	114° 22' 57.0"	738367E	3895695N	11	R
05	4.3	35° 10' 24.5"	114° 21' 27.0"	740657E	3895281N	11	R
06	7.6	35° 08' 46.2"	114° 22' 32.1"	739089E	3892207N	11	T
07	1.3	35° 09' 41.4"	114° 22' 34.7"	738978E	3893907N	11	S
08	4.5	35° 09' 21.6"	114° 25' 16.8"	734892E	3893189N	11	R
09	1.7	35° 10' 27.5"	114° 26' 02.2"	733691E	3895192N	11	L
10	3.7	35° 11' 07.1"	114° 27' 14.8"	731823E	3896364N	11	D

11. BACKWAY TO OATMAN

Wpt.	Mile	Latitude North	Longitude West	UTM Easting	UTM Northing	Zone	Turn*
01	0	34° 55' 39.5"	114° 31' 02.9"	726765E	3867633N	11	S
02	0.7	34° 55' 57.7"	114° 30' 22.6"	727773E	3868222N	11	L
03	1.2	34° 56' 07.3"	114° 30' 48.2"	727117E	3868500N	11	R
04	1.9	34° 56' 35.6"	114° 30' 22.4"	727748E	3869387N	11	L
05	2.4	34° 56' 53.0"	114° 30' 08.0"	728099E	3869935N	11	L
06	4.8	34° 58' 11.3"	114° 28' 21.0"	730755E	3872416N	11	S
07	6.5	34° 59' 01.7"	114° 26' 59.6"	732778E	3874021N	11	R
08	7.9	34° 58' 56.5"	114° 26' 01.5"	734256E	3873898N	11	L

12. MOSS WASH

Wpt.	Mile	Latitude North	Longitude West	UTM Easting	UTM Northing	Zone	Turn*
01	0	35° 01' 39.2"	113° 48' 46.2"	243369E	3879518N	12	R
02	1.8	35° 01' 35.8"	113° 50' 09.8"	241247E	3879475N	12	S
03	3.6	35° 01' 42.9"	113° 51' 23.7"	239380E	3879745N	12	R
04	6.3	35° 01' 53.6"	113° 53' 39.1"	235957E	3880176N	12	R
05	8.2	35° 02' 51.9"	113° 52' 46.5"	237341E	3881932N	12	L
06	9.7	35° 03' 51.2"	113° 51' 59.5"	238585E	3883727N	12	L
07	10.3	35° 04' 07.5"	113° 52' 06.9"	238414E	3884234N	12	R
08	13.5	35° 05' 33.1"	113° 52' 28.4"	237944E	3886888N	12	L

* R = Right   L = Left   S = Straight   D = Driver's Choice   T = Turnaround

Wpt.	Mile	Latitude North	Longitude West	UTM Easting	UTM Northing	Zone	Turn*
13. HUALAPAI MOUNTAINS							
01	0	35° 05' 33.7"	113° 52' 28.9"	237931E	3886906N	12	R
02	3.3	35° 04' 07.6"	113° 52' 07.6"	238395E	3884237N	12	R
03	16.4	34° 57' 35.6"	113° 54' 49.3"	233945E	3872276N	12	R
04	19.9	34° 56' 06.2"	113° 55' 00.8"	233572E	3869530N	12	S
05	34.1	34° 50' 58.3"	114° 06' 35.5"	215647E	3860570N	12	R
14. LOCKETT MEADOW							
01	0	35° 22' 19.5"	111° 34' 32.5"	447703E	3914262N	12	-
02	1.7	35° 22' 25.2"	111° 35' 51.7"	445707E	3914449N	12	R
03	4.5	35° 21' 37.8"	111° 37' 07.8"	443776E	3912999N	12	R
15. SCHULTZ PASS							
01	0	35° 14' 13.7"	111° 39' 58.5"	439377E	3899347N	12	R
02	6.0	35° 17' 18.4"	111° 37' 09.1"	443694E	3905008N	12	S
03	14.6	35° 22' 19.5"	111° 34' 32.5"	447703E	3914262N	12	-
16. ELDEN MOUNTAIN							
01	0	35° 14' 22.9"	111° 39' 38.5"	439886E	3899628N	12	S
02	6.3	35° 14' 45.4"	111° 36' 10.3"	445150E	3900285N	12	D
17. CINDER HILLS OHV AREA							
01	0	35° 19' 42.5"	111° 32' 40.6"	450502E	3909409N	12	R
02	2.6	35° 20' 00.5"	111° 30' 16.2"	454151E	3909943N	12	S
03	5.2	35° 20' 01.7"	111° 28' 01.4"	457553E	3909962N	12	S
04	6.3	35° 20' 04.7"	111° 26' 54.4"	459245E	3910049N	12	L
05	6.6	35° 20' 27.4"	111° 26' 59.9"	459110E	3910748N	12	D
18. SOLDIER PASS							
01	0	34° 53' 00.6"	111° 46' 58.6"	428452E	3860205N	12	-
02	0.2	34° 53' 11.4"	111° 47' 01.1"	428392E	3860539N	12	S
03	0.5	34° 53' 26.7"	111° 47' 08.3"	428212E	3861012N	12	S
04	0.9	34° 53' 46.0"	111° 47' 12.0"	428122E	3861608N	12	T
19. VAN DEREN CABIN							
01	0	34° 53' 16.0"	111° 49' 18.4"	424907E	3860710N	12	R
02	2.3	34° 54' 54.4"	111° 48' 31.2"	426128E	3863730N	12	L
03	2.7	34° 54' 59.8"	111° 48' 43.8"	425812E	3863899N	12	T
20. SCHNEBLY HILL ROAD							
01	0	34° 51' 43.8"	111° 45' 38.0"	430480E	3857823N	12	-
02	6.3	34° 53' 21.9"	111° 42' 08.5"	435820E	3860808N	12	S
03	11.9	34° 54' 43.0"	111° 38' 32.8"	441310E	3863270N	12	R

Wpt.	Mile	Latitude North	Longitude West	UTM Easting	UTM Northing	Zone	Turn*
21. GREASY SPOON							
01	0	34° 53' 09.7"	111° 53' 33.1"	418440E	3860570N	12	L
02	2.8	34° 51' 42.0"	111° 52' 04.8"	420658E	3857850N	12	R
03	5.8	34° 51' 20.1"	111° 54' 48.1"	416506E	3857211N	12	L
22. OAK CREEK HOMESTEAD							
01	0	34° 50' 38.9"	111° 50' 54.9"	422415E	3855890N	12	L
02	1.0	34° 49' 47.3"	111° 51' 11.6"	421979E	3854305N	12	R
03	2.0	34° 49'11.6"	111° 51' 42.7"	421179E	3853211N	12	R
04	2.4	34° 49' 03.2"	111° 51' 55.8"	420843E	3852956N	12	L
05	3.0	34° 48' 43.3"	111° 52' 07.5"	420542E	3852344N	12	L
06	4.0	34° 48' 03.2"	111° 52' 08.5"	420504E	3851109N	12	R
07	7.1	34° 49' 38.2"	111° 52' 55.2"	419344E	3854046N	12	S
08	8.0	34° 50' 06.3"	111° 53' 22.0"	418667E	3854919N	12	D
23. BROKEN ARROW							
01	0	34° 50' 45.8"	111° 45' 28.4"	430711E	3856036N	12	S
02	0.5	34° 50' 29.9"	111° 45' 15.5"	431035E	3855545N	12	L
03	1.0	34° 50' 14.7"	111° 44' 56.7"	431509E	3855074N	12	L
04	1.1	34° 50' 12.3"	111° 44' 53.6"	431585E	3854997N	12	L
05	1.7	34° 49' 58.5"	111° 45' 03.1"	431341E	3854575N	12	S
06	2.0	34° 49' 45.9"	111° 45' 13.6"	431071E	3854187N	12	T
24. HUTCH MOUNTAIN							
01	0	34° 45' 49.6"	111° 39' 17.1"	440080E	3846847N	12	-
02	7.9	34° 46' 47.7"	111° 31' 38.8"	451741E	3848567N	12	D
03	15.3	34° 47' 20.9"	111° 26' 37.7"	459397E	3849551N	12	L
04	0	34° 48' 24.1"	111° 26' 07.2"	460181E	3851496N	12	R
05	4.4	34° 48' 06.1"	111° 23' 22.2"	464371E	3850924N	12	T
25. SMILEY ROCK							
01	0	34° 45' 06.7"	112° 07' 00.6"	397775E	3845896N	12	-
02	0.9	34° 45' 26.9"	112° 07' 44.0"	396680E	3846531N	12	R
03	7.7	34° 47' 06.2"	112° 10' 20.0"	392749E	3849636N	12	L
04	14.4	34° 45' 47.8"	112° 13' 50.3"	387376E	3847286N	12	L
05	15.2	34° 45' 14.2"	112° 13' 27.0"	387955E	3846243N	12	S
06	16.1	34° 44' 49.7"	112° 12' 57.2"	388703E	3845480N	12	L
07	17.7	34° 44' 23.2"	112° 11' 31.6"	390871E	3844635N	12	S
08	20.4	34° 43' 20.5"	112° 10' 41.4"	392123E	3842691N	12	L
09	22.2	34° 42' 55.7"	112° 09' 34.4"	393820E	3841907N	12	R
10	22.8	34° 42' 26.1"	112° 09' 23.9"	394076E	3840992N	12	S
11	23.3	34° 42'26.8"	112° 08' 57.8"	394739E	3841004N	12	D

* R = Right   L = Left   S = Straight   D = Driver's Choice   T = Turnaround

Wpt.	Mile	Latitude North	Longitude West	UTM Easting	UTM Northing	Zone	Turn*
26. MINGUS MOUNTAIN							
01	0	34° 44' 16.1"	112° 02' 05.6"	405261E	3844258N	12	-
02	6.2	34° 42' 01.0"	112° 05' 46.1"	399609E	3840156N	12	S
03	17.4	34° 41' 53.0"	112° 08' 17.4"	395757E	3839952N	12	L
04	18.8	34° 42' 27.2"	112° 08' 55.2"	394806E	3841017N	12	D
27. CROSSMAN PEAK							
01	0	34° 25' 09.1"	114° 11' 54.8"	757472E	3812001N	11	-
02	5.2	34° 20' 12.8"	114° 08' 35.1"	762413E	3817803N	11	L
03	9.3	34° 29' 38.1"	114° 05' 28.4"	767101E	3820569N	11	L
04	14.1	34° 32' 25.2"	114° 06' 01.8"	766103E	3825694N	11	S
05	18.4	34° 35' 38.6"	114° 05' 53.0"	766154E	3831659N	11	L
06	25.2	34° 36' 36.9"	114° 10' 40.1"	758789E	3833248N	11	R
07	29.6	34° 39' 56.7"	114° 10' 44.4"	758508E	3839403N	11	L
08	36.3	34° 43' 59.2"	114° 15' 23.8"	751189E	3846677N	11	D
28. MOHAVE WASH							
01	0	34° 25' 09.1"	114° 11' 54.8"	757472E	3812001N	11	L
02	5.2	34° 28' 12.4"	114° 08' 35.6"	762400E	3817791N	11	L
03	9.3	34° 29' 38.0"	114° 05' 28.4"	767103E	3820564N	11	R
04	17.0	34° 25' 32.3"	114° 01' 07.6"	773981E	3813188N	11	R
05	18.9	34° 24' 07.2"	114° 01' 25.0"	773612E	3810553N	11	R
06	23.4	34° 26' 09.1"	114° 04' 24.4"	768922E	3814174N	11	S
29. VAMPIRE MINE							
01	0	34° 17' 41.3"	114° 05' 49.4"	767199E	3798465N	11	L
02	3.3	34° 16' 50.3"	114° 02' 53.0"	770796E	3796788N	11	S
03	6.8	34° 15' 17.2"	114° 00' 35.7"	775354E	3794258N	11	R
04	9.8	34° 12' 54.3"	113° 59' 53.5"	776563E	3789885N	11	R
05	10.5	34° 12' 36.1"	114° 00' 23.8"	775803E	3789302N	11	R
06	11.3	34° 12' 17.9"	114° 01' 00.7"	774876E	3788711N	11	R
07	12.1	34° 12' 50.3"	114° 01' 10.8"	774588E	3789705N	11	S
08	12.8	34° 13' 09.4"	114° 01' 05.4"	774711E	3790296N	11	S
09	14.2	34° 12' 36.3"	114° 00' 15.6"	776014E	3789313N	11	D
30. SWANSEA TOWNSITE							
01	0	34° 17' 40.7"	114° 05' 46.4"	767276E	3798448N	11	L
02	3.3	34° 16' 21.7"	114° 03' 09.9"	771349E	3796129N	11	S
03	6.8	34° 15' 13.6"	114° 00' 33.5"	775412E	3794146N	11	R
04	9.5	34° 13' 06.6"	113° 59' 56.8"	776466E	3790261N	11	L
05	10.7	34° 12' 31.9"	113° 59' 19.8"	777446E	3789220N	11	L
06	12.2	34° 11' 42.8"	113° 58' 07.3"	779346E	3787763N	11	R
07	17.4	34° 08' 16.3"	113° 55' 36.6"	783399E	3781514N	11	L
08	24.4	34° 10' 12.8"	113° 50' 44.5"	790772E	3785334N	11	R
09	18.4	34° 07' 28.2"	114° 04' 30.0"	769773E	3779630N	11	L
10	31.7	34° 07' 46.8"	114° 16' 43.3"	750965E	3779685N	11	D

Wpt.	Mile	Latitude North	Longitude West	UTM Easting	UTM Northing	Zone	Turn*
31. BUCKSKIN MOUNTAINS							
01	0	34° 15' 22.5"	114° 08' 44.5"	762841E	3794060N	11	L
02	1.0	34° 14' 43.1"	114° 09' 05.4"	762340E	3792833N	11	S
03	3.3	34° 13' 06.0"	114° 08' 30.8"	763310E	3789863N	11	S
04	4.0	34° 12' 51.2"	114° 09' 03.0"	762499E	3789385N	11	L
05	5.3	34° 12' 03.4"	114° 09' 08.5"	762400E	3787907N	11	L
06	5.5	34° 12' 03.3"	114° 08' 56.4"	762709E	3787915N	11	T
07	4.8	34° 11' 25.6"	114° 12' 33.4"	757185E	3786600N	11	D
32. CATTAIL COVE							
01	0	34° 19' 58.6"	114° 08' 08.1"	763533E	3802596N	11	-
02	0.3	34° 20' 14.4"	114° 08' 10.3"	763461E	3803081N	11	R
03	0.5	34° 20' 11.6"	114° 07' 58.6"	763764E	3803002N	11	S
04	1.6	34° 20' 35.1"	114° 07' 55.1"	763832E	3803727N	11	R
05	3.9	34° 20' 03.6"	114° 06' 02.1"	766749E	3802840N	11	R
06	4.2	34° 19' 50.7"	114° 06' 05.6"	766671E	3802441N	11	T
07	7.2	34° 18' 46.5"	114° 04' 38.6"	768953E	3800527N	11	D
08	8.8	34° 17' 57.8"	114° 05' 06.4"	768283E	3799005N	11	T
33. PRESIDENT'S CHOICE							
01	0	34° 11' 09.2"	114° 12' 06.2"	757896E	3786112N	11	R
02	0.1	34° 11' 08.2"	114° 12' 10.2"	757793E	3786077N	11	R
03	0.5	34° 11' 13.0"	114° 12' 36.1"	757126E	3786207N	11	L
04	1.0	34° 10' 58.9"	114° 12' 28.3"	757338E	3785779N	11	S
05	1.3	34° 11' 01.3"	114° 12' 18.1"	757598E	3785860N	11	S
34. BRADSHAW MOUNTAINS							
01	0	34° 08' 10.0"	112° 08' 49.4"	394237E	3777647N	12	-
02	10.5	34° 15' 21.4"	112° 10' 30.2"	391807E	3790965N	12	S
03	14.9	34° 16' 42.2"	112° 13' 56.6"	386558E	3793515N	12	S
04	28.8	34° 11' 57.1"	112° 20' 21.0"	376615E	3784860N	12	D
05	6.5	34° 09' 39.9"	112° 17' 30.5"	380923E	3780576N	12	T
06	14.1	34° 19' 12.1"	112° 22' 02.6"	374192E	3798292N	12	S
07	17.1	34° 21' 24.3"	112° 22' 24.9"	373679E	3802373N	12	R
08	29.0	34° 23' 55.2"	112° 13' 42.0"	387094E	3806849N	12	D
35. DESOTO MINE							
01	0	34° 19' 12.6"	112° 22' 04.3"	374151E	3798309N	12	L
02	2.1	34° 18' 15.5"	112° 20' 31.0"	376510E	3796516N	12	L
03	4.0	34° 17' 58.0"	112° 19' 19.8"	378324E	3795953N	12	R
04	4.7	34° 18' 01.8"	112° 18' 59.9"	378835E	3796066N	12	L
05	7.2	34° 17' 38.9"	112° 17' 22.6"	381312E	3795326N	12	L
06	8.5	34° 17' 08.6"	112° 16' 57.5"	381943E	3794387N	12	L
07	11.7	34° 16' 37.3"	112° 15' 09.8"	384685E	3793389N	12	D

* R = Right   L = Left   S = Straight   D = Driver's Choice   T = Turnaround

Wpt.	Mile	Latitude North	Longitude West	UTM Easting	UTM Northing	Zone	Turn*

36. WICKENBURG MOUNTAINS

Wpt.	Mile	Latitude North	Longitude West	UTM Easting	UTM Northing	Zone	Turn*
01	0	33° 58' 18.7"	112° 43' 21.6"	340849E	3760178N	12	-
02	8.6	34° 02' 32.4"	112° 36' 43.0"	351205E	3767827N	12	R
03	13.0	34° 02' 53.9"	112° 33' 22.1"	356365E	3768408N	12	L
04	16.8	34° 05' 03.2"	112° 31' 49.8"	358792E	3772357N	12	R
05	20.6	34° 04' 50.2"	112° 29' 35.3"	362235E	3771906N	12	S
06	23.2	34° 04' 17.6"	112° 28' 22.4"	364088E	3770875N	12	R
07	24.6	34° 04' 39.4"	112° 27' 54.1"	364823E	3771535N	12	T

37. CASTLE HOT SPRINGS ROAD

Wpt.	Mile	Latitude North	Longitude West	UTM Easting	UTM Northing	Zone	Turn*
01	0	33° 51' 12.4"	112° 37' 16.4"	350016E	3746896N	12	R
02	20.8	34° 00' 03.4"	112° 23' 47.6"	371024E	3762946N	12	R
03	23.5	33° 58' 59.8"	112° 21' 49.2"	374036E	3760944N	12	S
04	28.0	33° 56' 09.8"	112° 19' 26.2"	377637E	3755660N	12	S
05	31.0	33° 54' 29.6"	112° 19' 21.7"	377715E	3752573N	12	R
06	36.5	33° 50' 04.3"	112° 18' 53.3"	378340E	3744393N	12	D

38. BACKWAY TO CROWN KING

Wpt.	Mile	Latitude North	Longitude West	UTM Easting	UTM Northing	Zone	Turn*
01	0	33° 50' 04.0"	112° 18' 52.4"	378362E	3744382N	12	R
02	8.5	33° 56' 09.3"	112° 19' 25.7"	377651E	3755645N	12	R
03	16.2	34° 01' 10.8"	112° 20' 12.5"	376570E	3764947N	12	S
04	20.2	34° 03' 38.4"	112° 21' 53.5"	374040E	3769530N	12	R
05	26.4	34° 07' 44.7"	112° 21' 37.7"	374548E	3777110N	12	S
06	30.4	34° 10' 20.6"	112° 21' 36.9"	374632E	3781912N	12	R
07	31.3	34° 10' 14.5"	112° 20' 51.2"	375798E	3781709N	12	L
08	34.4	34° 12' 20.0"	112° 20' 12.7"	376835E	3785559N	12	D

39. NEW RIVER CANYON

Wpt.	Mile	Latitude North	Longitude West	UTM Easting	UTM Northing	Zone	Turn*
01	0	33° 58' 05.5"	112° 07' 34.3"	395956E	3759007N	12	-
02	4.4	33° 58' 20.0"	112° 03' 45.1"	401841E	3759388N	12	R
03	13.7	34° 00' 34.1"	111° 57' 14.0"	411918E	3763422N	12	R
04	19.5	34° 00' 32.5"	111° 52' 45.0"	418816E	3763310N	12	R
05	13.3	33° 52' 42.2"	111° 48' 54.0"	424628E	3748776N	12	S
06	26.3	33° 47' 57.7"	111° 57' 46.7"	410859E	3740131N	12	R

40. HARQUAHALA PEAK

Wpt.	Mile	Latitude North	Longitude West	UTM Easting	UTM Northing	Zone	Turn*
01	0	33° 43' 40.6"	113° 17' 34.9"	287546E	3734160N	12	-
02	3.8	33° 45' 49.7"	113° 19' 40.2"	284410E	3738208N	12	L
03	10.6	33° 48' 41.5"	113° 20' 44.8"	282866E	3743541N	12	T

269

Wpt.	Mile	Latitude North	Longitude West	UTM Easting	UTM Northing	Zone	Turn*
41. BELMONT MOUNTAIN							
01	0	33° 43' 04.5"	112° 52' 48.7"	325780E	3732273N	12	S
02	5.8	33° 38' 48.6"	112° 55' 24.6"	321620E	3724465N	12	L
03	6.3	33° 38' 35.2"	112° 55' 45.8"	321065E	3724062N	12	S
04	6.6	33° 38' 37.3"	112° 55' 58.2"	320747E	3724134N	12	T
05	4.6	33° 35' 11.1"	112° 55' 06.7"	321958E	3717756N	12	S
06	7.3	33° 33' 06.4"	112° 54' 05.7"	323459E	3713887N	12	L
07	12.3	33° 29' 38.2"	112° 53' 03.7"	324942E	3707443N	12	R
42. RENO PASS							
01	0	33° 52' 12.0"	111° 27' 50.9"	457072E	3747644N	12	R
02	1.1	33° 51' 25.2"	111° 27' 18.2"	457905E	3746199N	12	L
03	2.4	33° 51' 16.2"	111° 26' 11.7"	459614E	3745914N	12	L
04	5.7	33° 52' 50.2"	111° 24' 18.8"	462526E	3748798N	12	L
05	6.6	33° 52' 59.1"	111° 23' 31.2"	463749E	3749067N	12	S
06	9.3	33° 53' 02.4"	111° 21' 10.2"	467371E	3749157N	12	S
07	11.9	33° 52' 35.9"	111° 18' 54.8"	470848E	3748327N	12	D
43. SUNFLOWER MINE							
01	0	33° 55' 52.4"	111° 27' 48.6"	457162E	3754433N	12	R
02	3.8	33° 56' 29.0"	111° 28' 55.9"	455439E	3755566N	12	S
03	5.6	33° 57' 27.2"	111° 29' 27.6"	454634E	3757364N	12	S
04	6.5	33° 57' 56.2"	111° 28' 49.4"	455619E	3758251N	12	R
05	7.4	33° 58' 04.9"	111° 28' 13.1"	456552E	3758515N	12	R
06	9.5	33° 58' 03.5"	111° 26' 57.4"	458492E	3758465N	12	R
44. FOUR PEAKS							
01	0	33° 40' 41.3"	111° 30' 07.1"	453468E	3726388N	12	R
02	2.1	33° 40' 00.6"	111° 28' 24.0"	456120E	3725124N	12	L
03	11.1	33° 43' 31.7"	111° 24' 05.7"	462795E	3731598N	12	S
04	18.2	33° 43' 15.7"	111° 20' 12.8"	468789E	3731082N	12	L
05	23.4	33° 45' 05.8"	111° 18' 23.0"	471624E	3734465N	12	L
06	27.8	33° 47' 17.2"	111° 15' 53.8"	475473E	3738501N	12	D
45. TELEGRAPH LINE ROAD							
01	0	33° 52' 20.2"	111° 37' 22.3"	442393E	3747976N	12	L
02	2.4	33° 53' 25.2"	111° 39' 02.3"	439835E	3749992N	12	R
03	4.4	33° 54' 23.3"	111° 39' 51.6"	438580E	3751789N	12	L
04	5.2	33° 54' 35.0"	111° 40' 10.8"	438091E	3752153N	12	L
05	6.2	33° 55' 04.8"	111° 40' 42.4"	437285E	3753077N	12	L
06	3.2	33° 53' 16.1"	111° 42' 35.5"	434357E	3749748N	12	L
07	5.7	33° 51' 34.6"	111° 42' 12.7"	434921E	3746618N	12	R

* R = Right   L = Left   S = Straight   D = Driver's Choice   T = Turnaround

Wpt.	Mile	Latitude North	Longitude West	UTM Easting	UTM Northing	Zone	Turn*

46. BULLDOG CANYON

Wpt.	Mile	Latitude North	Longitude West	UTM Easting	UTM Northing	Zone	Turn*
01	0	33° 33' 03.6"	111° 34' 50.9"	446082E	3712332N	12	-
02	2.2	33° 31' 20.0"	111° 34' 27.9"	446657E	3709138N	12	S
03	5.5	33° 29' 19.9"	111° 33' 13.2"	448563E	3705427N	12	S
04	8.4	33° 27' 56.8"	111° 31' 52.9"	450624E	3702859N	12	R

47. APACHE TRAIL

Wpt.	Mile	Latitude North	Longitude West	UTM Easting	UTM Northing	Zone	Turn*
01	0	33° 27' 51.8"	111° 28' 52.6"	455276E	3702683N	12	S
02	17.2	33° 32' 15.3"	111° 19' 27.8"	469881E	3710739N	12	S
03	39.2	33° 40' 20.7"	111° 09' 08.3"	485882E	3725651N	12	D

48. MONTANA MOUNTAIN

Wpt.	Mile	Latitude North	Longitude West	UTM Easting	UTM Northing	Zone	Turn*
01	0	33° 18' 03.3"	111° 14' 38.3"	477285E	3684480N	12	-
02	9.4	33° 23' 54.6"	111° 11' 47.0"	481736E	3695291N	12	R
03	13.1	33° 25' 02.5"	111° 10' 25.7"	483840E	3697378N	12	R
04	22.0	33° 22' 08.0"	111° 06' 59.7"	489156E	3691995N	12	R
05	28.2	33° 17' 44.2"	111° 08' 51.4"	486256E	3683877N	12	R
06	30.0	33° 16' 51.2"	111° 10' 14.8"	484096E	3682248N	12	L

49. HACKBERRY CREEK

Wpt.	Mile	Latitude North	Longitude West	UTM Easting	UTM Northing	Zone	Turn*
01	0	33° 17' 54.4"	111° 03' 32.1"	494514E	3684183N	12	L
02	2.4	33° 16' 36.8"	111° 02' 28.3"	496164E	3681791N	12	R
03	5.1	33° 14' 47.4"	111° 02' 55.1"	495470E	3678422N	12	L
04	5.4	33° 14' 54.6"	111° 02' 35.8"	495969E	3678644N	12	L
05	6.1	33° 15' 25.9"	111° 02' 26.3"	496215E	3679608N	12	L

50. WOODPECKER MINE

Wpt.	Mile	Latitude North	Longitude West	UTM Easting	UTM Northing	Zone	Turn*
01	0	33° 12' 01.9"	111° 13' 22.2"	479230E	3673347N	12	L
02	0.5	33° 12' 17.3"	111° 13' 06.5"	479639E	3673822N	12	R
03	1.0	33° 12' 31.9"	111° 12' 51.9"	480017E	3674271N	12	S
04	2.3	33° 12' 50.9"	111° 12' 09.3"	481120E	3674853N	12	R
05	3.1	33° 12' 33.8"	111° 11' 37.1"	481954E	3674326N	12	R
06	3.4	33° 12' 22.1"	111° 11' 31.9"	482087E	3673963N	12	R
07	4.6	33° 11' 58.0"	111° 12' 28.9"	480611E	3673224N	12	S
08	5.3	33° 11' 50.7"	111° 13' 00.7"	479787E	3673001N	12	S

51. AJAX MINE

Wpt.	Mile	Latitude North	Longitude West	UTM Easting	UTM Northing	Zone	Turn*
01	0	33° 11' 50.2"	111° 12' 59.7"	479814E	3672986N	12	L
02	0.8	33° 11' 59.2"	111° 12' 32.7"	480511E	3673262N	12	R
03	1.2	33° 11' 55.2"	111° 12' 14.2"	480990E	3673138N	12	L
04	1.9	33° 12' 10.4"	111° 11' 42.0"	481824E	3673606N	12	R
05	2.0	33° 12' 13.2"	111° 11' 40.6"	481862E	3673692N	12	R
06	2.2	33° 12' 20.4"	111° 11' 33.4"	482047E	3673913N	12	D
07	3.0	33° 12' 26.1"	111° 11' 01.8"	482868E	3674085N	12	L

Wpt.	Mile	Latitude North	Longitude West	UTM Easting	UTM Northing	Zone	Turn*

52. MARTINEZ CABIN

Wpt.	Mile	Latitude North	Longitude West	UTM Easting	UTM Northing	Zone	Turn*
01	0	33° 10' 44.1"	111° 21' 04.4"	467255E	3670985N	12	-
02	5.1	33° 11' 35.3"	111° 16' 02.0"	475092E	3672538N	12	S
03	8.1	33° 12' 09.3"	111° 13' 26.8"	479112E	3673578N	12	R
04	0.3	33° 12' 01.5"	111° 13' 20.0"	479287E	3673337N	12	R
05	0.7	33° 11' 50.2"	111° 13' 01.4"	479769E	3672988N	12	S
06	3.0	33° 10' 26.6"	111° 12' 10.6"	481079E	3670409N	12	S
07	5.2	33° 08' 58.8"	111° 12' 02.6"	481280E	3667705N	12	L
08	6.4	33° 09' 29.4"	111° 11' 14.4"	482531E	3668646N	12	R
09	7.3	33° 09' 11.3"	111° 10' 34.0"	483575E	3668088N	12	L
10	7.9	33° 09' 29.5"	111° 10' 10.6"	484183E	3668644N	12	L
11	8.8	33° 09' 52.4"	111° 09' 37.2"	485051E	3669350N	12	T

53. MARTINEZ CANYON

Wpt.	Mile	Latitude North	Longitude West	UTM Easting	UTM Northing	Zone	Turn*
01	0	33° 09' 52.4"	111° 09' 37.2"	485051E	3669350N	12	S
02	0.5	33° 10' 02.8"	111° 09' 15.7"	485607E	3669671N	12	S
03	1.3	33° 10' 27.5"	111° 09' 25.1"	485364E	3670429N	12	S
04	2.0	33° 10' 18.1"	111° 09' 36.6"	485066E	3670141N	12	S

54. JACK HANDLE

Wpt.	Mile	Latitude North	Longitude West	UTM Easting	UTM Northing	Zone	Turn*
01	0	33° 09' 29.6"	111° 11' 14.5"	482527E	3668652N	12	L
02	1.2	33° 10' 14.7"	111° 11' 03.6"	482813E	3670041N	12	L

55. BOX CANYON

Wpt.	Mile	Latitude North	Longitude West	UTM Easting	UTM Northing	Zone	Turn*
01	0	33° 08' 58.6"	111° 12' 02.3"	481289E	3667698N	12	S
02	2.0	33° 07' 48.5"	111° 12' 23.0"	480748E	3665540N	12	S
03	5.2	33° 05' 48.8"	111° 13' 55.2"	478350E	3661860N	12	R
04	15.7	33° 03' 29.7"	111° 22' 41.1"	464702E	3657617N	12	D

56. COKE OVENS

Wpt.	Mile	Latitude North	Longitude West	UTM Easting	UTM Northing	Zone	Turn*
01	0	33° 09' 11.2"	111° 10' 34.3"	483569E	3668083N	12	R
02	2.7	33° 07' 31.1"	111° 10' 12.8"	484120E	3665000N	12	L
03	5.3	33° 06' 16.2"	111° 09' 50.8"	484686E	3662691N	12	T

57. WALNUT CANYON

Wpt.	Mile	Latitude North	Longitude West	UTM Easting	UTM Northing	Zone	Turn*
01	0	33° 10' 45.2"	111° 02' 19.6"	496385E	3670964N	12	R
02	1.3	33° 09' 49.3"	111° 02' 56.3"	495434E	3669244N	12	R
03	5.3	33° 09' 00.5"	111° 05' 32.5"	491385E	3667744N	12	L
04	8.3	33° 07' 59.2"	111° 04' 00.4"	493771E	3665855N	12	R
05	9.3	33° 07' 12.2"	111° 04' 10.8"	493500E	3664408N	12	R
06	10.7	33° 06' 58.9"	111° 05' 17.0"	491786E	3663998N	12	R
07	11.9	33° 07' 52.5"	111° 05' 04.8"	492102E	3665649N	12	L

* R = Right   L = Left   S = Straight   D = Driver's Choice   T = Turnaround

Wpt.	Mile	Latitude North	Longitude West	UTM Easting	UTM Northing	Zone	Turn*

58. PLOMOSA MOUNTAINS

Wpt.	Mile	Latitude North	Longitude West	UTM Easting	UTM Northing	Zone	Turn*
01	0	33° 46' 39.3"	114° 06' 43.1"	767446E	3741050N	11	L
02	0.5	33° 46' 45.8"	114° 06' 18.9"	768063E	3741270N	11	L
03	5.3	33° 50' 10.1"	114° 08' 16.4"	764865E	3747481N	11	R
04	7.0	33° 50' 31.3"	114° 06' 53.1"	766988E	3748192N	11	L
05	9.5	33° 51' 52.7"	114° 05' 25.3"	769174E	3750765N	11	S
06	10.0	33° 51' 31.6"	114° 05' 11.2"	769555E	3750125N	11	L
07	10.8	33° 51' 44.7"	114° 04' 42.1"	770292E	3750550N	11	R
08	11.2	33° 51' 36.5"	114° 04' 16.4"	770960E	3750317N	11	L
09	14.0	33° 52' 45.2"	114° 01' 54.5"	774546E	3752536N	11	D

59. SAND BOWL OHV AREA

Wpt.	Mile	Latitude North	Longitude West	UTM Easting	UTM Northing	Zone	Turn*
01	0	33° 36' 11.1"	114° 31' 29.1"	729674E	3720700N	11	L
02	1.0	33° 35' 23.8"	114° 31' 21.0"	729919E	3719250N	11	L

60. DRIPPING SPRINGS

Wpt.	Mile	Latitude North	Longitude West	UTM Easting	UTM Northing	Zone	Turn*
01	0	33° 40' 30.3"	114° 04' 38.7"	770969E	3729772N	11	R
02	1.0	33° 39' 49.3"	114° 04' 00.2"	771997E	3728537N	11	R
03	1.4	33° 39' 31.6"	114° 04' 08.0"	771812E	3727984N	11	R
04	2.4	33° 38' 52.0"	114° 04' 26.9"	771360E	3726752N	11	L
05	4.1	33° 37' 48.8"	114° 04' 32.4"	771273E	3724799N	11	L
06	5.1	33° 37' 15.0"	114° 04' 19.4"	771637E	3723767N	11	R
07	6.1	33° 36' 44.3"	114° 04' 46.9"	770954E	3722803N	11	L
08	6.3	33° 36' 38.8"	114° 04' 42.3"	771329E	3722949N	11	T
09	0.5	33° 36' 22.0"	114° 04' 59.4"	770653E	3722105N	11	S
10	2.8	33° 35' 41.7"	114° 06' 48.4"	767877E	3720786N	11	S
11	6.6	33° 37' 02.1"	114° 09' 60.0"	762868E	3723126N	11	S
12	9.9	33° 38 '59.0"	114° 12' 12.9"	759943E	3726636N	11	L
13	10.7	33° 39' 06.3"	114° 12' 58.2"	758172E	3726827N	11	D

61. PALM CANYON

Wpt.	Mile	Latitude North	Longitude West	UTM Easting	UTM Northing	Zone	Turn*
01	0	33° 23' 15.3"	114° 12' 55.6"	759024E	3697530N	11	-
02	3.4	33° 22' 18.1"	114° 09' 50.6"	763855E	3695897N	11	S
03	7.2	33° 21' 37.8"	114° 06' 19.7"	769341E	3694803N	11	T

62. CASTLE DOME MOUNTAINS

Wpt.	Mile	Latitude North	Longitude West	UTM Easting	UTM Northing	Zone	Turn*
01	0	33° 16' 01.3"	114° 14' 17.7"	757258E	3684100N	11	-
02	2.2	33° 14' 46.4"	114° 12' 35.8"	759957E	3681864N	11	R
03	5.1	33° 12' 38.4"	114° 12' 07.5"	760795E	3677940N	11	T
04	4.1	33° 14' 03.8"	114° 08' 47.9"	765893E	3680711N	11	R
05	10.3	33° 09' 14.8"	114° 08' 11.7"	767073E	3671832N	11	R
06	21.0	33° 02' 07.7"	114° 10' 55.4"	763184E	3658559N	11	L
07	37.3	33° 02' 03.6"	114° 05' 48.6"	771149E	3658649N	11	T
08	54.0	32° 57' 40.9"	114° 17' 32.1"	753101E	3650068N	11	D

Wpt.	Mile	Latitude North	Longitude West	UTM Easting	UTM Northing	Zone	Turn*
63. LAGUNA MOUNTAIN RIDGE							
01	0	32° 45' 31.8"	114° 25' 58.2"	740504E	3627277N	11	-
02	2.7	32° 46' 43.3"	114° 27' 32.2"	738002E	3629422N	11	R
03	4.1	32° 47' 00.0"	114° 28' 41.7"	736182E	3629893N	11	R
04	7.3	32° 48' 02.0"	114° 29' 55.2"	734225E	3631759N	11	D
64. OATMAN MASSACRE SITE							
01	0	32° 52' 34.9"	113° 13' 08.5"	292392E	3639574N	12	R
02	9.1	32° 58' 58.7"	113° 09' 21.5"	298536E	3651273N	12	L
03	10.6	33° 00' 09.1"	113° 09' 34.3"	298248E	3653448N	12	T
04	2.2	33° 00' 10.9"	113° 08' 29.9"	299920E	3653469N	12	L
05	3.0	33° 00' 15.9"	113° 09' 16.8"	298706E	3653649N	12	T
65. BUTTERFIELD STAGE ROUTE							
01	0	33° 00' 03.9"	112° 25' 15.6"	367250E	3652111N	12	-
02	1.4	33° 00' 49.5"	112° 26' 16.7"	365684E	3653540N	12	R
03	4.5	33° 03' 16.6"	112° 26' 41.2"	365109E	3658078N	12	L
04	8.3	33° 01' 49.3"	112° 29' 58.5"	359954E	3655461N	12	S
05	11.1	33° 00' 31.9"	112° 32' 10.7"	356489E	3653127N	12	L
06	12.5	32° 59' 35.5"	112° 31' 19.2"	357801E	3651370N	12	D
66. ORGAN PIPE CACTUS NATIONAL MONUMENT							
01	0	31° 57' 20.0"	112° 48' 10.6"	329602E	3536743N	12	-
02	22.2	31° 58' 01.1"	113° 00' 43.0"	309871E	3538356N	12	L
03	24.0	31° 56' 32.2"	113° 00' 40.1"	309897E	3535615N	12	L
04	32.6	31° 54' 01.8"	112° 52' 59.4"	321916E	3530767N	12	S
05	37.6	31° 53' 36.8"	112° 48' 41.4"	328680E	3529882N	12	L
06	0.0	31° 57' 13.1"	112° 47' 56.5"	329970E	3536521N	12	R
07	2.1	31° 58' 14.8"	112° 46' 27.3"	332344E	3538383N	12	L
08	11.0	32° 00' 57.8"	112° 42' 40.9"	338368E	3543306N	12	S
67. BACKWAY TO MT. LEMMON							
01	0	32° 35' 35.9"	110° 43' 10.5"	526316E	3606046N	12	R
02	5.1	32° 32' 15.4"	110° 43' 03.3"	526520E	3599875N	12	S
03	18.5	32° 28' 25.1"	110° 43' 32.8"	525769E	3592782N	12	L
04	25.1	32° 26' 53.6"	110° 45' 15.6"	523092E	3589958N	12	D
68. RICE PEAK							
01	0	32° 32' 15.4"	110° 43' 03.3"	526520E	3599875N	12	R
02	1.1	32° 32' 27.6"	110° 43' 56.0"	525143E	3600247N	12	R
03	2.2	32° 32' 13.6"	110° 44' 36.5"	524090E	3599813N	12	R
04	2.7	32° 32' 27.9"	110° 44' 53.5"	523645E	3600253N	12	L
05	4.5	32° 31' 16.3"	110° 45' 07.4"	523287E	3598047N	12	R
06	5.8	32° 30' 43.5"	110° 44' 57.5"	523548E	3597037N	12	T
07	1.9	32° 31' 15.5"	110° 44' 42.5"	523936E	3598023N	12	L

* R = Right   L = Left   S = Straight   D = Driver's Choice   T = Turnaround

Wpt.	Mile	Latitude North	Longitude West	UTM Easting	UTM Northing	Zone	Turn*

69. CHAROULEAU GAP

Wpt.	Mile	Latitude North	Longitude West	UTM Easting	UTM Northing	Zone	Turn*
01	0	32° 36' 42.4"	110° 46' 16.3"	521467E	3608082N	12	R
02	1.0	32° 35' 56.1"	110° 46' 17.8"	521431E	3606658N	12	R
03	4.5	32° 33' 55.5"	110° 46' 51.0"	520573E	3602942N	12	S
04	7.3	32° 32' 23.2"	110° 47' 07.8"	520143E	3600100N	12	S
05	8.2	32° 31' 51.9"	110° 46' 51.4"	520570E	3599135N	12	S
06	9.7	32° 30' 51.7"	110° 47' 01.7"	520307E	3597283N	12	R
07	13.1	32° 31' 04.5"	110° 48' 30.2"	517997E	3597672N	12	S
08	17.0	32° 30' 58.6"	110° 51' 22.6"	513500E	3597483N	12	R
09	19.3	32° 31' 13.6"	110° 53' 02.1"	510903E	3597943N	12	L

70. CHIMNEY ROCK

Wpt.	Mile	Latitude North	Longitude West	UTM Easting	UTM Northing	Zone	Turn*
01	0	32° 20' 25.4"	110° 32' 24.6"	543274E	3578071N	12	L
02	0.9	32° 20' 39.1"	110° 33' 09.7"	542094E	3578486N	12	R
03	3.8	32° 21' 05.3"	110° 34' 48.8"	539500E	3579281N	12	L
04	6.3	32° 20' 02.9"	110° 36' 20.2"	537118E	3577353N	12	R
05	7.2	32° 19' 56.8"	110° 37' 15.2"	535679E	3577160N	12	L
06	8.2	32° 19' 15.4"	110° 37' 11.7"	535776E	3575884N	12	L
07	8.4	32° 18' 24.8"	110° 36' 17.4"	537202E	3574333N	12	R

71. CHIVO FALLS

Wpt.	Mile	Latitude North	Longitude West	UTM Easting	UTM Northing	Zone	Turn*
01	0	32° 16' 52.7"	110° 37' 58.5"	534568E	3571487N	12	R
02	0.8	32° 16' 57.5"	110° 37' 31.6"	535272E	3571639N	12	D
03	2.2	32° 16' 30.4"	110° 36' 40.8"	536603E	3570809N	12	R
04	2.8	32° 16' 29.9"	110° 36' 11.2"	537378E	3570795N	12	R
05	3.2	32° 16' 08.2"	110° 36' 12.3"	537351E	3570128N	12	L
06	3.3	32° 16' 05.4"	110° 36' 08.2"	537457E	3570040N	12	L
07	4.4	32° 15' 34.0"	110° 35' 46.8"	538021E	3569074N	12	T
08	1.5	32° 16' 10.2"	110° 35' 48.5"	537973E	3570190N	12	S
09	2.4	32° 16' 31.1"	110° 35' 03.4"	539151E	3570840N	12	S
10	3.2	32° 16' 51.7"	110° 34' 31.8"	539975E	3571478N	12	S
11	5.3	32° 18' 21.1"	110° 34' 25.4"	540131E	3574230N	12	L

72. GUNSIGHT PASS

Wpt.	Mile	Latitude North	Longitude West	UTM Easting	UTM Northing	Zone	Turn*
01	0	31° 51' 01.7"	110° 41' 49.4"	528661E	3523715N	12	R
02	2.6	31° 50' 03.7"	110° 43' 54.4"	525380E	3521921N	12	R
03	3.3	31° 49' 57.7"	110° 44' 32.7"	524374E	3521732N	12	R
04	4.2	31° 50' 07.1"	110° 45' 20.7"	523113E	3522021N	12	R
05	5.4	31° 50' 42.6"	110° 45' 13.2"	523308E	3523114N	12	L
06	6.0	31° 51' 03.3"	110° 45' 39.3"	522621E	3523741N	12	S
07	6.6	31° 51' 16.1"	110° 45' 24.3"	523012E	3524145N	12	R
08	7.3	31° 51' 29.2"	110° 45' 03.0"	523573E	3524547N	12	L
09	9.5	31° 52' 26.9"	110° 45' 02.7"	523575E	3526325N	12	L
10	11.5	31° 51' 29.9"	110° 45' 52.5"	522272E	3524568N	12	R
11	13.2	31° 51' 28.7"	110° 47' 18.6"	520007E	3524527N	12	S
12	14.8	31° 51' 03.7"	110° 48' 27.8"	518190E	3523752N	12	S

Wpt.	Mile	Latitude North	Longitude West	UTM Easting	UTM Northing	Zone	Turn*
73. GARDNER CANYON							
01	0	31° 44' 14.7"	110° 39' 46.4"	531933E	3511193N	12	R
02	0.8	31° 44' 04.2"	110° 40' 32.7"	530716E	3510867N	12	R
03	5.3	31° 44' 52.9"	110° 44' 26.9"	524549E	3512350N	12	R
04	7.0	31° 45' 11.8"	110° 45' 48.2"	522409E	3512927N	12	L
05	8.4	31° 44' 13.6"	110° 45' 26.3"	522989E	3511136N	12	R
06	11.9	31° 42' 53.7"	110° 45' 49.7"	522380E	3508675N	12	L
74. BULL SPRINGS ROAD							
01	0	31° 41' 21.7"	110° 58' 25.7"	502483E	3505816N	12	R
02	4.8	31° 39' 29.6"	110° 56' 29.7"	505537E	3502368N	12	R
03	8.1	31° 38' 28.4"	110° 54' 41.1"	508401E	3500485N	12	S
04	12.5	31° 37' 12.4"	110° 52' 30.2"	511851E	3498150N	12	S
05	18.8	31° 34' 02.0"	110° 49' 57.5"	515883E	3492292N	12	R
06	24.1	31° 30' 55.6"	110° 47' 19.2"	520067E	3486562N	12	D
75. PATAGONIA MOUNTAINS							
01	0	31° 32' 29.1"	110° 45' 04.3"	523618E	3489448N	12	-
02	6.1	31° 29' 19.5"	110° 41' 31.2"	529255E	3483624N	12	R
03	8.0	31° 28' 03.6"	110° 42' 26.8"	527793E	3481285N	12	S
04	12.8	31° 25' 27.8"	110° 42' 16.1"	528089E	3476488N	12	S
05	16.6	31° 23' 11.1"	110° 41' 28.1"	529367E	3472284N	12	S
06	17.3	31° 22' 44.9"	110° 41' 11.1"	529818E	3471479N	12	R
07	19.1	31° 22' 03.2"	110° 40' 07.8"	531495E	3470201N	12	R
08	22.9	31° 19' 59.0"	110° 37' 17.5"	536007E	3466389N	12	T
09	18.8	31° 23' 18.0"	110° 52' 17.0"	512229E	3472462N	12	D

* R = Right   L = Left   S = Straight   D = Driver's Choice   T = Turnaround

Glossary

Airing down - Letting air out of your tires to improve traction.

ARB lockers - A brand of differential locker that can be quickly activated when needed but turned off when not in use. (See locker.)

Arizona Pinstripes - Brush marks or paint scratches from abrasive tree branches.

Articulation - The flexibility of your suspension system. Greater articulation means your wheels will go up and down more to better accommodate ground undulation.

BLM - Bureau of Land Management.

Cairn - A stack of rocks that marks an obscure trail.

Clevis - A U-shaped device with a pin at one end that is used to connect tow straps.

Come-along - A hand-operated ratchet that functions as a winch.

Cryptobiotic crust - A brown or black, jagged crust that slowly forms on loose desert soils. Nature's first step to controlling erosion.

Dispersed camping - Free camping on public lands away from developed recreation facilities. Usually limited to 14 days or less depending upon area. Camp near existing roads and use existing sites whenever possible. Pack out your trash.

Great Western Trail - A series of multi-use, connected backroads that runs from Canada to Mexico. Some areas are yet to be completed. Arizona's portion of the trail is nearly done. Some trails in this book follow portions of the Great Western Trail. For information call 1-928-567-4121 or visit Web site: www.azgwt.org.

High centered - When your undercarriage gets stuck on a rock, mound, log, or ridge. Usually requires you to jack up your vehicle to get free.

High-lift jack - A tool that allows you to quickly lift your vehicle high off the ground. Considered a necessity on hard-core trails. Also substitutes for a winch.

Javelina - A small pig-like animal that grows to about 3 ft. in length and weighs up to 60 lbs. They have poor eyesight but a keen sense of smell. They keep their distance from humans and are difficult to photograph up close.

Lift - A vehicle modification that raises the suspension or body of a vehicle to provide greater ground clearance.

Locker - Optional gearing installed inside your differential that equalizes power to wheels on both sides of an axle. Eliminates loss of power when climbing steep undulating hills. Not the same as locking-in your hubs.

Low range - A second range of gears that increases the power of your vehicle. Used for climbing steep grades, especially at higher altitude.

Petroglyphs - Indian motifs abraded into rock surfaces.

Skid plates - Plates that protect vulnerable parts of your undercarriage.

Snatch block - A pulley that opens so it can be slipped over your winch cable.

Suguaro -Arizona's largest and most recognized cactus. (See page 4). Starts as a single trunk and developes branches after about 75 years. Some live 200 years. Suguaro blossoms are the state flower. Grows at elevation of 700 to 3500 ft.

Switchback - A zigzag road for climbing a steep grade.

Tank - Cattle watering hole. May or may not include a metal collection tank.

Tow point, tow hook - A point on your vehicle that enables you to quickly and safely attach a tow strap. Considered a basic necessity for four-wheeling.

References & Reading

4 Wheel Drive Roads of Mohave County, Arizona, by Luis & Paula Vega, H & H Printers, Inc, Kingman, AZ. Guide to 15 Four-Wheel-Drive Trails around Kingman, Lake Havasu City and Bullhead City. Maps, photos and GPS waypoints. (2000)

Arizona Ghost Towns and Mining Camps, Text by Philip Varney, Prepared by Book Division of Arizona Highways, Phoenix, AZ. Photos, stories and maps of Arizona's famous ghost towns. (1994)

Arizona Handbook, by Bill Weir, Moon Publications, Inc., Chico, CA. Comprehensive recreation guide with photos and maps. (1999)

Arizona Place Names, by Will C. Barnes, University of Arizona Press, Tucson, AZ. Alphabetical reference of lesser-known places in Arizona. (1997)

(The) Back Roads, Prepared by Book Division of Arizona Highways, Phoenix, AZ. Twenty full-color, backroad tours for the whole family. (1999)

Back Roads and Beyond, by Pete Cowgill, Broken Toe Press, Tucson, AZ. Guide to southern Arizona truck and foot routes. (1997)

Crown King and the Southern Bradshaws: A Complete History, by Bruce M. Wilson, Crown King Press, Chandler, AZ. Photo illustrated history of Crown King mining days. (1999)

Desert Survival Handbook, by Charles A. Lehman, Primer Publishers, Phoenix, AZ. A basic guide to desert survival. (1996)

Deserts, by James A. MacMahon, Alfred A. Knopf, Inc, New York, NY., A National Audubon Society Nature Guide on desert plants and wildlife. (1998)

Explore Arizona, by Rick Harris, Golden West Publishers, Phoenix, AZ. A guide to lesser-known, remote places in Arizona. (1986)

(The) Four Wheel Drive Trails of Arizona, by Scott Deuty, 4x4 Travel, Gilbert, AZ. Guide to 12 back roads around Phoenix. Maps, photos and GPS waypoints. (1996)

Ghost Towns and Historical Haunts in Arizona, by Thelma Heatwole, Golden West Publishers, Phoenix, AZ. Guide to Arizona ghost towns with maps and photos. (1981)

Jerome—Story of Mines, Men, and Money, by James W. Brewer, Jr., Southwest Parks and Monuments Association, Tucson, AZ. Small pamphlet on town of Jerome. (1993)

Mountain Biking Flagstaff and Sedona, by Bruce Grubbs, Falcon Press Publishing, Inc., Helena, MT. Guide to 35 mountain biking trails around Flagstaff and Sedona. Maps and directions. (1999)

Roadside History of Arizona, by Marshall Trimble, Mountain Press Publishing Company, Missoula. History of places along Arizona highways. (1998)

Scenic Driving Arizona, by Stewart M. Green, Falcon Publishing, Inc., Helena, MT. Thirty scenic, mostly-paved drives. Includes maps and photos. (1992)

Stone Cabins, by Carol Nilson, Reader's Oasis Books, Quartzsite, AZ. Brief guide to 19 stone cabins around Quartzsite. Illustrated in pen and ink. (1999)

Addresses & Phone Numbers

Bureau of Land Management
Web site: www.blm.gov

Arizona Public Lands Information Center
222 North Central Ave, Suite 101
Phoenix, AZ 85004   (602) 417-9300

Arizona State Office
222 North Central Avenue
Phoenix, AZ 85004-2203   (602) 417-9528

Arizona Strip Field Office
345 East Riverside Drive
St. George, UT 84790-9000   (435) 688-3200

Havasu Field Office
2610 Sweetwater Avenue
Lake Havasu City, AZ 86406-9071   (928) 505-1200

Kingman Field Office
2475 Beverly Avenue
Kingman, AZ 86401   (928) 692-4400

Phoenix Field Office
21605 North 7th Avenue
Phoenix, AZ 85027   (623) 580-5500

Tucson Field Office
12661 East Broadway Blvd.
Tucson, AZ 85748   (520) 722-4289

Yuma Field Office
2555 East Gila Ridge Road
Yuma, AZ 85365   (928) 317-3200

Chambers of Commerce

Ajo- (520) 387- 7742
Apache Junction- (480) 982- 3141
Black Canyon City- (623) 374-9797
Bullhead City- (928) 754-4121
Casa Grande- (520) 836-2125
Cave Creek and Carefree- (480) 488-3381
Chloride- (928) 565-2204
Cottonwood- (928) 634-7593
Flagstaff- (928) 774-4505
Globe- (928) 425-4495
Grand Canyon- (928) 527-0359
Jerome- (928) 634-2900
Kingman- (928) 753-6253
Lake Havasu City- (928) 855-4115
Mayer- (928) 632-4355
Mesa- (480) 969-1307
Mohave Valley- (928) 768-2777
Nogales- (520) 287-3685
Oatman (leave message)- (928) 768-6222
Parker- (928) 669-2174

Payson/Rim Country Vis. Ctr.- (928) 474-4515
Phoenix- (602) 254-5521
Prescott- (928) 445-2000
Quartzsite (leave message)- (928) 927-5600
Sedona- (928) 282-7722
Sonoita- (520) 455-5498
Tucson- (520) 792-1212
Yuma- (928) 782-2567

Maps, Books & GPS Sources

4X4*BOOKS*.com
(308) 381-4410
Fax: (877) 787-2993

All Topo Maps (iGage Map Corp.)
P.O. Box 58596
Salt Lake City, UT 84158
(888) 450-4922, www.igage.com

Arizona Public Lands Information Center
222 North Central Ave, Suite 101
Phoenix, AZ 85004   (602) 417-9300

DeLorme Mapping
P. O. Box 298
Yarmouth, ME 04096
(207) 846-7000, www.delorme.com

Garmin International
1200 E. 151st Street
Olathe, KS 66062
(800) 800-1020, www.garmin.com

Lowrance Electronics, Inc.
12000 E. Skelly Drive
Tulsa, OK 74128-1703
(800) 324-1356, www.lowrance.com

Magellan Corporation
960 Overland Court
San Dimas, CA 91773
(909) 394-5000, www.magellangps.com

MAPTECH
10 Industrial Way.
Amesbury, MA 01913
(888) 839-5551, www.maptech.com

Micropath
2023 Montane Drive East
Golden, CO 80401-8099
(303) 526-5454, www.micropath.com

National Geographic Maps
375 Alabama Street, Suite 400
San Francisco, CA 94110   (415) 558-8700
www.nationalgeographic.com/maps

OziExplorer
www.oziexplorer.com
oziexp.html (in Australia)

Wide World of Maps, Inc.
2626 West Indian School Road
Phoenix, AZ 85017-4397   (602) 279-2323

National Parks/ Monuments
Web site: www.nps.gov

Canyon de Chelly National Monument
P.O. 588
Chinle, AZ 86503   (928) 674- 5500

Grand Canyon National Park
P.O. Box 129
Grand Canyon, AZ 86023
General Information: (928) 638-7888
Backcountry Information: (928) 638-7875
Web site: www.nps.gov/grca

Organ Pipe Cactus National Monument
10 Organ Pipe Drive
Ajo, AZ 85321   (520) 387-6849

Saguaro National Park
3693 South Old Spanish Trail
Tucson, AZ 85730   (520) 733-5153

Sunset Crater National Monument
Route 3 Box 149
Flagstaff, AZ 86004   (928) 526-0502

Tonto National Monument
HC 02 Box 4602
Roosevelt, AZ 85545   (928) 467-2241

State Parks
Web site: www.pr.state.az.us

Arizona State Parks, Main Office
1300 West Washington Street
Phoenix, AZ 85007   (602) 542-4174

Buckskin Mountain State Park
5476 Highway 95
Parker, AZ 85344   (928) 667-3231

Catalina State Park
11570 North Oracle Road
Tucson, AZ 85740   (520) 628-5798

Cattail Cove State Park
P.O. Box 1990
Lake Havasu, AZ 86405   (928) 855-1223

Jerome State Historic Park
Box D
Jerome, AZ 86331   (928) 634-5381

Lake Havasu State Park
1801 Highway 95
Lake Havasu City, AZ 86406   (928) 855-2784

Lost Dutchman State Park
6109 North Apache Trail
Apache Junction, AZ 85219   (602) 982-4485

Patagonia Lake State Park
P.O. Box 274
Patagonia, AZ 85624   (520) 287-6965

Red Rock State Park
4050 Lower Red Rock Loop
Sedona, AZ 86339   (928) 282-6907

U.S. Fish and Wildlife Service
Bill Williams River National Wildlife Refuge
60911 Highway 95
Parker, AZ 85344   (928) 667-4144

Cibola National Wildlife Refuge
Rt. 2 Box 138
Cibola, AZ 85328   (928) 857-3253

Kofa National Wildlife Refuge
356 West 1st Street
Yuma, AZ 85364   (928) 783-7861

U.S. Forest Service
Web site: www.fs.fed.us

Coconino N.F/. Supervisors Office
2323 East Greenlaw Lane
Flagstaff, AZ 86004 (928) 527-3600

Coconino N.F./ Mormon Lake Ranger District
4373 South Lake Mary Road
Flagstaff, AZ 86001   (928) 774-1147

Coconino N.F/. Peaks Ranger District
5075 North Highway 89
Flagstaff, AZ 86004   (928) 526-0866

Coconino N.F./ Sedona Ranger District
250 Brewer Road, P.O. Box 300
Sedona, AZ 86339   (928) 282-4119

Coronado N.F/ Supervisors Office
Federal Building
300 West Congress
Tucson, AZ 85701   (520) 670-4552

Coronado N.F./ Nogales Ranger District
303 Old Tucson Road
Nogales, AZ 85621   (520) 281-2296

Coronado N.F./ Santa Catalina Ranger District
5700 North Sabino Canyon Road
Tucson, AZ 85750   (520) 749-8700

Kaibab N.F./ Supervisors Office
800 South 6th Street
Williams, AZ 86046   (928) 635-8200

Kaibab Plateau Visitor Center
Hwy 89/AZ67
Jacob Lake, AZ 86022   (928) 643-7298

Kaibab N.F./ North Kaibab Ranger District
P.O. Box 248
Fredonia, AZ 86022   (928) 643-7395

Kaibab N. F./ Tusayan Ranger District
P.O. Box 3088
Tusayan,AZ 86023   (928) 238-2443

Prescott N.F./ Supervisors Office
344 South Cortez Street
Prescott, AZ 86303   (928) 771-4700

Prescott N.F./ Bradshaw Ranger District
344 South Cortez Street
Prescott, AZ 86303   (928) 771-4700

Prescott N.F./ Chino Valley Ranger District
735 North Highway 89
Chino Valley, AZ 86323   (928) 636-2302

Prescott N.F./ Verde Ranger District
300 East Highway 260
P.O. Box 670
Camp Verde, AZ 86322   (928) 567-4121

Tonto N.F./ Supervisors Office
2324 East McDowell Road
Phoenix, AZ 85006
(602) 225-5200

Tonto N.F./ Cave Creek Ranger District
40202 North Cave Creek Road
Scottsdale, AZ 85262   (602) 488-3441

Tonto N.F./ Globe Ranger District
7800 South Sixshooter Canyon Road
Globe, AZ 85501   (928) 402-6200

Tonto N.F./ Mesa Ranger District
26 North MacDonald
P.O. Box 5800
Mesa, AZ 85201   (480) 610-3300

Tonto N.F./ Payson Ranger District
1009 East Highway 260
Payson, AZ 85541   (928) 474-7900

Tonto N.F./ Tonto Basin Ranger District
Hwy. 88 HC 02 Box 4800
Roosevelt, AZ 85545   (928) 467-3200

Other State Agencies

Arizona Game and Fish
2222 West Greenway Road
Phoenix, AZ 85023   (602) 942-3000
Web site: www.azgfd.com

Arizona Office of Tourism
2702 North 3rd Street Suite 4015
Phoenix, AZ 85004   (602) 230-7733
Web site: www.arizonaguide.com

Arizona State Land Department (Permits)
1616 West Adams
Phoenix, AZ 85007   (602) 364-2753
Web site: www.land.state.az.us

Other Helpful Numbers:

Arizona State Association of 4-Wheel Drive Clubs
P.O. Box 23904
Tempe, AZ 85285   (602) 258-4294
Web site: www.asa4wdc.org

Arizona Site Stewards
To report vandalism call 1 (800) VANDALS

National Forest Service Nationwide Camping Reservations
(800) 280-2267

Tread Lightly
298 24th Street, Suite 325
Ogden, UT 84401   (800) 966-9900
Web site: www.treadlightly.org

4-Wheel-Drive Shops

4-Wheelers Supply & Off Road Centers
3530 East Washington
Phoenix, AZ 85034   (602) 273-7195

Desert Rat Off Road Center
10701 North 19th Avenue
Phoenix, AZ 85029-4903   (602) 973-9697

Desert Rat Truck Centers
3705 South Palo Verde Road
Tucson, AZ 85713-5401   (520) 790-8502

Flagstaff 4x4
2920 East Route 66
Flagstaff, AZ 86004   (928) 527-0270

Fly-N-Hi Off Road Center
3319 West Mcdowell Road
Phoenix, AZ 85009-2415   (602) 272-2433

Iron Springs Four Wheel Drive
925 Hinman Street
Prescott, AZ 86305   (928) 778-0320

Lee's 4-Wheel Drive
3127 North Stone Avenue
Tucson, AZ 85705   (520) 624-0851

Offroad Unlimited
821 West Broadway
Mesa, AZ 85210   (480) 833-4999

Parker Auto and Marine
908 Joshua Avenue
Parker, AZ 85344   (928) 669-6104

Tucson Differential
1102 South Venice
Tucson, AZ 85711   (520) 750-1309

Western Differential
3825 East Kleindale
Tucson, AZ 85705   (520) 327-1747

Willy Works, Inc.
1933 West Gardner Lane
Tucson, AZ 85705   (520) 888-5082

Index   (m = map page,   p = photo page,   mp = map & photo page)

About the Author

Charles A. Wells graduated from Ohio State University in 1969 with a degree in graphic design. After practicing design in Ohio, he moved to Colorado Springs, CO, in 1980 and worked 18 years in the printing business. Over the years, he and his family enjoyed a wide array of recreational activities including hiking, biking, rafting, and skiing. He bought his first SUV in 1994 and began exploring places he was previously not able to reach in the family sedan. He later joined a four-wheel-drive club and learned about hard-core four-wheeling. This book follows three successful backroad guidebooks—two on Colorado and one on Moab, Utah.

All of the trails in this book were driven by the author in the vehicles described below. He wrote the trail descriptions based on his own observations, shot most of the photographs, and created all the maps. No sponsors were involved. The result of this hands-on approach is a valuable and unbiased reference for both novices and hard-core four-wheeling enthusiasts.

Author with Jeep Grand Cherokee on Schnebly Hill Road above Sedona. Equipped with automatic transmission, factory skid plates, tow points, CB radio, and LT235-75R15 BFG all-terrain tires.

Jeep is a registered trademark of Chrysler Corporation.

Author's Jeep Cherokee on President's Choice. Equipped with Tomken 5″ lift, bumpers, rocker skids, tire carrier, and brush guard; 8,000 lb. Warn winch; Dana 44 rear axle; 410 gears; ARBs front & rear; Tera Low 4 to 1 transfer case; skid plates; stock 4-liter engine with 5-speed; K&N air filter; interior roll cage; 33 x 10.50 BFG A/T tires; tow points; fold-in mirrors; and CB radio.

Order Form

Phone orders: Call toll free 1-(877) 222-7623. We accept VISA, MasterCard, Discover and American Express.

Postal orders: Send check, name, address, and telephone number to: FunTreks, Inc. P.O. Box 49187, Colorado Springs, CO 80949-9187. If paying by credit card, include your card number and expiration date.

Fax orders: Fax this order form to 1-(719) 277-7411. Include your credit card number and expiration date.

E-mail orders: Our e-mail address is *funtreks@pcisys.net* Include phone number so we can call to determine payment method.

Please send me the following book(s):

I understand that if I am not completely satisfied, I may return the book(s) for a full refund, no questions asked.

Qty.

❏ *Guide to Arizona Backroads & 4-Wheel Drive Trails,* _____
      ISBN 0-9664976-3-5, 286 pages, Price $19.95

❏ *Guide to Moab, UT Backroads & 4-Wheel Drive Trails,* _____
      ISBN 0-9664976-2-7, 268 pages, Price $19.95

❏ *Guide to Colorado Backroads & 4-Wheel Drive Trails, (Original)* _____
      ISBN 0-9664976-0-0, 248 pages, Price $18.95

❏ *Guide to Colorado Backroads & 4-Wheel Drive Trails Vol. 2* _____
      ISBN 0-9664976-1-9, 176 pages, Price $15.95

Address:

Name: _____

Address: _____

City: _____State: _____Zip: _____

Telephone: (_____) _____

Sales Tax: Colorado residents add 3%. (Subject to change without notice.)

Shipping: $4.50 for the first book and $2.00 for each additional book. (Subject to change without notice.)

Payment: ❏ Check   ❏ VISA   ❏ MasterCard   ❏ Discover   ❏ Am. Express

Card number:_____Exp. date:_____

Name on card:_____

Call toll free 1-(877) 222-7623 -Thanks for your order